How world demographics, human greed, central bankers, and politicians, all aided and abetted by the ideas of the progressive left, created the illusion of continuing and robust economic growth as well as material wealth. And what, perhaps, can be done.

Prologue

The American dream can be summarised in a rather simple statement; 'That our children will have a better standard of living and quality of life than we did'. It is what many say made America great and it is a dream that is currently shared by much of the world's population. It is a natural dream that we can essentially end our lives with a surplus amount of wealth that can be passed onto the next generation and therefore, over time, a multigenerational family can grow and prosper.

There is nothing wrong with this dream in and of itself per se and it is, in theory, and sometimes even in practice, an attainable one. However, it is a dream that can only be accomplished through making certain sacrifices, and in this book, we show how the first world, having embraced post modernism and therefore abandoned Judeo-Christian values, now finds itself unable to make those sacrifices. We furthermore will explain why the current makeup of the first world necessitates that even if we wanted to make them it would not be possible to do so without a coherent change in the way the world functions. It is an interesting dynamic created by the greed, compromise, and flatly the incompetence of individuals, and would be something that was academically fascinating to me, if I could divorce myself from thinking about the consequences for so many human beings that this problem poses. As things are, I feel a huge amount of indignation regarding this because this is a deception that has been perpetrated by governments and institutions across the world. And we the people have ultimately been the ones who brought it upon ourselves because as a group we have not been willing to save in order to achieve our hopes, but we have tried to do everything the quick and short way. This of course does not apply to everyone, but as a group, consumers have driven our collective economies into the jaws of death with only a tiny sliver of a chance to bring things back.

I wish, however, to highlight what that minute opportunity is and to make us think about how we can take it and begin to reverse the things that have brought us to this position. I hope to also impress it up everyone who reads this that if we took the issue of fiscal responsibility as seriously as politicians seem to take the issue of Climate Change, we would never have got into this mess. And when I say **we**, I mean it. It is certainly incumbent on all of us to take responsibility. We need to be accountable because it is us, the people, who demanded handouts and tax breaks and never paid attention to the real cost of the things that we wanted. I still meet people who genuinely believe that governments could simply create more money to pay for every program or benefit that we could wish for. Indeed, there are people in the US congress that have this sort of naïve idea about the world[1]. In that sense, there are still a good many people who think like a relative of a very good friend of mine. This relative, when told by their financial advisors that they would need to budget better and cut down on expenses because they were running out of money simply turned to the banker and said; "That's alright I can just simply write a cheque – who do I make it out to please?"

But we will think more deeply. We will look at the real workings of an economy and at the balancing of the budget. There will be some economic numbers that we won't care about one bit because, in truth,

---

[1] In that sense, it would behove all freshman Congress members and Senators to have a "bootcamp" that should end up looking pretty much like this book only with a few more equations... I would volunteer to teach those classes for free every 2 years for the good of the world, when you consider how much power those few people weald.

they are at best, a smokescreen. There will be some statistics, however, that will be of immense importance. We are going to do nothing less than understand how economies work and what is needed in order to keep them going and to make them viable. Let me from the outset say one thing. This work in no way whatsoever is against capitalism in its purer forms. It is clear to me, that capitalism is a system that has brought by the far the largest number of human beings out of poverty over time. What I am against is not capitalism at all, that is doing just fine. However, the books of every company or institution have two sides. One is the asset side, and capitalism is the single best way we have seen to grow the asset side. What we are going to be concerned with is the side of the equation that is almost never properly considered and that is the liability side. Or to put it another way, when it comes to the first world, we need to understand "How do finance our engine of growth that is capitalism – how do we pay for all this in a way that is sustainable?".

To do this, we will need to study a little bit of everything from basic mathematics all the way through history to economics. At this point, some of you might be falling asleep, but I promise everything that we will go through, is simpler (and far more interesting) than you might have been led to believe. I don't care if you think you are the worst person in the world at mathematics, I guarantee that you will be able to follow the mathematics that we use. It doesn't matter how bored the history of the British Kings or American Presidents made you because the history we will be talking about is far more interesting and colourful than that. Finally, even if you have never heard of a single economic theory you will be able to follow the train of thought that I will present here. I am not trying to persuade you. As Saint Augustine may (or may not[2]) have said; "The truth is like a lion. You don't have to defend it. Let it loose and it will defend itself". I want to equip you with a way to look at finance that allows you to draw your own conclusions and not be mired in the idea that just because a Nobel prize winner, an "expert" with 50-years of experience, or even a person with a doctorate from Cambridge University says so.

As with all understanding, by far the best way to approach it is to research it yourself. But the second-best approach is to learn about it from someone who is arguing from entirely the opposite perspective to your initial point of view. Looking at it from the perspective of someone who agrees with your initial inference usually adds no direct value and if you look at everything by considering only those who have the same perspective as yourself you will very soon find that you are in an intellectual "echo chamber" where all you end up hearing is your own voice reverberating ever surrounding you and engulfing any pushback. But what we are going to do is follow the first method and we will study everything together.

The lessons of History

As we begin thinking about the issues surrounding the "American dream" we will start with history and we do so on the other side of the Atlantic Ocean with Western Europe in general, followed by the United Kingdom. Just as a caveat though, this is not a history book, so our study will flip back and forth between epochs and will also not be comprehensive in any way; we will pick only the most relevant parts to understanding the economic position of the world (and particularly in the west). With Europe we will begin by looking at a couple of case studies of hyperinflation. These are pertinent because they will allow us to begin thinking about how such events could happen and we will also ask if we are close to such things happening in the west right now. We won't do this until later though. What we will do now is simply look at what they are and begin to understand them. With the UK, we will take this as the case study for many of the social welfare programs that exist today and see what the pros and cons are. Think about it in this way. We are flipping back and forth throughout history as if we were Time travellers in some extremely contrived modern sci-fi movie although without the moral judgement. We will just look

---

2 The attribution is to St Augustine of Hippo (as opposed to St Augustine of Canterbury), but I have been unable to definitively verify it. A similar quote came from Spurgeon, but whatever the provenance it doesn't stop it from being true.

at what happened along with a few anecdotes, so we can begin to understand the present age that we occupy.

The early part of the 20th century was, for most of Western Europe at least, all about the First and Second world wars. Both these events were in each of their times the greatest war that had ever occurred on earth with casualties in the millions. In addition, the First World War (which had been billed as the War to End All Wars) germinated the seeds of the Second World War as Germany had been forced to pay reparations to the Allies that were exceptionally punitive. The 5 Mark coin was composed of 1.7921 g of gold meaning that the nominal reparation amounts of 132 billion gold marks was equivalent to just over 1.5 billion ounces of gold or in today's money 1.8 Trillion dollars. To put it into context that is just a little under 9% of the current US debt which, as we shall soon find out, is literally of Biblical proportions. It should also be noted that at that time the population of Germany was around 60 million people, so even without accounting for the increased productivity in the world in the 100 years following we are looking at 60% of current US debt population adjusted. That is a simply stunning number for reparations.

Now all is not what it seems because, unbeknownst to the general public either in the UK or Germany, Germany was only compelled to pay around 50 billion rather than the full amount with the rest being a brilliant smokescreen of PR to convince the people that Germany had been heavily punished. But that still represents almost 700 Billion dollars and to put it in context the entire Troubled Asset Relief Program that the US set in motion in 08 only invested a total of 426 Billion USD (even though it was authorized up to 700 Billion). We could further comment that Germany post 1918 had effectively come off the gold mark standard and so, in the end, the amount that Germany had to pay was somewhat less than even the above numbers. However, the point is, that both in truth and much more importantly, in the perception of the German public, Germany was paying a crushing amount of reparations to the victors of WWI. And the German people, in general, felt that this was too high a price to pay for a war that they both didn't feel that they had lost or that was mostly their fault.

Yet it is not just this perception of an unfair bargain that led to WWII. More it is the events that happened afterwards that set into motion the chain of tragedies that led, eventually, to the horrors inflicted on the world *ut totum* (very much including Germany itself) by Adolf Hitler. One case specifically will be very useful to us in this context and it is the case of hyperinflation in the Weimar Republic. Inflation is something that we will talk about a lot later. But for now, it suffices to say that inflation is something that is generally regarded as bad. Not everyone thinks it's bad, and you would certainly be forgiven for thinking, having seen on the news the aggressive attempts that various central banks have made to fuel inflation, that inflation was a very good thing. Well I hope to convince you over time that it is not a good thing, but something that is agreed by almost everyone is that hyperinflation is a very bad thing. And when we talk of hyperinflation, we mean extreme levels of inflation - virtually unimaginable price increases in the basic goods of life. As we shall see the definition of "basic goods of life" is something very important to properly and rigorously define, but for the moment let us just say that hyperinflation is one of the real evils that exist in the world and the worst thing that could ever happen to a country - do not let anyone deceive you - hyperinflation is far, far worse than a recession or even things like the Global Financial Crisis or The Great Depression that occurred in the US in the 1930's. Yes, hyperinflation is literally the Ebola of financial maladies, a truly malignant and festering destruction of wealth and prosperity as well as social cohesion. Ultimately it was this utter evil that planted the seeds which made the German people say enough is enough and grab onto the promises of a demagogue who openly declared his hatred for the Jewish people as well as virtually everyone else who either believed in Jesus Christ (over the state), or somehow didn't conform to the perfect (but manufactured) definition of the Aryan race in the diseased mind of this dictator and his cronies.

The Rise of hyperinflation in Weimar Germany and the Spectre of the valueless[3] Pengo.

The Weimar Republic was ushered in around the 11th of August 1919. It wasn't technically called the Weimar Republic during its lifetime (with the name taken as canonical only after 1933 and the advent of the Third Reich) and it was declared as a Republic before even the armistice of 1918; 2 days before to be exact. On the Wikipedia entry for the Weimar Republic is a photo taken of Philipp Scheidemann declaring (pretty much unilaterally) at the Reichstag that the Republic had been established. The Communists (formally this was the Spartakusbund, or the Spartacus League) then declared the emergence of a "Free Socialist Republic" just a couple of hours later.

In the two weeks prior to this, the Socialist Revolution spread throughout Germany. This was nothing less than an attempt to copy the Soviets who successfully undertook the Russian Revolution of 1917 and over those days it spread like an inexorable fire across the whole of Germany. There was huge concern amongst ordinary people that this really would be a full Communist takeover, and there indeed might have been if it weren't for the fact that one of the main leftist parties (the Social Democratic Party of Germany – the SPD) supported the creating of a parliamentary democracy and was able to effectively control the narrative and the course of the demonstrations through people like Gustav Noske[4], and also because the focus of the rebellion was more directed at workers' rights and trades-unionism rather than a fierce revolutionary outlook.

Nevertheless, there were still various minor rebellions and scuffles extending all the way past the middle of 1919. But as usual with these things, those that come later are merely aftershocks and are never quite as bad as the big quake. And therefore, over the course of 1919 things became calmer and clearer. Most people simply wanted to get their lives back together following the War to End all Wars, and so the SPD got the most votes at the elections in January. The reason the Weimar Republic came to be known as such was because the National Assembly first convened in Weimar because there was still unrest in Berlin and other areas and because the Constitution of the Parliamentary Republic was written there. The future looked better and more optimistic for the middle class – more than 80% of parliamentary seats had fallen to democratic parties – and workers got significant fundamental concessions and rights that they did not have under the previous Monarch. But all was not well. Due to some exceptionally idiotic economic management along with a president of the Reichsbank (the precursor of today's Bundesbank central bank) that would have been a staunch advocate of Modern Monetary Theory if he had been around today, the spectre of hyperinflation reared its ugly head.

There are many much more comprehensive books[5] on how hyperinflation really got going and what it meant for the country. I would recommend every reader study this in great depth because it is a very interesting story and really shows how financial conditions could have such an effect on a country. However, for our purposes we will just quickly go over what happened as an overview. Unfortunately, the reason for hyperinflation boils down to only one thing. That thing is the unchecked printing of money in the financial system of a country. This can stem from a lot of different reasons. For example, if the currency itself is restricted to such an extent that no one outside the country will accept it as payment, leading to a black-market rate that is far higher than the given rate, or if the government decides it needs to grow the money supply exponentially to pay off its own debts. This might seem obvious, but we need to remember this because over the course of our studies we will find that some very intelligent people don't agree with this, and in fact believe de facto that this sort of hyperinflation is

---

[3] To quote the movie Short Circuit, "Newton we are wasting valueless time here!"

[4] The revolution had begun in Kiel where a group (composed mostly of workers as well as the army and the navy) had tried to follow in the footsteps of the Russian Revolution. Noske had been sent to calm the situation down, and the rather naïve would be revolutionaries accepted him as their negotiator even though he was mostly self-proclaimed as an expert on military strategy.

[5] If you are struggling for a specific book, I can say that "The Downfall of Money" is a good one, giving strong insight into the phenomenon.

no longer possible in the western world. I don't think they could be more wrong in that idea, but I will leave it for you to decide as we continue our journey. In this case the villain of the piece was one Rudolf Havenstein who was the previously mentioned President of the Reichsbank. He seemed to channel the ideas of the recently assassinated socialist industrialist Walter Rathenau who had some, shall we say, mystical ideas of utopia, and had claimed that Germany could not be ruined by printing money. Havenstein took that philosophy to its ultimate end, proudly boasting in August 1923 just a few months before his death that he could increase the money supply in Germany by two thirds overnight, presumably due to his ultra-efficient printing capabilities, which consisted of 2000 printing presses and 30 paper mills working 24/7. Of course, this was essentially a death nail in the value of the Mark. When the President of the Central Bank basically says your currency will almost halve in value overnight, well don't be too surprised if it does just that. Havenstein was a typical bureaucrat, a lawyer by profession who had no business being a financier much less a President of one of the most important central banks in the world, and it was clear that he didn't understand the first thing about money. Unfortunately, as we shall see, this is still the case amongst many supposedly educated people today and something which is exacerbated rather than helped by modern technology.

What must be realised, however, and this is key and fundamental to the entire thesis of this book, is that printing money is a hidden taxation on the country. Nothing more, and nothing less. If you double the money supply, you have essentially devalued all the cash in the bank accounts of savers by 50 percent. Those who were prudent and saved their money, end up paying for the spendthrifts who ignored the future and lived simply for today. Oh well this might not be noticed at first, because, regardless of anything you say, the markets are not "efficient". The prince doesn't suddenly move to reflect reality. It is more like the way streams trickle down a mountain, eventually coming together and forming a torrent of a river. The "real" market takes time to come to a full head. And by the real market I mean the basic prices for the consumer, not the stock market or anything similar, but the real price of food, living space, and services such as transport or medical care. But the problem, of course, is that by the time that hyperinflation is really seen, it is too late, far too late, to do anything to stop it without immense and costly sacrifices of both treasure and blood, sweat, and tears.

Whilst there are many anecdotes regarding the catastrophic collapse of the paper Mark, perhaps the most whimsical was that people found it cheaper to take notes from the bank to paper their walls than to buy wallpaper made for that very same purpose. Then there were the practical considerations which often required people to carry their daily spending money in suitcases, or at the height of the crisis, wheelbarrows. The lower denomination notes eventually became so worthless that sometimes people would drop them from their wheelbarrows and not even bother to pick them up again. Then there was the fact that you had to rush your wage to the nearest store the minute you got it because if you didn't do it right away the price of bread or eggs might go up again (a loaf of bread went from 4 paper marks in 1921 to 2 billion marks in 1923 meaning that on average such a loaf cost around 2.8% more per day).

Can you imagine that happening today in the US or the UK? Can one even begin to comprehend the carnage that this would lead to and the pain and suffering this would cause? The same thing that happened in Weimar would occur. First people would desperately try to sell any property they didn't need, but very quickly there wouldn't be anyone to buy that. Then in order to feed their families, all the gold and silver at hand would be sold as well as every heirloom of value. But very quickly even these would not be enough, and you will see that property will be the next to collapse. It might seem that property should be going up a lot when there is such bad inflation, but the fact is that it won't for various reasons. Firstly, interest rates will go up spectacularly in a desperate attempt to reduce inflation. Secondly, there are relatively few properties compared to the 1920's that are not mortgaged. This means there is more leverage in the system which in turn means that the housing market is more susceptible to precipitous drops. In addition, as everything else turns sour and even people who were considered rich before have to cut cost to make ends meet, there will be significant selling of property assets. Property prices will go up at least in nominal terms but not even close to compensating for inflation. Most notably property prices will collapse versus gold, silver, and other commodities, and especially food. We shall see later that this is exactly what is to be expected to happen across the developed world in the coming years, and we shall also see why this is so.

And just in case you are tempted to think that hyperinflation is unique, Weimar was not even the worst case of hyperinflation that we saw even in the 20th century, even in central Europe. The devaluation of the Hungarian Pengo[6] after the second world war was simply the worst example in history that we know of. It may be of course that Venezuela manages to beat this, but this hasn't happened yet. The Pengo started life at the beginning of 1927 with a healthy exchange rate of 5.26 Pengo to one US dollar. It remained quite stable for the next 15 years or so, even appreciating to 5.06 against the USD by the end of the first quarter of 1941. However, by the middle of June just three years later in 1944 it had devalued to 33.51 per USD. That basically means if you had converted your money in 1941 to Pengo from USD and then converted back in three years you would have got back just 15 percent of your dollars back assuming you hadn't received any interest. But that was not hyperinflation, by any means. What came next was astounding. Little over a year later in August of 1945 the Pengo was now trading at 1320 to the dollar a further essentially meaning that any cash that was kept in Pengo would have been wiped out in terms of hard (gold or silver standard[7]) currency. But worse was to come, and this time it was truly pathological. In the year from August of 1945 through to July 1946 the exchange rate was to reach 4.6×10^{29} Pengo to the dollar. That is written down in long form as 460,000,000,000,000,000,000,000,000,000 a figure that certainly boggles the mind in trying to understand its size. To give you an example, the estimated number of grains of sand on earth[8] is around 10^{20} which is less than a trillionth of the dollar to Pengo exchange rate. Or to put it another way, the entire value of Pengo in circulation in the entire country at the pathological end of that currency was less than a single cent of one US dollar. This means that the quote from EuroTrip "A Nickel! Now I open my own hotel!" was at this time an understatement for the purchasing power of the dollar. And remember, that the number of people alive today who experienced this number in the 100's of thousands if not millions.

So, anyone with any cash had simply had it wiped out to zero with no recourse to anything at all. This was despite a desperate measure undertaken at the end of 1945 to tax the entire populace on a one-time basis at **75% on their net assets.** That was a demented idea in, and, of, itself but it still had next to no effect at all. Why did it have no effect at all? Because inflation had skyrocketed to such a degree that the entire extant money supply was effectively worth zero in "hard" currency like the US dollar. This is a key point to note; that under extreme inflation even the state appropriating pretty much everything does very little to stabilise things because confidence in the currency is essentially zero so no cash confiscation measures that are not in a hard currency[9] can possibly be effective. Such is the absolute demon of hyperinflation, and that is why deflation whilst being nothing to write home about, is not even a footnote when compared to extreme levels of inflation.

---

[6] I am using the English term for the currency as a convenience which is not written with an accent. In Hungarian the Pengo was written as *pengő* and meant "ringing".

[7] This is a key point which will dominate much of our discussion later on. For now, let's just say that gold or silver standard is a term that applies to a currency is backed one for one by gold or silver.

[8] If you are wondering how I know, I used to ask people that I interviewed for Goldman Sachs this question. You can take some estimate for the area of desert and beach that exists in the world, come up with some idea for the depth we are talking about and then multiply those together to get a total volume. Then divide by an estimate of the volume of one grain. To be honest, you can easily be off by 10 or 100 times in these estimates in aggregate and at Goldman I would have accepted any answer from around 10^{16} through to 10^{22} as the logical process and arithmetic was more important than the exact answer.

[9] This being for our purposes simply any currency that is not subject to significant (greater than say 7% a year) amounts of inflation.

But at this time there are those amongst you who will say something like the following. "Well everything you have said thus far is all well and good, but Weimar was 100 years ago and even the Pengo crisis ended over 70 years ago. Since then we have seen so many developments that the economies of today are utterly alien to those 70 years ago. How can we compare these crises to those of the past? Furthermore, you have said little about how these crises came about. Well you would be right but this is quite deliberate because as we spend more time looking at these things, we will need to remember is that whilst technology has developed a lot, and economic theory has also developed, human psychology and gullibility is something that has not changed, and nor has human greed and avarice. If anything, it has grown due to problematic education systems (particularly in the west) which have significantly reduced emphasis both on logic and on mathematics as well as academic discipline, and have descended into politically correct quagmires that would have their place only in the midst of Dante's inferno. In addition, the access to credit has increased dramatically, and what credit does is amplify economic mistakes aggressively. It also allows significant growth almost magically manifest itself in otherwise weak economies because of course it amplifies success. We will say more about credit as we examine the situation of today in detail, but for now we simply note that credit is both astonishingly easy to understand and simultaneously, often rather misunderstood. By the same token it is also both incredibly useful but is also responsible for terrible suffering. It should also be noted that there was hyperinflation in Zimbabwe just over a decade ago, to the extent that the country was forced to dollarize in 2015[10]. The highest denomination note that Zimbabwe issued was 100 trillion Zimbabwean dollars and at the time of dollarization, you could get 40 US cents for it[11]. We will not talk explicitly about Zimbabwe because I am concerned with discussing developed countries because the mantra exists that this could not happen any more in developed countries, that this was a phenomenon of yesteryear. But to allow us to understand this properly, we need to study some more. So, this is how we will continue to progress. We will consider later whether these examples of hyperinflation scenarios could possibly happen today because of things like the Quantitative Easing programs conducted by the Federal Reserves and other Central Banks. For now, we move on to consider the case of the UK.

The UK, a former glorious Empire on which "the Sun never set", and the Welfare State.

The UK, or as it was known in the 19th and early 20th centuries, the British Empire was the dominant power in the world before the US. Whilst the US has probably been the great superpower for around 100 years (basically since the end of the 1st world war), the British Empire was preeminent in the 100 years before that. The UK was the "forge" of the industrial revolution and became so powerful in the 19th century that by 1900 it had obtained an Empire on which "the Sun never set" because, of course, it was so global that it was always daylight somewhere within its environs. In 1900 the UK represented and commanded around 25% of the world's GDP with the US and China each at around 12 percent. It was a force to be reckoned with and was probably the first truly global superpower (depending on how this is defined Spain might claim that honour, but this is contentious). If we now zoom back to the present day, the UK represents just 3 or 4 percent (depending on whether we are looking at things on a fully loaded PPP basis or just in terms of USD optical GDP) of the world economy. The massive relative contraction of the UK's economy by almost 90% is beyond the scope of this book (clearly making various once colonies such as India independent had a huge effect etc.) but the key here is that the UK was essentially the embryonic model for many of the worlds modern democracies, and therefore there is instruction to be found from studying its policies and fortunes over the 20th and the early 21st centuries. More specifically, we will focus on the various social programs that the UK (as well as other democracies) pioneered. We begin by considering the welfare state.

The idea of a Welfare State is very simple. It is exactly like insurance was when it was first conceived. You take a pool of people and combine a certain percentage of their earnings (the taxes) and in

---

[10] It has since tried to reintroduce its own currency but with inflation at 200% at this point in time, it is unclear whether this will succeed.
[11] Ironically however, these days you can get 20 US dollars or more for one in good condition on eBay!

exchange if one of them gets sick and cannot contribute to the economy, some of these taxes are used to pay for their care and livelihood. In addition, if anyone is unable to work at a given time due to illness or simply just unemployment, the state provides several benefits to allow them to survive. Finally, the system is designed to protect individuals who are elderly and therefore unable to contribute either. It's a good system, and despite what some of the naysayers will say, it **can** work at least in principle.

The reason for this is that there should be very little "friction" in the system as there are few additional costs. If it turns out that the statistical assumptions are not working for example (e.g. there is a new epidemic of some disease that was otherwise unknown) then the costs of welfare become a little bigger collectively, but this would hopefully be somewhat mitigated by savings made during periods that were relatively quiet when no great plague broke out. However, because there is no one trying to make a profit here and taking money out of the insurance ecosystem there is no real loss on average. The savings that are made during the quiet periods can be invested in a waterfall of assets which will provide income and allow for additional protection when there are more issues and more people suffer. This is exactly how things like fire companies started in England. Post the Great Fire of London in 1666, the various fledgling insurance societies created brigades to deal with fires of buildings that they insured (in the first instance, they did nothing about fighting fires that were not at buildings that they covered), and then this was eventually taken over by local councils and then the government. Again, the absolute risk of fire for insured buildings was not particularly large, but it made sense to pay for someone to protect the portfolio of buildings insured by a specific insurance society.

In theory, a government providing pensions, healthcare, and national insurance should work exactly as described above, but the weakness is as follows. Suppose you don't want to work but are otherwise perfectly healthy. Or you feel that you don't want to go for a higher paying job that is double your current hours because you would lose your benefits and hence your incremental increase in salary is close to negligible for a much worse quality of life. With regards to insurance this is analogous to conducting an insurance fraud such as claiming you are disabled when instead you are perfectly well. However, with insurance the company has assessors whose job is to ferret out those that wish to commit fraud. Not only that, but once a fraud is identified, insurance companies often exchange information on those who are potentially causing issues. You also have serious penalties, both criminal and civil that can result in exceptionally bad cases here.

But with a welfare state it is your choice – not that of the state. Whilst you are supposed at least to show evidence that you are looking for a job to qualify for unemployment benefits, there are many ways around this rule and enforcement is extremely lax. Thus, when the UK government capped the maximum benefits that could be received by any household to 26,000 pounds (it then reduced this cap just recently at the start of November 2016 to 23,000 and 20,000 for those in London and outside London respectively), this by itself resulted in a significant number of people returning to work according to the bank of England[1]. Human beings do tend to mostly take rational actions when confronted with this kind of dilemma.

Also, going back and looking at insurance for a moment, you are generally obliged to take a medical and the cost associated with the insurance is also based on your lifestyle choices but with the welfare state there is no requirement to behave in a certain way. Welfare overall therefore doesn't have the checks and balances to allow the money to be used efficiently and therefore the friction that exists is very high. There is a huge benefit when buying insurance in being a person who has never smoked, doesn't drink, and is not particularly overweight. But when it comes to the national health service, there is no assessment of lifestyle for coverage or any payment to be made and therefore there is no financial incentive at all to live a lifestyle that is less likely to mean significant hospital costs.

Finally, there is a very controversial subject which is the issue of providing the very best possible care in terms of things like the latest medication. This is a major issue because the simple fact is that medicine on the very edge of knowledge is expensive in the extreme. This does mean that an effective and inexpensive health system would, by definition, need to exclude the most radical experimental programs from being made available. This is a very clear issue because where would one morally draw the line? However, the simple fact is that resource usage would dictate that these remedies are not available. A related point is that for experimental medicine to be affordable, a necessity is that considerations for the side effects of a potential drug are curtailed from the formidable hurdle that they present today. I.e. there should be some balance struck between the risks of side effects and the benefits of getting a medicine out of testing sooner rather than later, and therefore with far less R&D cost leading to lower cost for people. One could argue that it is here where individuals who are of sound mind should have some flexibility to be able to go for the option that makes the most sense. If one is mentally capable of assessing the risks associated with the side effects of a given drug when supplied with the relevant information, then one should have the option to take part in a clinical trial that might otherwise be regarded as being unsafe. Whilst it is true that a physician must follow the oath of Hippocrates to do no harm (something that Google fails to properly take to heart), people should have the choice to attend experimental programs even if they are potentially dangerous, if they assess that this is the best choice for them. We cannot let health and safety guidelines infringe on the basic freedoms that humans have at least with regards to choices that might lead to a better outcome - assisted suicide being one that clearly doesn't fall into this category given that result of going down that path is already known.

But as human life expectancy improves in part because of the high quality of medicine that we have today, we see a situation where the demographics of the world are working against us. Manifestly people are living longer but they are not necessarily active at full capacity for much longer. That is, many people, more than 50% of people in the west whilst they may have a life expectancy of 80 years still retire around the age of 60 or 65. This means that their pensions are required to fund, on average, their lifestyle for around 15-20 years. As we shall see very soon, this would imply that they should have been setting aside something like 30-50 percent of their income for their pension on the basis that they would have a 40-year working life and need to be able to cover 60 years of expenses on average from that work.

However, the average pension saver does not set aside anything close to this amount of money for their pension, which means, on balance, most people will have exceptional shortfalls to deal with. This is especially true of those who will begin to retire in the next 15 years. These are the people who are following the so called "baby boomers" This, in turn, puts further pressure on the workforce as pensioners are forced to work to support their meagre income. This also puts additional stress on the workforce system because those who are coming close to pensionable age will be disincentivised to retire on time due to the fact that it is always extremely difficult to restart a career once the decision to retire has been made. In general, human beings try to be safe rather than sorry and therefore would push to stay in employment for the longest possible time. This in turn reduces the chance for promotion for younger employees who are themselves forced into retiring later which further propitiates the paradigm. And this brings us neatly to the next bugbear of modern-day demographics and that is pensions.

I would bet my pension on it...

The pension system worldwide is very similar to the welfare state in that the intended structure is that a group of people put away some percentage of their wealth today in savings in order to fund their life post retirement. Again, the idea is simple and could work. During ones working life, one puts aside a certain percentage of their income pre-tax into a fund which is then administered actively to be able to have a decent return. At the end of ones working life, one uses the money in the fund to provide for the needs of the individual. It should be possible to work out quite quickly the amount of money that should be saved in a pension. For example if one needs X dollars to live on per year and their expected lifetime beyond the retirement age is say 30 years, they would need 30X (on average it would be less than this because the part of their investment not being used could earn a return during the 30 years - however if we adjust for the costs of inflation and also note that the fund would have to be placed in the most conservative assets during that time to ensure that there was no capital deterioration, then the approximation is, if anything, aggressive). Now if their expected working life is for example 40 years, they would need to save ¾ X every year. That would be a large percentage of their income. If their working life were only 30 years instead (i.e. they needed to get advanced degrees before starting their careers and wanted to retire at say 60) they would need to save X every year. The reality is that the majority of people in every country in the world do not save even close to 20% of their salary every year and therefore, without working post their retirement, would have to live on a very small fraction of what they lived on during their working lives after they retire.

In the past, this was not the case. The reason was simply because people died much earlier. When the UK passed the Old Age Pensions Act of 1908 this initially led to pensions of 5 shillings (per week) to those over 70 who had a yearly income of less than 31 pounds and 10 shillings who were also of good character (yes there was, apparently, an exam). In the context of today's money this is equivalent to around 15 pounds a week (although one should adjust for costs[12] which meant that its equivalent buying power was higher) and was deliberately selected as a very low number as the government wanted people to continue to provision for their own pensions. However, it should also be noted that at that time, the life expectancy in the empire was 47. This meant that the cost to the state was very low relatively speaking at the outset at least. Whilst it is true that certain professions (such as policemen who had pensions from 1890) particularly in the public sector had pensions in the 19th century, the reality is that a full pension system has only been functioning in the UK for 70 years. This follows the National Insurance Act of 1946 being the advent of a universal contributory state pension system which was, and still is, funded by National Insurance Contributions. The interesting thing here is that new-born boys when universal pensions first started in the UK would have been drawing them for less than 10 years by now. This illustrates one very concerning thing about any pension scheme – that they need to survive many different changes (since that Act the UK has both voted for a Common Market and has now voted to leave the EU, lost an empire, and fought in two world wars to name but a few events) in politics and demographics to be called successful. Unfortunately, however, most pension schemes globally speaking are massively underfunded currently. This applies to both public and private schemes. The picture looks even grimmer when we consider that this is the case **after** a period of exceptional demographic growth and before a prospective time of potentially disastrous demographic stagnation. Not provisioning well enough for the long term is a result of what I call the "Steady State Fallacy" which is something we will discuss in more detail later.

Thus, it simply beggars' belief that the pension funds are so ill prepared and poorly funded for the demographic paradigm that is to follow. But again, this stems mostly from the fact that human beings are very bad at thinking about things on scales that are not within their day to day experience – i.e. any time scales that cannot be conceived as a few weeks or a few months at the most. The reality of financial planning is that it should be prudent and robust over 50 and 100-year timeframes, but very few funds and pension funds care at all about these considerations because they pay bonuses to employees every year and not every 20 years or more. This means that the managers of a pension fund are not at all aligned to the needs of the investors. They therefore make decisions that may or may not work in the short term but regardless are very unlikely to work in the long term.

They make some assumptions about long term returns and then proceed to sort of ignore them by liquidating stock assets during market dips and buying up such assets during rallies. This ends up costing pension funds far more money than if they were simply to passively invest and fund themselves very well. The same is true for governments, who fail to plan or provision over a long period of time because, typically speaking, they have an election to fight every four or five years and therefore their

---

[12] Today the number of available resources, assets, and services is much higher, and generally to do almost anything you need at minimum a mobile phone and an internet connection as well as electricity, to pay VAT, and a number of additional taxes.

efforts tend to be very tactical rather than strategic. A quick fix rather than something permanent and therefore likely to be a poor solution.

The "culture of now".

Because we live in a society which is addicted to immediate gratification (you must have the latest Iphone now rather than when your old Iphone stops working, you cannot do without the latest flat screen TV immediately rather than when you have enough to afford it from your savings), very few people are willing to work for a pension fund that won't pay bonuses until 20 years of provable successes have been realised. What they do instead is work for the fund that pays bonuses now because they have lives to live and bills to pay now and, of course, because they are also people who have been affected by the prevailing culture of "now".

The entire developed world has become obsessed not just with materialism and things, but with immediacy. Gone are the days where one would work hard, scrimp and save for a specific purchase, now more than ever before people are encouraged to purchase things to make their lifestyle "complete" regardless of the quality of their financial position. Whether it is the latest smartphone or a new car, or even a beach house, there is a sense in which people are far less happy to slowly work towards a specific goal. As such, not only have many material goods become overly inflated to due to demand fuelled by the overborrowing that came out of such tribute to immediacy, but these material possessions have also become far less satisfying when achieved.

This should not be surprising to anyone, as the satisfaction of a long-term project is an entirely natural thing. The human condition is such that the anticipation of something is often much more enjoyable than the thing itself. All of us suffer from this to a lesser or greater extent. In fact, much of our happiness is anticipatory rather than existential. By this I mean the following. Suppose that you are looking forward to going on the holiday of a lifetime to somewhere that you always wanted to go. In the days and weeks before your departure you spend time imagining how much fun you will have. You joyfully pack your bags thinking of exactly what you will be doing with every piece of clothing or bottle of sunscreen that you place in your luggage. Eventually the day itself arrives and you excitedly board your plane ready to have the best time ever. If you look back on how you felt before going on holiday you will find that you were indeed very happy during the weeks before the trip despite the truth that you were not actually on holiday at the time, you were simply looking forward to it. At the same time on the holiday itself, even though you do enjoy the experience a lot, you might find in the quieter moments that your thoughts drift to coming back home and having to go back to work and spending time catching up and how hectic things will be. When you look back on your time particularly just before you leave for home, you will find that you were potentially even less happy when you were on holiday than when you were not on holiday but anticipating what a good time you would have. This is far more than simply optimism taken to the extreme, it is a necessary part of the human experience to be able to look forward to things. We need to be able to do this because otherwise we cannot psychologically survive things that are traumatic or stressful. This has been well known since ancient times, but William Shakespeare put things far better than anyone as was his tendency:

"The happiest youth, viewing his progress through. What perils past, what crosses to ensue, would shut the book and sit him down and die."[13]

---

[13] Henry IV Part 2: Act 3 Scene 1

And arguably the most succinct and palpable description of the remedy for this comes from the words of Jesus Christ as written in the book of Matthew[14] 1500 plus years before the play Henry IV was penned:

"Take therefore no thought for the morrow: for the morrow shall take thought for the thing of itself. Sufficient unto the day is the evil thereof."

So, something that is intrinsic to the human condition is that we cannot look at the totality of the bad things in our lives and genuinely just take them on the chin. The only way to deal with them is to regard things each day at a time and deal with the issues that arise there. If we can manage that, then we will find ourselves surviving first a day, then a week, and then months, and then years, and finally decades. This may seem paradoxical because now we appear to be arguing completely against the previous idea that the "culture of now" is a bad thing but really this is not the case. You see, many have pointed out the problem with this cultural phenomenon which is more commonly known as short termism. There are people who have argued that this short termism is the single greatest threat to the west, but they fail to realise something very important that the "culture of now" is not simply dangerous because it leads to tactical decisions, it is toxic because it seeks to take a process that is well understood (e.g. saving money for some purchase) and collapse it to nothing. It is not wrong to make decisions that solve a problem triage style, but it is wrong to look to make gains without the required sacrifice i.e. to expect something genuinely for free.

There are also many situations where looking at things over the long term does not work at all. These include situations where predicting developments over a great timeframe is just too hard to be done. When this is the case, the value of a long term view is almost nothing because there is just no way to simulate things forward in a way that is definitive for us mere mortal humans[15] and therefore any conclusions we come to that is based on our estimates may be wildly wrong, and any strategy we might choose to adopt now is unlikely to be effective. So, when many of today's philosophers argue that we need to somehow think and consider of the needs of those living 200, 300 or 1000 years from now, they are right only technically. Yes any analysis should take this into account but the ability of a human being (or any intelligence with the exception of that of God Himself) to see what the issues would be even in 50 years from now is so limited that trying to look at the long term when it comes to grandiose ideas is the very definition of folly, and anyone who claims that we can do so has far too much hubris for their own good.

To put it another way, short termism is actually very useful as long as those using it obey one golden rule which is to take into account both the cost and the benefit of the tactical decision, as well as the potential benefits of waiting for things like technology to improve. As a simple example for this, it would have been possible for the US to have gone to Mars in around 1990 if it had continued to develop various technologies at the pace that it was developing them for the moon landing. However, the cost to do this would have been extraordinarily expensive, at many multiples of the cost of the moon landings, and therefore it made sense to wait for technology to develop organically and have a chance to do this more (relatively) cheaply, 50 years later. Simply put, the benefits of doing it were no longer manifest. The US had won the space race, and the Soviet Union would never recover from that defeat, so there just wasn't the appetite to mount such an expedition at the time.

Taking the potential for improved technology into account is always something worth doing, as the US itself found out in a very small matter with the aluminium lightning rod atop the Washington Monument. The 100 oz pyramidal structure was made of Aluminium and at that time it was the single

---

[14] Matthew 6:34 as written in the King James version of the Bible. Not the best translation by any means given that it was published in 1611 and we now have access to far better as well as far more manuscripts in the original Greek. However, it is without a doubt a masterpiece of the English Language in its lexical beauty.
[15] And despite what you may have heard, the classic example of this is Climate Change. We will discuss this ourselves later on.

biggest Aluminium object ever created as Aluminium was very difficult to extract, meaning that Aluminium was worth as much as silver (and on the day of purchase it ended up being significantly more than if it had been silver). The year was 1884 and just two years later, two different scientists Charles Hall in the US, and Paul Heroult in France would independently come up with the same electrochemical method to extract it from Bauxite for a fraction of the previous cost. If the builders of the monument had waited, they would have been able to save significant costs (although in the context of big government spending this nowadays would be regarded as a mere trifle). There are many, much more significant examples of tactical mistakes, but you get my point. Short termism is not a bad rule of thumb, assuming we properly take costs into account. And this is a critical thing to consider.

There is one other truth about human beings that should be self-evident if you think about yourself whoever you are. Human beings are, in general, lazy. Humans are, ironically speaking, extremely industrious at being lazy. This may seem like a contradiction in terms, but it is true. If you consider the lengths that some people will go to just to avoid doing their homework or to evade certain chores, you wonder whether it would not have been far better to simply do the work that you were supposed to in the first place. But this laziness has consequences. And these consequences are everywhere in life. This indolence stems from something inextricably linked to the human condition which is evil. But that is something we need to talk about later.

Why supermarkets and Airlines love to give you "Loyalty Points".

Almost everyone belongs to some kind of "points club". Most of us belong to multiple clubs with accounts and passwords, and club cards. And very few of us really make good use of these points in an efficient manner. We may ask why not? Surely, we should be very excited to do this. But the fact of the matter is that we very rarely have enough time or desire to properly and aggressively make use of all our points. This is because we don't really see them as something valuable in any real sense and that is because we are lazy. We are continually weighing up the hassle of trying very hard to use our airmiles in a way that properly benefits us versus just letting them lapse or using them to enhance a flight that we have already bought instead. Most of us only see them as a bonus, and we never spend any time thinking about our points. And that suits the airlines just fine. They factor in our laziness into the points that they give us, expecting that we will not use them completely and let most of them lapse. They appear to be very generous in dishing out points because they know that we feel good about point when we get them but that we will never use them. Another secret that the airlines have, is that in order to balance the planes, it is most convenient to have people evenly distributed between the front, the centre, and the back of the plane. In order to do that, they are often willing to upgrade people for free into Business or First class if those classes are empty. But this encourages several people to book economy flights and then just spend time angling for an upgrade. In order to deal with this, it makes sense for airlines to offer upgrades based on a miles spend. This maximises the number of people paying for a premium seat, because people no longer expect to be given a free upgrade, but it also gives the airline a way to balance the plane as it were without getting a reputation for free upgrades.

Now why have we discussed this? This is simply to show that human beings really are lazy in their actions especially when it is to do with things that they didn't really see as being earnt in the first place. If the points were simply a sum of money that was paid into a separate account where the point holder was given an ATM card and was able to decide when to take that money out, they would be far more careful with their points. Instead, as they stand, people's psychology is such that they don't see it as money not just because it is harder to spend that particular money, but because people didn't ever see it as money in the first place because people don't value points and didn't set out to generate them with that purpose. When you don't earn something over time and strife, you do not tend to value that thing very much. This is one of the reasons why lottery winners are disproportionately likely to bankrupt themselves compared to those who have earned their wealth or windfalls. Whilst studies have also shown that winning the lottery makes people happier (which seems to be a foregone conclusion), there are many examples of those who simply could not manage such money, and that should not be surprising either. When something is the result of blood, toil, and tears it means just too much to you for you to lose it. But if it is a result of a chance event, you are far more likely to throw caution to the wind with regards to trying to keep it.

Demographics in the land of the Rising Sun.

In order to illustrate some of the effects of the demographic problem that we have described it is pertinent to consider the situation of Japan which is already suffering from exceptional demographic issues and China which probably will see the worst ever demographic collapse in history towards the end of the first half of the 21st century (unless one rather grizzly factor prevents this). Let us begin, however with post war Japan.

With the enforcement of the Constitution of Japan on the 3rd of May 1947, the sun finally set on the Empire of Japan (which arguably had become one in 660BC even if that is somewhat of a stretch). The country still had a nominal Emperor (Emperor Showa better known as Hirohito in the west) who had remained installed throughout WWII and would continue to reign until 1989. However, with the new constitution Japan had become a democratic state. For almost another 5 years until the San Francisco treaty of April 28th, 1952, Japan remained occupied by the US. It was not until a decade post the end of the occupation that Japan began a period of very rapid economic growth continuing over the next 30 years ushering in an era of exceptional prosperity during which time it grew from a GDP that was approximately 3% of the world to almost 10 percent. During this time, Japan created the Shinkansen which became the preeminent rail network of the world. Starting with the Tokaido Shinkansen with a line from Tokyo to Osaka opening just 10 days before the start of the 1964 Olympic games, to the hosting of the 1970 expo in Osaka, and the creation of a whole host of exceptional companies and products, Japan raced towards the future faster than even its own rail network could carry it.

At the end of the 1980's Japan appeared to be at the top of the world. The Nikkei had hit 40,000 and the mantra in the west was that Japanese was the most important foreign language to learn. In addition, scores of companies in the west actively tried to emulate that which was perceived as the vastly superior Japanese business model. There were countless books and documentaries published to explain how Japan had effectively taken over the world and furthermore how to emulate it. There was never any talk of a bubble, just a new and exceptionally powerful way to do business. But, sadly, a bubble it truly was.

Anecdotally speaking (and yes you will have noticed that I love these little vignettes here and there) the bubble economy of Japan is best represented by the situation in Roppongi the famous entertainment district of Tokyo where on Friday nights the only way to get a cab was to hold out your hand and show with the number of fingers you were sticking out how many 10,000 Yen notes (at the time around 80 USD) you would be willing to give the driver in addition to an already very expensive metered fare for the privilege of getting home in his standard Taxi. Remember this was in the late 80's so people were willing to pay up to 1000 USD or more in today's dollars just for the benefit of being able to go home in a very cheap and cheerful Toyota Crown. Any betting man that saw this would have to have concluded that the economy was, at the very least, overheating.

Very quickly after this the metaphorical dams burst. Firms in Japan had indeed been growing, but that is all that was going on. There was no underlying profit to that growth it was simply production of goods for the sake of production. The grand house of cards finally began to collapse at the start of the 90's with several high-profile corporate failures. Over the next three decades (up to and including today) there was a continuous attempt to stimulate the Japanese economy all to no avail, and whilst it was initially not obvious why all attempts had failed, it soon became clear that there was never going to be strong underlying growth to the Japanese economy because the Japanese were simply not having enough babies.

Some quite radical economists have argued that the BOJ was essentially the cause of the property bubble that was the real harbinger of the overall bubble in Japan and that they were essentially responsible for bursting that bubble too. This isn't particularly radical – it is just very sound economics. But the radical bit is that the argument then goes on that the BOJ should have fixed the problem by injecting a massive amount of liquidity into the economy and essentially using it to recapitalise the banks who were in dire straits following the initial meltdown of the property market. Unfortunately, this then becomes genuinely bizarre as if right out of a manga cartoon strip.

If that were indeed what the BOJ did, it would not simply just have kicked the can down the road, but it would also have turned the can into a kettle bell. What it would have meant would be that every man, woman, and child in Japan would have effectively paid for the recapitalisation by the purchasing power of their capital and salaries going down. If, for example, the cost of recapitalising the banks had been, say 10% of GDP, the BOJ would have had to create 10% of the GDP of Japan. It would do this by "printing money" either literally via the printers or in cyberspace (by simply creating whatever it needed and taking it to deposit). So now if the total money supply in Japan were before this 90% of GDP as an example, the money supply would now be 100% of GDP, meaning that any individual who had money in a bank would effectively have a reduced share of the money supply. If this sounds simply as if it is socialising losses into the general population it is because this is *exactly* what it is. It is a way of making the public pay for the problems of the government. It is, however, much less unpopular than taxation because human beings are usually bad at really understanding the mathematical implications of an increase in money supply on anything other than a theoretical basis, and because we are inherently not good at spotting things when they are gradual and don't appear right away, and as we shall see this is exactly what the west has been doing since the Global Financial Crisis hit.

Remember the old anecdote about a frog in water. If that frog is thrown into hot water right away it will likely fight continually to escape. But if that frog is put in water that is only very gradually heated up, the frog doesn't notice at least for a while. Well human beings are like that when it comes to their purchasing power. If their food costs a very little bit more year in year out, it will take a while for them to notice. This is where increasing the money supply can appear to be fine and even reasonable even though it is, in fact, a massive redistribution of wealth from savers to the government. We will consider this in more detail because the above is an example of an utterly deleterious concept (more of a notion really) that is called Modern Monetary Theory.

But Japan is lucky.

However, you might say to yourself; "well I've recently been to Japan and it is an exceptionally well-functioning place" For a country which has had several "lost decades", it does not seem so much the worse for wear. You can roam the streets of Tokyo and very seldom see any real indication of the lack of affluence. Sure, there are some places with homeless people and some poor areas but, by and large, Tokyo is more impressive than any of the big metropolises of the west with regards to the apparent quality of life of its citizens. Furthermore, the countryside sports probably the best infrastructure in the world for that sort of environment. Things certainly don't seem that bad, at least on the surface. And, in fact, after a more thorough investigation we find that things are much better than would be predicted simply by looking at raw economic numbers.

Well this is all at least partly true, but unfortunately this is due to a few factors where Japan is a very special case. The first factor is simply the overall national identity and social coherence. The national identity in Japan is so strong that there are huge swathes of the population that are perfectly willing to do things that are truly altruistic for the good of the whole populace. This is pretty much unique to Japan as a function of the percentage of the population and is manifest in various ways. We see this to an extent in shops like the 7 elevens which almost universally across the world are filled with sullen, disinterested people who are, quite understandably focussed somewhere else entirely. On occasion, you do see some exceptionally service minded workers in these shops but rarely. In Japan, however, it is almost the exact opposite. Whether the cashier or worker are in their last year of high school, or aged 90 or almost any age in between, there is a politeness and a focus that I have never seen anywhere else. Almost every woman or man work cheerfully and diligently in every job that exists in Japan focussing on doing the job to the very best of their ability. And when it is investigated as to why there is this meticulous attention to detail, most often cited is the sense of not wanting to let people down; whether it is parents or friends, themselves, or simply "the nation of Japan", there is a huge sense of pride and of belonging in the country. Another example was the response of a group of old age pensioners to the Fukushima disaster who volunteered for the clean-up of the Number one reactor on the basis that they had already lived most of their lives and therefore radiation would be of much less relevance to them as compared to younger people who still had their whole lives ahead of them. It is exceptionally hard to see this happening in almost any other country in the world (certainly not voluntarily – I would not be surprised if this was imposed in North Korea, but it wouldn't be because the people felt comfortable doing this) and is a testament to the unique (amongst such a large population) feeling of Japanese-ness that exists in the country. This general cohesiveness that comes from such a tangible feeling of Japanese identity should not be underestimated when it comes to the behaviour of the Japanese in the financial markets and elsewhere. Such a close knit "face" of a country is only usually seen during times of acute stress such as wartime in most countries but in Japan it mostly stays this way.

The national identity and feeling the need to do their bit for their country has led to an environment where the response to chronic financial stress is almost identical to what it would be if there was acute financial stress. This has meant that citizens, and domestic pension funds and other entities, were all willing to purchase government bonds whenever called upon. Not because there were consequences to not doing so but because it was the "Japanese thing to do". As such this has continually put pressure on the yields of government bonds supporting the ability of the government to issue at reasonable yields even as the debt to GDP ratio ballooned higher and higher. Some have argued that the Japanese show of "face" is simply a veneer, but it does seem to be far more than that and if it is a veneer it is robust and of high quality and little of this has flaked off since the start of the difficult times in the 90's.

The next important factor that has prevented Japan from imploding has been the fact that, of the main G7 countries, Japan has been the first in the world to go down the twin paths of extremely low rates and thoroughly weakened demographics. With regards to low rates, Japan began on a path of rate cutting at the start of the 90's. The bell-weather five-year interest rate swap rate (basically the deposit rates one would expect to receive over a 5-year period if a financial institution lent its cash to a strong Japanese bank) hit their highs at 8.5% on the 19ths of September 1990. There followed a protracted total collapse of the rate down to 2% at the end of 1995. From that point it steadily decreased (with a few reversals but never back above 2%) to a rate in 2016 of a measly -0.2%. Yes, that's right, minus 0.2%. That means over a 5-year period one would expect uncollateralised cash to return minus 0.2% per annum from being left on deposit with a bank. So, you could leave your cash under the mattress and do better than putting it in a bank account – at least if you are a bank. We will talk a lot more about negative rates and what they really mean later, but for now we should note that Japan was the first to see these typically far lower medium-term rates. As a comparison, at the end of 1995, 5-year swap rates in the US were just below 6%, in the UK around 7%, and in Australia they were at 8%.

The consequence of a protracted period of lower rates in Japan meant that the Yen became the funding currency "de choix" as the market for borrowing in Yen was deep simply because of the fungibility of borrowing. As long as the currency you need to borrow is deliverable (i.e. there are no currency conversion or any such restrictions), you can simply borrow in a different currency[16], convert it to another, and so now you have the currency you wanted in the first place. Investment banks since the early 1990s could transform borrowings in Yen into much cheaper borrowings than you could otherwise get in other currencies. The way they did this was through a structure which was called a cross currency swap. Now many people will tell you that cross currency swaps are very complex instruments which

---

[16] Often but not always in the currency native to whichever country happened to have the most accommodative lenders for you.

require a lot of expertise and time to understand. These people are categorically wrong – either they themselves never really thought about the product and don't understand it, or they know exactly what it is and are scared that people will come to understand just how simple it really is.

The best way to understand a cross currency swap is by example. Let's say for example that you are a company and want to borrow 100mm USD for say 5 years. Let's say furthermore that you are a company of very high quality and your bank has no problems lending at the risk-free rate that it lends to other banks. This means that you can borrow money at Libor flat i.e. libor +0%. This libor rate is an acronym for the London Inter Bank offered rate and represents as we have mentioned before the rate at which the highest quality banks would lend cash to each other uncollateralised. The expected rate of Libor over a 1year or a 5year or a 10-year period trades as the 1year 5 year and 10-year swap rate respectively and as we have seen the US 5-year swap rate at the end of 1995 was 6%. This means that you would have to pay 6% every year to borrow USD.

What if you wanted to pay a lower rate was there something you could do? Well if you were willing to borrow in JPY as you have seen you could borrow at 2% instead over a 5-year period. Now actually the rate wasn't really 2% as being a US company you would only be at the highest possible credit rating in your home currency at least in theory, but let's ignore this factor for now as it can be shown to be relatively small versus the big picture that we have here. One strategy that you could do to cheapen your borrowing is to borrow in JPY and swap it out back into USD. This means that you go to a Japanese bank and borrow for 5 years at 2% fixed and then you would have a much lower interest loan. Furthermore, it would be several times lower than the US loan so that even if the Yen strengthened versus the USD, the interest payments would still be substantially less than if they were in USD because you would be paying 3 times the USD amount so the Yen would have to triple in value for the payments to be the same which is unlikely. Looks like a perfect deal, right? Well as we know there is no free lunch and I am sure that you have seen the issue with this type of deal. Whilst the interest payments are clearly preferential, the principal payments would be where you could lose your shirt. Because you still have to pay back the full amount of the loan that you borrowed so if you converted it to USD to buy your asset you have essentially made one very big bet that the JPY would not appreciate. Of course, you could be right in this bet and be totally fine, but that is where the risk is.

So now we have Japan, with intermittent ultra-low or even negative yields on its debt and swap curve but with a debt to GDP that has never been seen in the history of the world for any state that is not in default. Historically speaking, most states would have failed by the time that they had accumulated such a big amount of debt. In fact, states in general would historically have failed far before any such level of debt was attained. It is simply the reasons that I have highlighted above that have meant that Japans debt bubble has not exploded with nothing left to be seen. There are indications though that this may be beginning to change. When it finally does it will have consequences for far more than Japan and far more than just Asia. In fact, the bond bubble in Japan could burst more powerfully in terms of tangible impact on the populace than either of the bombs that caused such devastation and destruction in Hiroshima and Nagasaki (as an aside in the continuing debate of whether the US should have exploded the bombs to end WWII my view is definitely not and that a show of force in devastating, for example, mount Fuji would have saved 200,000 lives potentially but we can never really know). In a cruel twist of irony, it could be a different kind of "nuclear" explosion that could destroy the economy of the US coming from an ally that used to be a deadly enemy, and in this case, entirely unintentional. But there are other pockets of danger waiting to destabilise the world economy even more concerning than Japan, and one of these is China.

China

China is a truly fascinating place. It is a plethora of contradictions and can be viewed through an almost infinite number of different lenses, but one thing that is not deniable is that the country has succeeded more than any other so far in taking vast tracts of people out of poverty and providing them with the basics of first world living (proper sanitation, white goods, the internet, and all other modern conveniences). This success is unprecedented in time not only in terms of the number of people who have been moved out of poverty, but also in terms of the speed that this took. Many families were transformed within the space of a single generation or even quicker than that. Of course, this titanic task involved a cost and that price was many different things including the abomination that was termed "the cultural revolution" by those that advocated it. Another part of the price that was paid was simply the pollution that China took on by becoming the manufacturing engine of the world. Cheap goods come from abundant and plentiful labour, but they also come from buying the cheapest possible fuels (no matter what toxic substances remain after their use) and incorrectly disposing of by products and spent equipment. Thus, China has stored up very long-term problems that need to be addressed. The government there recently agreed to spend 1 trillion RMB to begin to deal with this issue (even the government admits that 20% of the rivers in China are toxic and another 40% are seriously polluted[17]). The question, however, is addressed by who?

And here we come again to demographics, and specifically for China the One Child Policy. The One Child Policy (or OCP). This policy was created only recently, in 1979 (three years post the death of Chairman Mao who was an advocate of the opposite). The idea was initially that this policy should only be extant for a generation, but it is still in place today (although slightly relaxed). It is possible for people to pay a fine to have a second child, and those in the countryside are allowed a second automatically (minorities also have even more lax rules), however overall for China the average birth rate is 1.4 per couple. This is still significantly below the rough rate of 2.1 which is necessary to maintain a population for the long term.

Yet the Chinese population continues to grow – but the number is not all it seems. The population of China is growing simply because of the dramatic changes in life expectancy from 36.3 in 1960 through to 75 in 2011. This is over a doubling of the life expectancy and has meant that the population has continued to grow. But the population pyramid doesn't look like a pyramid anymore and by 2050 it will be a mushroom with a huge percentage of the population over 60. And there is no going back to the population pyramid precisely because so many people have been taken out of poverty, and with this there is now no pressure to have a large family. In the past the pressure had been out of the need to have others to till the land. Now with a huge generation of aspirational Chinese who want their children to do better than they did we see choices made to limit the number of children to allow those children to have the best. This means that, in line with the mathematics of population dynamics, we have crossed the Rubicon and China is likely to see probably the worse demographic distribution of any country ever with roughly ¼ of the population supporting the rest. Of course, there are mitigating factors as always (those whose life expectancy is 80 are often able to work until their 70's etc.) but the rub of this is that China will simply not be able to support a middle class by the middle of this century. Couple this with an already massive and widening gap between the rich and the poor and we have all the ingredients for a civil war. One might say – well China and Japan are very different to the United States, and this is certainly true indeed. However, as we shall see the mathematics is genuinely the same for almost everyone and that is because maths is universal and not subject to the social, political, and philosophical policies of any country no matter how powerful it is.

The US – unprecedented unfunded forward liabilities.

The US is already bankrupt under any reasonable set of assumptions or metrics. Just as it is impossible for a corporation to remain solvent if it loses money year after year, it is not possible for the US to have a budget deficit year after year and claim that it is somehow going to be okay down the line due to economic growth. The analogy here is a company that has a negative profit margin claiming that

---

[17] https://www.chinadialogue.net/blog/6726-China-s-water-pollution-will-be-more-difficult-to-fix-than-its-dirty-air-/en

selling more of its goods will make it more profitable – selling more of its goods will, in fact, accelerate the path to bankruptcy. Of course, an economist would argue that debt by itself is not the problem and that it is the percentage of debt to GDP that is the problem, but the US is already at many times its nominal GDP in terms of both its bond debt as well as its unfunded liabilities which come in the form of welfare, pensions, and medical assurances and benefits.

In the US, the concept of the American dream is breaking down. Whilst this is going on, a sort of welfare state has been conceived this is leading people to the most destructive behaviours. Due to the lobbying of the car companies, it is extremely easy to borrow to buy a car and so we see towns like Detroit with people having brand new cars but living in rented houses paid for under Section 8 with rents going to landlords that are seeing up to 50% yields as returns depending on exactly where these properties are.

The fundamental breakdown in substantially all current welfare states is simply this. The entire idea is predicated on the assumption that people who are physically and mentally capable of working hard are willing to work hard. This, however, is not the truth of this world. Whilst there does exist tenderness, empathy, sympathy, and people who are willing to help those who cannot help themselves, the system is abused by those that could help themselves but choose not to because the system is there to protect them. For example, the current super high rates of unemployment amongst the young in Europe[18] are exacerbated by the fact that whilst there are low level jobs available, the availability of unemployment benefit means that many are unwilling to take these entry level positions because the initial net benefit to them is relatively low. This has the double effect both of impoverishing them faster, but also affecting their future earnings. If you have no employment history or experience, you cannot command better salaries going forward. Heck, if someone were simply to start working in McDonald's they could be a manager at the same organisation within 10 years at the very latest, and then 10 years further down the line they could easily become an executive or a franchise holder. But if they do nothing for 10 years, they would still not be qualified for the McDonalds manager position as they have no experience. And of course, when someone is 10 years older, they are even less attracted to an entry level position than they would have been a decade before. This has the effect of keeping them in a perpetual benefit trap.

What this means is that an entire generation in the first world is growing up addicted to benefits. This leads to an even bigger dependency going forward and we see a two-tier system basically in existence with a small group of "elites" that are very well off and the vast quorum of the world basically failing to make the middle class. Those that could still be regarded as in the middle classes are also disappearing with taxes so high that it is almost impossible to maintain a middle-class lifestyle. As such many who would regard themselves as middle class drop out during their lifetimes, whilst a very small proportion manage to stay there, and an even smaller fraction break out into the elite class.

Now to some extent one can argue what is wrong with this setup and this book certainly is not attempting to make a judgement on this, but I am pointing out a simple fact. The entire system of welfare currently in the majority of first world nations is an engine for destroying the middle classes and engendering dependency in those with few resources. This would certainly not have been the design at all, but this is the simple result of the policies that were followed; policies that gained an increasingly large number of votes in elections.

Unfortunately, this means that there is now a new version of the serfdom of the middle ages in existence which is functioning. We are all "free", but we still must pay very large percentages of our income to the state who provides the basic benefits equivalent to what the lord of the manor did in the past. Some would say that the analogy is somewhat stretched but it is a good one because there is no ability to opt out from the system. There is no ability to say; "I will provide all my own support and pay for everything

---

[18] https://www.spectator.co.uk/2017/07/spains-lost-generation/

that I use but you should not tax me". Exactly because of this, the analogy is not simply that it is the modern-day equivalent of serfdom for a large proportion of the world's population. The only ones that are not affected by this are the "lords of the manor" who are those who have sufficient wealth that they can avoid paying a large amount of the taxes that would be owed through creative accounting and other techniques, and especially because they are subject to capital gains rather than income taxes. But again, this leads to more inequality and a polarisation of society causing the exclusion of the middle class. If, by some good fortune or other way you manage to break into a group that has 10-20mm USD income consistently, you have a good chance to be able to grow your wealth aggressively. Anything else, and no matter how much you try you will eventually fall away and out of the middle class.

With regards to the much-discussed Affordable Care Act, the legacy of Obama is being destroyed even as we speak. Donald Trump has quite rightly assessed that Obamacare needs to be changed but the issue is that there cannot be a good and cheap healthcare plan in the US anymore because the US is so litigious that doctors have to charge outrageous amounts of money to see patients because the premiums that the average doctor has to pay for liability insurance is now in the millions of dollars. This makes everything a lot more expensive with the only beneficiaries being lawyers that don't add any sort of value to the whole sorry affair. The biggest issues with the affordable care act itself that I personally have is that it provides care to a whole bunch of able bodied people whilst reducing care for truly disabled people[19] many of whom would have loved to have a job and pay their own way in life but can do very little due to their disabilities as well as prejudices and other issues.

The mathematical fallacy of human demographic assumptions.

Human beings have a problem. We only live for around 80 odd years. There are some exceptions like my grandmother who is 99 (I hope and pray, of course, that she will live to be 119) but this argument works well enough over a 100, or 120-year lifespan also. This is one of the great problems that human beings have. Not only because it would be great to live longer to accomplish far more than you could with your given years, but also because it leads to a terrible mathematical fallacy. Or to be more exact this is not a fallacy, but more a problem with perspective. Human beings are often good and analysing things which occur on the scale of a few days or even a few months. We are much worse at processing and dealing with things which occur in a few years, and we very often fail to predict or pre-empt things which occur over a period of years of the same order as the length of our lifespans.

Why is this? Well there are many reasons, but the most obvious is simply that we often understand phenomena and cycles better if we experience them and that experience remains fresh in our minds. This does make sense especially as our memories tend to fade aggressively over even the period of a decade. And that means that our assumptions about what things are unlikely to change over a specific period of temporal measurement that is far longer than that of our usual experience are often wildly inaccurate. It explains much of the short termism that we have talked about and the dangers associated with it. This also explains why I found 2008 much easier to deal with and less surprising than almost of my colleagues. Most of them worked in G7 currencies and did not trade the emerging markets very much if at all; even those that did only traded one or two markets and not the entire gamut as did I. As such they were unaccustomed to events such as the global financial crisis. However, I had been trading the markets in Poland, Hungary, Turkey, South Africa, Brazil etc. In these countries, a crisis was far more common than in the G7 with such events happening so often that, on average, I had seen more than one country in crisis every year of my trading career before the financial crisis. In fact, the events of 2008 were only surprising in that they affected almost every G7 market but fundamentally, I was trained

---

[19] https://www.foxnews.com/opinion/obamacare-medicaid-expansion-hurts-people-with-disabilities-and-the-seriously-ill

to expect crises relatively often and therefore was able to deal with one better than those for whom it was truly a "black swan" event.

This issue also applies to other phenomena particularly in science where we must do extreme amounts of work to analyse those events which take place over much longer time periods but for which we only have a small amount of extant data. This touches all sorts of areas and the more perceptive of you will have recognised that "climate change" is likely to fall into this category. This is one area where our computer models are trying to predict changes over 100s of years but without that data being already there. We do have data from the past, but the data even 75 years ago was far less accurate than it is now. This would be fine if we were seeing average temperature changes of multiple degrees, but when the issues are over fractions of a degree, we need to be very careful indeed when looking at old data. The fact is that there is no one alive today who was taking temperature data as their job 75 years ago, and so we don't have perfect assurance of what those numbers were during days when much more manual work was needed to get a good reading. The same thing will apply in 75 years unless we take special care to document today all our processes and ensure they are compensated for in minute detail as time goes by. And when our politicians seem to be making decisions based on theoretical changes of fractions of a degree, we are required to be certain of our findings before we make a declaration. But much more about this later.

To look at an even more striking example just look at the explosion of data storage capabilities that we have witnessed over the last 50 years or so. In 1962 Phillips created compact cassette tapes. That was not even 60 years ago. Yet today how many of us has a tape player in their home? I certainly don't. Maybe you do, but you can see my point. Larger cassettes were used to store data for computers. Since then data storage has gone from that to 8-inch floppy disks (created in 1967 by IBM[20]), to the 5.25-inch floppy (invented in 1976), via 3-inch (in the 80's prevalent on Macs and IBM PCs), through compact disks, to DVD, and finally to various solid-state devices, breaking into the cloud that we have today which uses servers with hard disks and other solid state storage methodologies. You can clearly see the issue. In 100 years whatever medium is used to store data is likely to be very different to what we use today (although it may well still be some kind of solid state device and some version of the cloud but not necessarily the same as today– if you don't believe me just think of a time in 50 years when viruses on the net abound and the cloud 3.0 storage system exists that has quantum virus protection that is AI guided.) with different protocols and is very unlikely to be backwards compatible. If we cannot even store data over long periods of time using a universal medium, how much harder is it to think about and understand phenomena that take place over many years?

Now what we really do when we fail to appreciate phenomena on a scale of our lifetimes is make assumptions about the so called "steady state" situation and assume that because we see little change over a number of years or even a couple of decades that we should be in the steady state situation even though we know this steady state situation is only manifest over many years. So, we will call this phenomenon the failure to identify the steady state or SSF (steady state fallacy) for short. We will see the importance of this fallacy later when we discuss socialism and communism and their abhorrent consequences.

Sitting pretty in the bosom of the Middle Class

An interesting phenomenon tends to happen when people have some money especially if this is sufficiently abundant for them to be considered middle class in the west. Instead of displaying a tendency to have more kids because they can look after them better, they tend, if anything, not to have more kids, but to educate those kids and build for the future. They also now have access to better medical services and therefore they tend to live longer. This means that a country with a large percentage of the population joining the middle class tends to then have problems subsequently in

---

[20] https://en.wikipedia.org/wiki/History_of_the_floppy_disk

terms of the demographics of that country. Some countries notably the United States and the UK have had liberal immigration policies which have cushioned this blow, but Japan has had a very restrictive immigration policy, and this has led to the demographic issues that they now have.

At the start of the 20th century the fertility rate in the developed world was far greater than it is now. Consequently, we saw the world population jump exponentially because at the same time standards of living were improving and now people were living longer and almost all children survived to adulthood. At this point in time, every country in the western world is either in the stages of population peak or even over the hump. The state furthest along the road of depopulation is, of course as we have already discussed Japan. The Land of the Rising Sun being so homogenous and coherent has refrained from supporting its population through immigration and has accepted an ageing and dropping population. Around about 2010 the number of people in Japan peaked at just over 128 million[21] and began to drop slowly but surely to reach 126.7 million as estimated for 2017. Now this is hardly a precipitous drop, but this was the first drop over a 5-year period since the Second World War which took its toll on population. Unless there is some significant change in policy within Japan, the population will continue to drop to below 100 million by 2100[22], but more importantly the population will continue to age as Japan already has over 26% of its population over the age of 65.

So, for the world population we expect linear growth until we reach a steady state world population in around 30 years at around 11 billion people at the very most, and probably somewhat less than this maybe around 9 billion. This is a huge number but let us be clear on things. At that point, without fertility rates increasing we expect the population to remain constant and even begin to fall. If it does so, we should expect world GDP to go down all else being equal. No longer will an increasing population be able to mask economic failures. We will see GDP under pressure, and we will have to look to Improvements in productivity to be able to take us to higher levels of GDP. And yet, there are many who are concerned about a world population "bomb". That the world population will simply explode out of control. And these people are falling into the steady state fallacy. For the most part people have assumed that because the world population has been growing significantly in their own lifetimes, that this will continue ad infinitum. And yet fertility rates in the west are such that this cannot be the case, and even in the third world things are changing radically in the direction of stabilising population. The data is clear. World demographics as a result of more and more people leaving poverty are beginning to turn.

The replacement rate for the human population is for every woman to have around 2.1 babies. This is firstly because it takes two humans, one male and one female[23], to make a baby and therefore you need two of them to replace the two humans over the long term. The reason the .1 is there is simply because there are accidents and other things which mean that some offspring do not make it to sexual maturity in order to reproduce. And the problem is, as we have mentioned, as soon as people do make it to the middle class, they do tend to stop having many babies due to costs and because the probability of survival of offspring is incredibly high in a modern society. This is also because the states in the west now have so many entitlement policies, that it is no longer the case that the average citizen feels the need to have children to help them when they are old. The government now is the carer and therefore why have children? And in case you thought that this applied only to the first world, the fertility rate in India at 2.2 essentially means that the population there is going to stabilise and that in a country where there is still a lot of poverty and incentive to have children. The same is true in almost any country in the world where the middle class is growing or substantial. In fact, Africa is the only continent where there are significantly high fertility rates such that the populations will be growing substantially even in

---

[21] https://en.wikipedia.org/wiki/Demography_of_Japan
[22] I simulated the population forward in time myself having made certain assumptions regarding the behaviour of families and assuming that Japan is already basically fully developed in terms of the middle class.
[23] And no, a man cannot be a woman and a woman cannot be a man at this stage of scientific developments. Changing the DNA of a human isn't currently possible in situ to go from male to female or vice versa.

the medium term. The top 20 countries in terms of fertility rate are almost all (18) in Africa (with Afghanistan being the big outlier)[24], but Africa is coming from a relatively low population base (at 1.1 billion), and even there, fertility rates are dropping very quickly. There is no reason not to expect that, as quality of life, access to birth control, and other factors continue to improve Africa will also fall to the demographic challenge of being in the bosom of the middle class.

This will have an impact on everything. This will have an impact on assets such as houses. You see this already in Japan. Real estate has stagnated since 1990 in Yen terms and generally the only places that have seen significant price improvements have been areas that are truly exclusive in Japan. These include the very best areas of Tokyo as well as unique places like Niseko (where Hirafu village is tiny but offers the best skiing in Asia). But overall if you were a property owner in Japan over the last couple of decades you would not have done well from the price appreciation point of view. The lack of growth in house prices in Japan is a direct result of the demographics that exist in Japan. Houses simply cannot grow, unless you invest significant money in them, and apartments certainly can't so therefore their prices (at least versus inflation) cannot be significantly higher because housing stock would have to go down in a country with demographics that are negative for house prices to go up. And this of course is extremely unlikely because owners generally do not tear down their buildings due to lack of demand. After all, land is strictly less valuable than land with a building on it and therefore it is extremely unlikely that a housing glut would be resolved quickly unless the population resumed an upward growth cycle. And in Japan this is very unlikely indeed.

Don't hesitate, emigrate?

In general progressives on the left are very quick to advocate for any immigration at all as the "golden cure" for any and every demographic issue. They are so militant about this that they are even prepared to argue that illegal immigrants should simply be given a path to citizenship despite the obvious problem that they committed a crime to become illegal immigrants in the first place, and thus are quite unlikely to make the fine, upstanding citizens that a country might desire. It should be of no surprise that progressives want this, because if there is something that they desire even more, it is power, and with illegal immigration comes illegal voting which almost always favours the left. But let's pretend that their argument that any immigration at all works to alleviate demographic pressure has some merit and investigate it shall we? We soon see that it doesn't work in many obviously pathological cases. For example, a large influx of very low skill immigrants into Japan would not help its economy much at all. Those immigrants would find it almost impossible to find jobs suitable for them in Japan given that even the lowest skilled jobs require strong Japanese language skills and a customer service ethic that is second to none. It is ironic that it is the innate Japanese identity that would get in the way of foreign unskilled labour from working in Japan, as this makes the homogeneity of the country both its greatest weakness as well as its biggest strength. So, the only hope that Japan has in terms of demographics would be for highly skilled immigration to take place. And if fact this is what we see happening right now. However, this solution is only going to limit the demographic drop and not stop it entirely as Japan is, quite rightly in my opinion, focused only on those with the greatest skill sets. This has the advantage of meaning that the demographic issue is somewhat mitigated but without any deleterious effect on its support systems. Quite the opposite in fact; immigrants with significant skills sets brought in to fill specific jobs are very unlikely to ever need things like unemployment benefits and so will be net benefactors rather than beneficiaries. In this way, Japan hopes to convert a destabilising force which is immigration (due to the immigrants and the natives having quite different philosophies and ways of life as well as upsetting the balance of the jobs market etc.), into one that stabilises and serves its own ends.

This is not the only trick that Japan has up its sleeve to deal with its demographic peculiarities. The country has made one of the most aggressive pushes towards the technological development of things

---

like robots and automated systems that will allow the elderly to be cared for without the need for carers per se. Whilst the country has been close to the leading edge of robotics and high end electronic systems pretty much since the end of the 1970's, the direction now is very clearly towards this end given the demographic issues that Japan currently faces. Of course, whilst it is tempting to believe that automating a nursing home will solve many issues, all of us who have spent some time working in such places either professionally or as a volunteer, will know that sometimes people just want the human connection; somebody to listen to them, someone to talk to, and to seem important to others. Whilst the people of Japan will, no doubt, soldier on even if they are forced to live out their old age in something akin to a hospital staffed entirely by robots and AI, no doubt this solution wouldn't work well for other countries which are likely to have similar problems. For them immigration might be the only solution, but this comes at an exceptional price and unless it is done right it will lead to far more harm than good. Even in situations where the people immigrating somewhere are culturally similar, great issues can arise if the sheer numbers (relative to the size of the place in question) are substantial enough and this can have unintended consequences such as the issues that affected the German economy post reunification. But immigration is not the only destabilising force that is in the present ecosystem of the world economy. Another extremely important one is the presence of debt which tends to blur the lines between what we call money and real, substantive, assets.

What is debt, and for that matter what is money?

Well we have been talking about assets, and we have been talking about keeping an economy going and demographics, but we haven't really talked about what money is and how it parallels with debt. Debt is one of these things that very few people properly understand, but again, it is not something that is inaccessible to logical thinking. At its most basic form, debt is an IOU. It is someone either a person or an institution promising to pay a certain financial sum at some point in the future. In fact, these days, the currency of most countries is simply debt in a different form. What do we mean by this? Well originally, when coins were first created, they were made of precious or semi-precious metals and their value was simply the value of the metal contained in the coin itself. So, the currency of a given country or state could be compared directly with that of another simply by looking at the metal content of each of the relevant coins. Thus, merchants from all over the world were able to trade with each other relatively easily knowing that they could measure the weight of the coin they received to verify its value. This meant that for a king or an emperor to issue coins, they were obliged to have the gold, silver, or other metals to produce the coinage and thus there was a universal value ascribed to any given currency. Of course, coins made of gold were worth much more than coins made of silver which, in turn, were costlier than coins made of copper, this being simply a function of the difficulty of being able to find the ore and refine the metal. It is worth noting that this generally meant that there was some stability between the effective exchange rate of the different metals as, for the most part, it was difficult to bring more of the precious metal into the market due to lack of modern machinery and refining techniques. These days, according to the world gold council[25], around 2750 tonnes of gold are mined each year which add to around 190,000 tonnes currently above ground in circulation. This being just under 1.5% of the total circulation, it's clear that more than half of the world's gold was, in fact, mined during the industrial age. So, in ancient times, gold was indeed exceedingly rare, as was silver, and their effective rate of exchange was almost fixed. This is first documented during the reign of Sargon of Akkad[26] 4000 years ago where 8 pieces of silver were worth 1 piece of gold. And throughout ancient history, this was roughly the case. This fact is something that will be very important to us later in our journey, and something of a "canary in the coalmine" with regards to the global economic situation. But for now, let's continue our story.

---

[25] https://www.gold.org/about-gold/gold-supply/gold-mining/how-much-gold
[26] And I mean the original Sargon of Akkad not my favourite youtuber

Money continued in this way for a couple of thousand years at least, and then, during the Tang dynasty (618-907AD), merchants in China found that it was not highly convenient for them to carry coinage about their person[27], so they began to keep their money with a trustworthy person who would issue them a receipt saying how many coins they had with the person (who in turn would charge a small fee for safekeeping). This became what we call a promissory note. Eventually, by the 11th Century during the Song Dynasty "Jiaozi" or paper money was created. This money was still a Promissory Note but issued by the government, and these promissory notes are what we call paper money at this current time.

If you don't think modern money is a promissory note, then just look at any British piece of paper currency[28] such as the five-pound note. Above the signature of the Chief Cashier of the Bank of England, there is the statement "I promise to pay the bearer on demand the sum of five pounds". Well what does that mean? This IS a five-pound note, why does it say it promises to pay five pounds? This is because all British currency isn't really currency at all. It is a debt. It is saying that the government will use some of its income from taxes to pay you that debt if called upon in the future and therefore you can use this note as money to pay for the services of others by giving the note to them and thereby handing over the debt. The whole world now functions on promissory notes.

In the past, this was not a problem. For example, in the US you had the Federal Reserve[29] issue silver certificates (between 1878 and 1964) that were redeemable in silver in the form of say a Morgan dollar. This meant that owning these promissory notes was equivalent to owning the silver in a dollar coin because the government would exchange one for the coin for you. However, beyond 1968, they were redeemable only as Federal Reserve notes which essentially converted them back to simple promissory notes. However, scroll forward to 2019 and we now have a world where every G7 currency (and pretty much every other one also) is fiat and not backed by anything. Currencies are literally only worth the paper (although usually has cloth mixed in) that they are written on and therefore currencies only retain value based on the confidence that people have regarding the credit worthiness of the issuing country.

In the past, you kept paper notes for convenience because (like the Tang dynasty merchants) it was simply easier to store notes upon your person if you wanted to carry a lot of money. You never worried that the notes were not worth anything because you could walk into a bank whenever you liked, give in your notes, and walk out with a bag of silver or even gold coins. Each dollar was around ¾ of a silver ounce and just under an ounce of gold was a 20-dollar coin (the famous double eagle). Because of this, the US was always obliged to have enough gold and silver reserves to cover the money that was in circulation in the form of notes. Note that they weren't obligated to have all this precious metal in coins that were readily available, simply they needed to have the gold and silver in bars so that coins could be produced if required. And because everyone knew that the government had the metal available, there was relatively little demand for the coins because of convenience.

So, we can essentially consider debt as a promissory note, and consider real money or cash as something which is backed by something tangible, such as gold. Notice that even if the money is the form of a note, as long as the government or entity that has issued it has the gold or silver (or any other physical object backing it) in their coffers and is keeping it safe for you (such as in a depository receipt[30]) this is still money. It still has the backing of something real, something solid, something that has intrinsic value to it.

We have been talking about money and now we have a robust understanding of it. It is a means by which we value all goods that exist and the work of the labour force. But for us to see how genuinely

---

[27] They were obviously so successful with so much turnover that they felt all this coinage was far too burdensome. This, in the present, would be called a first world problem.

[28] Now plastic, sadly.

[29] Prior to the creation of the Federal Reserve it was, of course, the US Treasury that issued the silver certificates

[30] As long, of course that there is a one depository receipt for every piece of gold that exists in that depository.

strange Modern Monetary Theory is, we need to obtain more intuition about it. To do this, it might be helpful to think about it with an analogy from the world of Particle Physics. It might seem counterintuitive to think about something relatively simple by considering an analogy with something complex, but we will be able to obtain more insight in this way.

Money; The Higgs Boson of Finance.

The discovery of the Higgs Boson was a great moment in the history of Particle Physics. All those who were involved in both the theory predicting its existence, and in the experiments that were developed to prove that it was a real thing, rejoiced at the discovery. The reason that the Higgs Boson was so very important, was because, in the theory that we call the Standard Model in physics, there is a requirement in the mathematics for the Higgs Boson to exist in order to effectively define the masses of a cornucopia of elementary particles that have already been discovered. For this reason, the Higgs Boson was nick-named the "god particle" as it was effectively a master-key that could be used to define all the other masses of fundamental particles through its interaction. How exactly this works is beyond the scope of this book[31] but I might write something about it at some point.

Money is analogous to the Higgs Boson in that it is the metric by which value is ascribed to everything in the world. It is what makes it possible to compare the value (or cost) of a massage versus say the price of a movie ticket, against the price of a car. When barter systems existed, there was very rarely a price for everything that was consistent. Prices were not transparent because it is hard to value say the cost of a wooden house in terms of the number of pigs that the house might buy. If you weren't a very good negotiator, or just not savvy enough, you might not get sufficient value for whatever you brought to the table. But with money you suddenly have a much better benchmark to work with and you no longer have to be so careful in conducting your business because value is just that much clearer when there is a universal scale out there as a metric for comparison.

The relative value provided by money has made things much more efficient overall and has been the medium by which Capitalism has worked. You no longer needed to have the gift of the gab to be able to negotiate a good barter deal for whatever you wanted. Because of money and capitalism, you are able to get a deal without really trying. You have much better sense now of the absolute value of things and you are also able to get things cheaper because everyone else can assess the value of things and a successful business breeds competition from others who want their "piece of the pie". This competition gives you the best and most transparent pricing for any purchases that you want to make. The advent of money was far more effective at equalising prices at least locally than even the internet revolution, simply because of the ease of having a single base to view value. What the internet did was make everything effectively local, but it didn't tighten local pricing in many areas all that much. It was money itself that did that a very long time ago.

But of course, money is different in each different country, so it is quite natural to assume that over time the world will progress towards one currency. But the wind of change is not inexorable as some might think, and the world ebbs and flows in terms of this goal. In fact, it can be argued that the world functioned much better when everyone was on the Gold Standard but had separate currencies that could be repegged at certain times if necessary. We will talk about what this means and the implications for the financial future of the world later in our thinking. For the moment, let's consider what money means for the individual countries and their ability to provision for their citizenry. How are we supposed to think about that?

A country as a company

---

[31] Maybe one day, I together with my father should write a book to explain what the Higgs Boson really means in much greater detail and to give the history of its prediction and discovery.

In many ways we can regard a sovereign nation as a company. A company has shareholders and a country has citizens. Aside from the fact that citizens of a country cannot sell their shareholding, and they are also the clients of the company, and hence pay in money (in the form of tax) for the services that they receive (such as the roads, medical insurance if it is supplied, state pensions etc.) Just like any company, the directors (the government) are entitled to change aspects of the operation and are responsible for keeping the company solvent. One big difference between a country and a company is that the country can, if it has its own unique currency, print its own money and therefore could, in theory, remain solvent whatever the situation that takes place. Whilst that might seem to be a solution to many of the problems that a country might have, in fact it isn't. You see, for a country to have social stability it needs to maintain confidence amongst investors and the public in general in terms of the purchasing power of its currency. As we have seen in the example of Weimer, citizens become very stressed indeed when they feel that they cannot purchase basic commodities that they need to live on at an at least relatively stable price. If, for example, the price of eggs was to double every six months, the average person living in a country would worry that they would not be able to afford to live in the long run and therefore they would get stressed. If enough ordinary people get sufficiently concerned about such matters, they will begin to at least think about protesting. If the issues of prices of basic goods continue to manifest themselves, then even very otherwise law-abiding people will start to complain leading to civil disobedience and even rioting eventually. In addition to local price stability, there is the requirement that the currency of a country remain stable versus those of other countries. This might not seem to matter initially, and indeed it does not with the specific proviso that the confining country in question is both self-sufficient, and none of the inhabitants feel the need to travel. For the US, for example, the value of the USD in other currencies matters relatively little – the US is able potentially at least to feed itself and provide its own energy autonomously, and in addition, relatively few people are travellers to outside the US except for tourism (which is a luxury experience and therefore far less likely to lead to significant frustration should it become prohibitive for individuals to undertake). However, for the vast majority of countries where these conditions do not apply, a weak currency versus others will not be good and will lead to various social and economic issues.

But why does printing more of its own currency lead to a weakening and unstable currency and unstable prices? Well simply because if you double the money supply at will and all else is equal, each unit of the currency that you increased should halve in value both at home and abroad. In practice as many (in fact pretty much all countries that are not on a specific commodity based standard such as the silver or gold standard) nations print money all the time, continually increasing the money supply, there is a sort of race going on between governments as they print money at different rates and this leads to the appreciation and depreciation of one currency versus another with a few different other things going on such as investment to and from individual countries etc These complications allow certain currencies to remain strong relative to their true value even as they print and print huge amounts of money. Post the global financial crisis, we saw much of this money printing in China without any noticeable weakening in the value of its currency because of all those reasons as well as the fact that the CNY is effectively fixed daily by the State Administration for Foreign Exchange (SAFE). We also saw this somewhat in Argentina, though over time the extent of the problem became manifest and 2017 through to 2019 saw huge amounts of both inflation and currency devaluation in that country.

Therefore, there is indeed no such thing as a free lunch. A country is free to print its own currency and that might seem an attractive option if that country has overborrowed, but again this ends up leading to much bigger issues going forward that could end up destabilising it. This is all just as we observed with the Weimar republic. The printing of money ended up destroying the value of the mark which was no longer backed by gold, and this led to the bad people seizing power. They got the power not because they were perceived as being good (most politicians for most of their careers are generally seen as untrustworthy, and at best neutral), but specifically because they were seen as agents for change and that change was needed at any cost. When you need and desire a transformation to happen, you often are willing to put up with barbarities that you would never even have dreamed of in the past as long as the person who has promised this change actually delivers it and this is especially the case when you have extreme inflation because there is nothing that you can do to protect yourself from it unless you have exceptionally good financial resources. And of course, this leads to the hellish ideas of Fascism and Socialism or Communism. But as finance has evolved, so have the tricks that central banks and desperate politicians use to print more money without appearing to print it. Which leads us to a very recent phenomenon which even 15 years ago would have seemed to almost everyone to be a flight of fancy. That of negative interest rates.

Negative rates and the obsession with GDP.

The new bugbear of the financial system is negative interest rates. We are all familiar with positive interest rates. Whether they are rates that you pay when you take out a loan, or those (increasingly meagre) rates that you receive when you leave your money on deposit the concept is very clear. Negative rates are just that. If you invest 1000$ at 1% a year in a bank account and revisit it in a years' time you would see that you have 1010 $ in your account at that time. If your account bears -1% however you would expect to see that you have 990$ in the account at the end of the year. This means that you pay the bank for the privilege of keeping your money (and use it to lend to others etc.)

This essentially acts as a tax on the wealth of anyone who retains savings for later use. However, the magnitude of that tax isn't just the negative amount of interest, as inflation itself is also a tax on wealth. Inflation, simply defined, is the average increase over a year of the cost of living as defined by an index that measures the increases of prices of a basket of goods and services such as the price of oil at the pump etc. This essentially means that the growth of ones' savings is always discounted by the increase in prices from inflation. So essentially, when inflation is, say 3%, the risk-free rate should always be above 3% in order to ensure that it is possible to see some sort of return over and above the inflation rate.

But when interest rates are negative, you need negative inflation to even break even in real terms. And in general, inflation is very rarely negative for any length of time. So, when the head of the ECB Mario Draghi announced on the 5th of June 2014 that the interest rate of its deposit [32] facility (with effect from the 11th of June 2014) would be negative (initially at -0.1%), there was certainly some concern in the markets. Whilst the deposit facility was only really relevant for banks[33] (and the ECB claimed that the negative rate was to encourage banks not to horde cash and lend it out), the overall benchmark rate of the ECB was also lowered and eventually went to zero. The lowest the deposit facility rate reached was -0.4% where it remains until the time of writing (Sep 2018).

Now this was the first time that such a large economy had any sort of negative rate. Negative rates were used before in Switzerland in the 1970's but this was specifically due to the status that Switzerland had as a "safe-haven and a tax haven" at that time. But the ECB did not have to impose such rates and their reason for doing it was quite unclear at least if you looked at what they themselves were saying about the matter. If Draghi genuinely was so concerned about getting inflation up, the ECB could have done other things. They did use Quantitative Easing later, buying a great deal of not only government bonds issued by EU members, but also corporate paper and other slightly riskier assets. So why would they impose negative rates?

There have been a few hints coming from the central banks, but the true reason is really something like this. Negative rates basically prevent long dated rates from getting too high. This is because if rates are negative, someone with cash is very worried about losing money simply from holding it. However, the person was probably holding cash because they wanted to save the money rather than investing in something riskier. So that person is concerned about losing money, and the result is that they look at government bonds and try to buy the shortest maturity of bond that is available with some sort of positive yield. This in turn begins to pull down the yields of short dated bonds, and as a result,

---

[32] https://www.ecb.europa.eu/press/pr/date/2014/html/pr140605_3.en.html
[33] https://www.ecb.europa.eu/stats/policy_and_exchange_rates/key_ecb_interest_rates/html/index.en.html

companies like insurance companies and banks are no longer getting an attractive enough yield on their investments. For insurance companies that generally need to earn enough return to cover their liabilities in the form of guaranteed returns as well as event pay-outs, this means that they are forced into looking at longer dated bonds. The same is true for banks and investment managers who weight up the balance between the yield offered by the bonds and where they can finance such assets. Banks will find it more attractive to purchase long dated bonds because their money would otherwise be doing nothing and earning a negative return, so they are willing to take a lower yield on their bonds.

What does this all mean? Well it means that government bonds become more expensive as more people are willing to buy them. As they do so, the government is able to issue its bonds at lower yields and hence higher prices. This means that they can get away with paying a smaller coupon on their bond and so their borrowing costs become much less. And this is the real gimmick of the protracted exercise. A negative rate is as if your local bank required you to put your money with them and then decided to charge you for the privilege.

There is also the view common amongst too many economists some of whom are central bank rate setters (such as Gertjan Vlieghe of the Bank of England's Monetary Policy Committee[34]), that negative interest rates should have been used during the time of the Global Financial Crisis. This is yet another indicator that the Central banks know that they are in trouble. The idea that rates should go negative is both abhorrent and unconscionable. There is never a situation in a functioning economy where you should not be able to get interest for your money. Not just because it is unfair to lend money and pay for the privilege, but because of the fact that negative rates imply that the Central Bank of whatever country is issuing a currency is unwilling to stand by its own currency even to such an extent that it is unprepared to provide even a zero return. It will only store your money for you if you accept to lose some of it and thus this is yet another tax on the populace in an unacceptable fashion. Not only does this tax the populace as a whole, but this unfairly penalises those who saved carefully in order to provision for the future. It disincentivises responsible citizenry. These people are the ones that have to suffer the most because they are essentially compensating the state for the bad decisions of others. They are paying for the financial incontinence of individuals that borrowed too much and didn't have their financial houses in order. They are paying for a group of supposedly intelligent financiers who care more about of the values of their houses than they care about the individual who has just a little money available and wants to try to save something for their retirement. In resulting to negative rates, the Central Banks have basically given up, and as we shall see, they really don't have very much left to fall back on and so perhaps giving up is really the right thing for them to do. That is exceptionally sad, but perhaps this was inevitable when almost no one in economics looks at anything other than a single figure that is represented by three letters; that of GDP.

Ever wondered why pretty much the only metric of economic growth that governments, and even the press, seem to look at is the Gross Domestic Product, or GDP for short? Well if you have, your wonderings are spot on. On the face of it, GDP would seem to be something which is a good quick way of measuring the health of an economy, but unfortunately it doesn't really hit the spot in terms of assessing how things really feel to the average person or family. The reason that governments and central banks appear to be almost singularly obsessed with GDP to the exclusion of all else is because the perceived wisdom is that GDP encapsulates in a single piece of data everything about the prosperity of a country. The problem with this is that GDP doesn't seem to really indicate how happy, contented, and prosperous the population really is. Why is this? Well for a start, GDP of a country is not per capita. Therefore, population growth by itself is more than enough to increase GDP even if wages do not go up and even if the productivity of each individual person does go down. Furthermore, GDP growth is only properly relevant when inflation is also taken into consideration. Obviously if GDP goes

---

[34] https://www.telegraph.co.uk/business/2016/04/22/interest-rates-could-go-negative-says-bank-of-england-rate-sette/

up by 5 percent but inflation is 10 percent one cannot argue that things are better because the cost of living has gone up by more than the increased economic product per person.

We also then need to ask why it matters that Japanese GDP is not growing if the population is also going down? Surely the GDP per capita is more relevant? However, the reality is that governments are not prepared at all for the demographic shift that is coming to almost the entirety of the developed world and, even more scarily, to the quorum of the developing world as well. These developing countries will, like China, experience a very fast collapse in demographic stability over much shorter periods of time than western countries did. This is because we already know how to make people live longer – access to medicines, good quality food, and decent living spaces with central heating and, where necessary, air conditioning. These things are achieved the minute people enter the middle class. In the past, all the necessary technology was not there so the middle class only gradually transitioned to being long lived (and therefore no longer needing to have as many children). The middle class that will emerge from the developing world will transition to averaging 1.5 children almost in a single generation. This might lead to crisis levels in the developing world before those countries have a chance to have any of the "good times" that the developed world has enjoyed. It isn't fair, but this is the world we inhabit. The question for the developing world is how best to manage this transition. And my answer would be aggressive capitalism without opacity – where prices are clear at all times and where the money supply is very carefully controlled in such a way that it is never allowed to expand exceptionally, and where social programs are focussed on those who cannot help themselves. And that bit about prices being clear, that may seem like it is self-evident, but we shall shortly show that it is not by any means a given that this is the case at all.

Sears anyone? Price discovery in the Soviet Union

Jump with me now to the time of the old Soviet Union as it was known, the formal name being the Union of Soviet Socialist Republics and hence USSR. Alan Bennett a man whose opinions are almost as orthogonal to mine as that of anyone alive nevertheless has his characters show some exceptional wisdom at certain times. Two quotes that come to mind are that "...Our perspective on the past alters. Looking back, immediately in front of us is dead ground. We don't see it, and because we don't see it this means that there is no period so remote as the recent past[35]." and "there is no better way to forget something than by commemorating it[36]." Now the first quote applies very well to what we currently remember of the Soviet Union. Few except the older generations who live in Russia and the Old Satellite states today really remember what the Soviet Union was really like. Even we in the West really bought into much of the propaganda that was floating around at that time regarding how advanced the economy was and how powerful their Space and other tech programs were. The CIA bought into this propaganda also having been under the impression that the GDP of the USSR before the fall of the iron curtain was around two thirds of that of the USA. They were wrong, very wrong. In fact, the best estimate of the GDP of the USSR just before the end was around fifteen percent of that of the US, representing at least a fourfold exaggeration by the best spy agency in the world. Everyone had bought into the idea that because the USSR was so comparatively successful in space and in the Olympics that it was in some way homogenous enough that it would be okay in terms of the standards of living of its populace, or the quality of their industry, but it was not true at all. We still even today do not quite realise how bad the old USSR does, and nor do the socialist loving left who quite happily would protest some topic whilst walking around carrying the old Soviet flag.

But what was the problem with the Soviet Union? Why didn't it succeed as a state the way that it succeeded in space and in Athletics or Chess? Well one of the most important reasons was touched

---

[35] Alan Bennet, "The History Boys"
[36] Alan Bennet, "The History Boys" – this quote is less apt regarding the USSR, but I still like the quote.

upon by Bruce Fairchild Barton, a two term US congressman[37] and an almost legendary advertising executive, the creator of Betty Crocker no less, who suggested that communism could be entirely dispensed with in the USSR if only the US would "Give every Russian a copy of the Sears-Roebuck catalogue and the address of the nearest Sears Roebuck outlet." There was a huge amount of truth to this with regards to the Soviet Union, because the fact was, that whist the top down direction construct was able to facilitate a few things at a high level, it was simply not adaptive enough to dictate everything because the free market didn't exist to properly price the value of goods and services. There was essentially no price discovery in the USSR. Oh, they bought various things from the west, but no one in the Soviet Union properly understood the mechanics of general prices for things and for services. One of the beauties of capitalism is simply the ability for the market to adapt according to changes in preferences and demand. But what people don't realise is that there is a corollary to this, and this is that prices are extremely transparent in a capitalist economy. In a capitalist modern economy, there are now literally apps such as Honey[38] that you can embed to find the best price at any time over the entire internet for a certain product. Now this wasn't the case of course during the Cold War, but the humble Sears catalogue was the forerunner to this. It was a brilliant idea for its time. The Sears catalogue first came out in 1895[39] and this, in tandem with an increasingly sophisticated US mail service was able to provide a retail solution to people in the US outside the cities. This debut was a game changer in the US and led to a massively increased uniformity in prices. Other things that contributed were the emergence of company branded products particularly starting in the British Empire. Prior to the 19th century if you went to your local grocer, they would generally have whatever they had purchased from various suppliers, but you had no knowledge of who those suppliers were. Going forward, as the industrial revolution began to allow improved transportation links and therefore the possibility of centrally sourced produce became realistic. From the middle of the 19th century onwards, manufacturers began to brand their products in order to demonstrate a uniform quality and therefore improve their reputation and insure increased sales. This again meant that price discovery was significantly Improved. Now you knew if you were buying "Mr Colman's mustard" that this was of a certain consistent quality and every consumer could now compare prices anywhere in the country, and eventually as transportation continued to improve, the world. Now you could purchase "Mr Cadbury's cocoa" both in the tiny grocery stores of villages in the Cotswolds but also in Singapore for example. You therefore began to have price comparisons across the world starting locally but becoming increasingly more global. This continued to improve throughout the 20th century with technology, and you ended up with every capitalist nation essentially having very similar products available at quite similar prices all things considered. In fact, even today there is such a thing as the Big Mac index[40] which is the USD equivalent price of a Big Mac in all the countries around the world that is used as a (semi) serious indicator of the fair value of various currencies across the world in terms of Purchasing Power. The idea is that a Big Mac is essentially the same everywhere (and as someone who has consumed this product in about 50 countries, I can say this is true) and therefore it is a uniform commodity for which to make price comparisons.

But in the old Soviet Union, they had no price discovery mechanisms at a time which was before the creation of the world-wide web. In fact, as noted by Michael Rieger in his essay "A world without Prices:

---

[37] Barton, a Republican, represented the Manhattan house district between 1937 and 1941 at a time when Republicans still had a shot in the Big Apple.

[38] And no, Honey don't sponsor me, but I like their product.

[39] Richard. W. Sears did have a mail order business before this, but it was somewhat limited in scope being focused on watches and jewellery until Julius Rosenwald bought out the interest of Roebuck who had been a partner with Sears.

[40] In my opinion, the single most important contribution to Economics by the Economist publication created back in 1986 by Pam Woodal. It was initially created as a sort of joke, to demonstrate Purchasing Power Parity, make of that what you will.

Economic calculation in the Soviet Union", Cato scholar Andrei Illarionov[41] who was studying economics under that regime categorically stated that there was no concept of even trying to look at prices at all – that the entire matter was somewhat taboo. This is not surprising as the entire economic system was designed in a way that made prices irrelevant. The idea was that a certain amount of a given product was to be made, and that this was the target regardless of how much effort was needed and of what resources had to be redirected to the cause. This is the very definition of a centrally directed economy but is clearly utterly inefficient. The entire thing could only work if there was a benign omnipotent being who could just immediately understand both the requirement of the people at a given time in terms of services and the resources available in terms of man hours. This is clearly something impossible, exactly in the prevue of God and therefore beyond man. But as we shall see later, this is perhaps what a lot of futurists are looking for in the future to come out of their idea of an AI "controller". This should be anathema to anyone, but some of the smartest people in the world do consider this to be a potentially ideal way to go.[42] Pricing will be very important in our discussion just a little bit later, but for the moment it is simply worth noting that the lack of price discovery is an obvious inefficiency and does not make for a very strong economic foundation. However, we should, at this point address the "tweepadok in the room"[43]

The Rhinoceros in the room

The big question that most readers would be asking themselves by now is something like this. "If you are right in asserting that most of the governments in the developed world are effectively bankrupt why is the market not reflecting this in much higher yields both for domestic debt and debt in other G7 currencies? This is indeed an extremely deep and pertinent question. At its heart, it is also really asking why the markets which are claimed by so many economists to be efficient are certainly not efficient in their behaviour in the real world.

This is partly to do with perception and partly to do with the way the central banks have been behaving. We have already talked about negative rates and how the western central banks have been using them post the Global Financial Crisis to supposedly prevent negative inflation. But this is only one of the tools of stealing money that the central banks have been using to try and get their governments out of the debt hole that they are in. Central banks have been buying an unprecedented amount of their own debt. This basically is a "Robbing Peter to pay Paul" strategy overall for the country concerned but has the added "benefit" from the view of the central banks of generating two very important phenomena. The first and most important is the increase in price of their own debt which leads them to be able to fund at better levels going forward hence reducing the cost of borrowing for new loans etc. and making their bonds appear healthier than they are. You may be thinking that a government might prefer to see cheaper debt so that they can buy back their liabilities much more cheaply in the future. This is correct but only if the government is truly solvent and has cash to do so. That is if it could liquidate its assets and have enough money to buy its own debt back then in theory it should always be doing this. However, the fact is that there are almost no "first world" governments now able to do this because they are all insolvent. Therefore, a much better strategy is to try to artificially raise the price of their debt so that they can issue more debt at much cheaper levels and then try and grow or otherwise spend their way out of trouble. The second benefit that is gained from the very balance sheets of the central banks going up in value – they will appear to be making a profit from buying their own bonds.

But it is not all good for them. Central banks get very scared as their balance sheets increase in size. They are not generally run by the best traders in the market because they don't pay even close to the compensation that the hedge funds or Wall street pays, and almost no central bank "traders" really look

---

[41] Sometimes economic advisor to Vladimir Putin. Not sure I would like that job.

[42] Images of the Samaritan AI in the series "Person of Interest" spring to mind.

[43] This coming from an episode of the Big Bang Theory when it was still just about funny i.e. before the writers turned the entire show into an exercise of the best practice of cultural Marxism and political correctness.

at anything except the longest term trends. Thus, they do become very uncomfortable as their balance sheet increases because even central banks are required to announce their P&L. Take for example the SNB, the Swiss National Bank which was forced to declare a big loss in 2015 as it failed to prevent its currency from appreciating against the EUR when it stopped defending the peg in January. The loss was around 23BN CHF which represents around 3.5% of the GDP of Switzerland. The loss came simply from its investment portfolios denominated in currencies other than CHF.

So, central banks are not very good at holding large balance sheets and their balance sheets are huge. If the Fed were to lose 1% of value on its holdings this would mean a loss of 35BN dollars – this happened on a single day in 2016. The 25 basis-point intraday move on the day after the US election for 10- year treasuries when applied (with some assumptions as the Fed doesn't tell us its P&L exactly) to the balance sheet of the Fed would have been a staggering 80+ Billion dollars in value change in mark to market. The exposure that the Fed has to a 1 basis point move is around 3.5BN USD! Given that the most senior market makers on Wall Street might have at most 3.5 million (and nowadays even less given the restrictions banks are under) this is an exceptional and unprecedented position and the Fed has almost no one who would count as being in the top rank of risk-taking traders.

It is the enormous unprecedented balance sheet positions that the central banks have accumulated that, more than anything else, are currently dictating the position of rates. Janet Yellen doesn't want to raise rates not because her economic analysis indicates that it is not a good idea but because she doesn't want to continue to lose money on her exceptionally large investments. If we are talking about Too Big to Fail, it is not the retail and investment banks that we need to worry about but the Federal Reserve, the Bank of England etc. And what is most scary is that there is no one else. The IMF has a healthy balance sheet but not even a percent of what is necessary to prevent the collapse of the central banks should confidence in them wain. And believe me, it is only confidence that holds them together because, whilst they can print money, that money is only fiat currency and not hard currency. And that applies right now to almost all central banks in the world

And much of this is because of the adherence to various pet theories of Economics that have been created to try to explain economic behaviour. Much of economic theory ranges from the truly evil to the downright stupid with a very small fraction of theories that make some sense and have a modicum of practical use in the world. I exaggerate, of course but only a bit. Frankly, most of the time I am tempted to think exactly like Katie Hopkins who, quite brilliantly described Economics as being "essentially wild guesswork articulated at authoritatively as is humanly possible in order to convince the maximum number of people you are right"[44]. Most of Economics is either a bunch of truisms knitted together in what often seems like just an attempt to make the resulting pastiche seem coherent, or some (usually quite basic) mathematics that is so far from modelling the real world that it might as well be trying to simulate the path of Voyager One using some marbles and a football tied with string. And now, I want to discuss one of the current darling theories of Economics that, in my opinion, has done more to damage the developed economies of the world than any other as it would appear to permeate much of what Central Bank thinking that is currently extant.

Modern Monetary Theory

Modern Monetary Theory is a relatively new pile of garbage added to the increasingly large number of very unfortunate and dubious ideas that increasingly mathematically illiterate[45] economists have come up with to try to explain the supposed economic miracle that has taken place over the last 20 years.

---

[44] Katie Hopkins, Rude (not that I am suggesting that she is rude although she might agree that she is. And in any case Hopkins wouldn't care less whatever I called her as she would simply get back at me with some, well chosen, quip.)

[45] Or, if you wish to be rather more charitable, Economists increasingly enamoured of mathematical formalisms rather than theories tied to reality.

The basic thesis of this theory espoused by a number of people who really should know better, is this; The central bank of a given country (assuming that country has its own currency and it is not at a currency board or a peg against another currency) can basically create as much money as is needed for the government to spend and thus the government of a country does not need to actually balance the books. Therefore, it is not possible for any government who can print its own money to go bankrupt. It is so simple; effectively Modern Monetary Theory is saying that you really can get something for nothing. It is saying that despite what we saw with Weimar, with the Pengo, and more recently, with Zimbabwe and Venezuela, that "This time it's different." It is saying that all my arguments of a country being like a company or a family are just simply wrong. Now let's mathematically destroy this "theory" without even resorting to anything that complicated.

Let us imagine a country that has basically provides the bare minimum of services in that country and therefore has a very small rate of tax indeed. Such a country might provide for basic sanitation and water services, roads, and a bare bones military and security complex. Let us also assume that the budget is balanced as it could quite easily be if just these standard savings were provided. This state would only need to increase its money supply as GDP went up; let's call this country Conservia. Furthermore, let's have another country that follows Modern Monetary Theory and therefore is increasing its money supply at will and call this country Momontia. Now let's just say that the trading ecosystem that each of these two states existed in was just these two currencies for the sake of simplicity. So, we basically are pretending that these are the only two countries in the world. No matter how many countries we use, we could make the same argument as we are going to make but it is instructive to use just two. What do we expect to happen as these two states evolved over time? Specifically, what should happen to the exchange rate between these currencies? The value of Momontia's currency would devalue significantly versus that of Conservia and over time the devaluation would be catastrophic. And obviously, all else being equal, if the money supply in Momontia were to double, then the exchange rate should also halve. After all, the value of the goods and services in one country in absolute terms really hasn't changed. What has changed before and after is the number of monetary units that explicitly represent the value of assets, goods, and services in that country. And this is all that has changed, just a number. At least from those looking in. And thus, someone in Conservia looking to buy a service looks at the cost of the service in terms of the currency of Conservia and will only buy that service in Momontia if the currency has adjusted to reflect the fact that the money supply has changed or if the price of that service in the currency of Momontia has not gone up. However, from the perspective of those in Momontia, they still think nothing has changed. They are still (for a very short time) willing to give their services and assets at previous prices. But suddenly people begin to realise that they are mispricing their own goods and services. Unexpectedly the government has a lot of money and therefore can afford to spend more, and this spend begins to drive up prices. Eventually, prices do adjust to reflect the increased money supply and then the damage is revealed. All the savers in Momontia have had the value of their savings halve in real terms but because the government didn't spend all the money it created right away, they didn't realise this till it was too late and their losses have been reflected in a massive inflationary spike. No one lost a single Momontian dollar nominally speaking, but the value of that Momontian dollar is now half what it was.

But, wait, the Modern Monetary Theorists do have a solution to this, and it's truly amazing (not); they say that inflation doesn't have to be created here! The principal argument as to why inflation will not appear, is that the government is able to control the demand side of inflation through taxation and through the issuance of bonds which effectively will remove excess cash from the system. The idea is that demand side and thus inflation can be fully controlled and therefore the government can just run any deficit it likes ad infinitum on proviso that it takes care to sterilise the excess cash that is not currently invested.

Now this would be all very well and good except for big swiss cheese type holes in this argument. The first major foible here is that this process is simply theft. You can indeed essentially tax ad nauseam anything to slow down the economy and keep a lid on inflation, but you have to do this so aggressively that you are just stealing from people for the privilege of simply being citizens, and that tax is used just to pay for a bunch of programs that are designed only to get votes to allow you to print more money, and the hubris of this leads to exactly the hyperinflation scenarios that we have seen before in currencies like the Pengo. Only with MMT, the taxes are sort of hidden at least for a while - and that is the point. Even if following the policies of MMT doesn't lead to immediate inflation as given by the indices, it will lead to massive inflational instabilities over time as no one can be certain how much money supply really is in the system and how much an aggressive government will push the limit in order to try and buy votes with gifts, or what the velocity of money really should be. In some ways MMT is just a modern version of Marxist theory but more insidious because it doesn't openly claim that the government will own the means of production. However, they really will in that they can simply increase the money supply at will and purchase any asset they would like. This is modern age Marxism, because if you can just create money to buy any asset that you feel like, you essentially own all these assets de facto and are effectively giving them to be run by the "owners" for as long as it is economically convenient for you. We will talk more of this when we discuss Socialism and Marxism.

But things are potentially even worse than this, and this is the second big cheese hole. Because with MMT, prices will now not really exist with certainty. The market will no longer really be able to put a price on anything because of the lack of certainty as to the value of a given amount of cash in terms of real goods and services. This is particularly the case in the situation such as that of the US today where a huge amount of money has been printed but it has been effectively sterilised by the Federal Reserve as bonds. This has led to asset inflation without "inflation" from the indices which are constructed to specifically exclude the value of certain assets such as your home etc. Thus, what the prices of all assets *should be* are extremely unclear in our current economic situation. I mean this very specifically because prices in the age of the Internet of Things are very precise indeed and very homogenous. However, the irony is that there is a massive increase in the opacity of the true value of money. And what tends to happen in this situation, this being the *critical* point and the crux of the matter, is that the natural effects of supply and demand are accentuated to an extreme level by the uncertainty with regards to where prices should be. This "feature" of MMT is something that cannot be swept under the carpet. And thus, you see things like property bubbles occur well beyond any reasonableness in places like Hong Kong or New York city, with prices ratcheting up on any positive news and staying put with any negative news. We will talk more about this later.

Mathematically speaking, we can frame this issue with MMT in a different way. Whilst prices today are essentially very well known, if a market is to follow the doctrine of MMT, future prices are much less certain. If the Fed were to effectively release their balance sheet and invest in real world projects tomorrow, this would lead to a massive spike in inflation. MMT theory says that this is the only situation where that would happen, but the point is virtually trivial that even if the money is retained by the Fed, at some point the market will begin to price in that money being put to work. It may not happen right away, but it will have this ratcheting effect as more and more of the market participants across the market realise that they had better spend their money now because there is much more money already created waiting in the wings to be used. The problem with MMT is that in this framework money now no longer functions as the Higgs Boson of finance but essentially becomes useless. The practices associated with modern monetary theory do nothing except add opacity. Whilst it is true that this may mean that in the short term some of the market fails to notice the precipitous nature of a failing economy, this only serves to make the reckonings worse when they do come. It is highly ironic that in a time and place where data is basically available to everyone through the internet, and markets are in constant contact with each other that the pursuit of MMT type principles by the central banks has made prices of things highly uncertain and has led to what I call "lavish inflation". We will say more about what lavish inflation is and why it matters later.

Many people are very suspicious of bankers (to some extent quite rightly so), and many will also know that bankers can end up in jail if they try to "front run" their clients orders. Front running is when you being a trader have been told to execute an order that is of a large size compared to the market and you know that this will have the effect of moving the market in the direction of the order (if it was a buy it will move the price up and vice versa), and therefore trade ahead of their order on your own account in order to personally (either for yourself of for the financial institution that you work for) profit from the power of that large order. Front running is illegal, and several bankers have e gone to jail for that crime. However, what MMT asks an economy to do is to put a huge order (in terms of increased money supply) in the system of the economy and somehow the proponents of this idea see no instability in prices generated by this order. It is patently crazy on the face of it. And it is the knowledge that there exists already pre-created excess liquidity in the system that makes more and more people gradually increase the price they are willing to buy assets at even as nominal inflation doesn't do anything because that money is not being released into the system. Another way to view this is that the "velocity" of that money is essentially zero right now and therefore doesn't generate any inflation, but that this velocity can be subject to an infinite acceleration at some given time when the Fed actually does something with the balances that are extant.

So, to summarise. The only real advantage of MMT for the modern government is that by employing these "economic principles" it is far easier to disguise a failing economy. MMT brings opacity by blurring where prices really should be and making it easier for corrupt or simply inefficient economies to hide their failings and appear far more prosperous than they are. Worse than this, the premise makes it easier to con the public into accepting a passive and highly insidious tax on their wealth through the significant increases in money supply. The vast amounts of uncertainty that any economy based on MMT generates should already be enough to make it utterly invalid, but we should also note that this also minimises the efficacy of standard monetary and fiscal policy tools with regards to stabilising negative scenarios as when prices are extremely opaque, the consequences of any action are usually far from those that were desired. And the consequences of MMT are apparent everywhere throughout the developed world. Their manifestation is different in each country, but they are there. We will discuss two of them in some detail these being the rise of the populism of Donald Trump, and the issue we will talk about now being the phenomenon of Brexit.

Good morning, Brexit is ready!

June the 23rd 2016 will be a date which will remain in memory for some time. This happened to be the occasion of my birthday but this was relevant to just a handful of people. For the majority of the British population, however, this will (maybe forever maybe not) be regarded as either the day that Great Britain declared its Independence from a gargantuan pariah state that has been sucking the life blood of the country for almost half a century, or the day on which the curtain finally set on the role of the UK as a nation of significance in the world. What had once been the greatest economy on earth suddenly went overnight from the 5th to the 7th as a result of the biggest short term drop of all time of the Pound. The vote came after long and certainly quite bitter campaign which climaxed in the death of an MP who was by all accounts both highly competent (brilliant even) and principled (making the loss an even more bitter pill to swallow). Ultimately, however, the Leave vote triumphed taking just under 52 percent of the vote.

This led to markets nosediving in what was described by most commentators as an "extremely turbulent day". Were the markets correct to have such an extreme reaction to what was essentially an advisory vote won by a slim majority and so badly understood by the British public that over 4million people had signed a petition within 2 weeks calling for a re-vote? As an aside the petition on the parliamentary website was actually started by a Leave campaigner prior to the referendum who complained that it was hijacked despite the fact that one would have presumably thought he would still be in favour of it if he believed exactly what he had stated on the petition itself.

Post Brexit the ugly underbelly of the UK was reportedly revealed with various racially motivated attacks (mostly verbal) across the country reported. Whether it was simply a case that post the vote the press was most sensitive to events that were racially motivated, or whether suddenly it became acceptable to express such feelings it remains unclear (the evil of it certainly was though), but what is certain is that this showed a very disturbingly divided society. It was even clearer when one looked at the geographical and demographic distribution of the voting as well as the wealth gap between those that voted to Remain and those that voted to leave. The fact was that those who suffered the most from the unfettered immigration into the UK since the borders were effectively opened by the New Labour party of Tony Blair and retained until this day. These immigrants were often relatives of immigrants that were already in the UK and were overwhelmingly low skilled and disproportionately settled in the inner cities rather than in the country, and because the education levels were low, they caused huge headwinds on salaries. Thus, the working class in general tended to vote for Brexit due to their concerns regarding jobs, but there was another reason that people were very concerned, and that is multicultural concepts that were being ushered in.

Ultimately, multiculturalism in the truest form is an extremely bad idea. This is because countries exist generally because people enjoy the culture unique to their country. That does not mean of course that if you are English and an immigrant you are expected to abandon the culture of your background, not at all. But you are also not expected to live as if you were still in your country of origin; you are supposed to be in a country because you actually like that country and not because it simply provides additional "lebensraum" for your culture to breed in. We can argue that for cultures that are close enough together, it is still possible to live as if you were in your previous country because there are enough places of commonality. This is mostly but not completely true in Europe, but for cultures that are very far apart, the decision to move to a country by construction needs to come with the idea that you are to adapt to the culture that you are going to be living in. It simply cannot be the case that the country you are moving to has to be the one to change. After all, they did not ask you to come, you had to apply. No country ever goes "recruiting" for people like a company does except under specific situations (for example during WWII, or Japan right now) and even then, they only generally look for the very brightest and the best, and still require a certain amount of assimilation.

There are those that love to argue (as we shall see this is generally those on the left) that the US is a "nation of immigrants" and has therefore embraced multiculturalism but this shows a profound lack of understanding of two things. The first is that the vast majority of those who came to the US in the past embraced the constitution of the United States, and especially the freedom that it demanded as being of paramount importance and aspired to become as American as possible. The second is that most of those immigrating into the US pre the middle of the 20th century, were fully ensconced in Judeo Christian values and certainly did not have a difficulty in accepting the rule of law and other precepts at all. Even those who were not quite as familiar with all of these things did generally embrace them over time; for example, many Chinese or Japanese immigrants converted to Christianity or were coming to America because they had become Christian and wanted to be free to worship as Christians in their new country. And even those that didn't still aspired to the values that were and are enshrined in the Constitution of the United States. At the same time, we should also note that the US was not the richest nation on earth at the close of the 19th century. In fact, Argentina was the richest country in the world in terms of GDP per capita in 1895[46]. Buenos Ares was more attractive to some even than Paris or Rome. How quickly that country fell, and the US exploded. Was it because Argentina did not have enough resources? Not at all, the country had plenty of land, plenty of natural resources including iron ore, uranium, and even petroleum, and the region of Patagonia has some of the most fertile grazing and growing land in existence even today. The country rapidly developed in the early part of the 20th century eclipsing almost all nations in terms of GDP per capita including many European countries and all

[46] https://panampost.com/marcelo-duclos/2018/04/14/in-1895-argentina-had-the-worlds-highest-gdp-per-capita-what-went-wrong/?cn-reloaded=1

looked rosy until it abandoned the gold standard in 1929. Whilst this initially helped with exports, this was a hefty price to pay. The seeds of political instability were sown from that time, and the country never properly recovered post the Great Depression due to its political troubles which allowed a significant amount of corruption to evolve in the country. Whilst Peron after the second world war was able to stabilise the economic situation temporarily, the seeds of corruption had already taken such root that it became almost impossible to properly grow the economy from the mid fifties onwards. Even today Argentina continues to underperform due to these same issues corruption now being ingrained even into the economic data.[47]

So, the economic incentives to come to the US at the start of the 20th century were ones of opportunity and not just of extant wealth. However, in the last 50 years, there has been a lot more immigration in the US of those who simply saw themselves as economic migrants and had no wish at all to adapt to the culture of the US. It is particularly difficult for those who hold to a religious belief that is also a political system. This is most stark in Islam. The Sharia law of Islam mandates itself as the law of any land of the Muslim people. This is certainly not the case in Christianity where the New testament demands that Christians obey the authorities of any land that they live in and where rising up against the temporal authorities without exceptional circumstances is considered an afront to God Himself (the idea being that all worldly authority is God given). Sharia law is very different indeed to the Judeo-Christian ideas of justice and is highly authoritarian with value attributed to someone because of their status rather than because of the content of their character. Thus, it has been extremely difficult for Muslims to assimilate into the culture of the US, not just because they have a different religion, but because that religion is also a social and political system that demands compliance.

But we don't even have to argue about culture here. The problem overall with immigration is that when it is allowed on masse with people who do not have significantly enough enhanced skill sets, you end up in a "race to the bottom" in terms of the standard of living of the poorest unskilled labourers in the economy of a western nation. Now whilst it is true that western nations generally have a very good amount of schooling and education, there are still significant numbers who are not skilled enough to have a sophisticated job. This is just the truth of human intelligence. I will show why this is later, but the point is that there are unskilled jobs to be done and these jobs are not much fun. Now if you had a single developed country in a vacuum, the pay associated with unskilled jobs would initially start low (they are unskilled after all), but over time the pay would rise dramatically. This is because less and less people would want to do these jobs, and in a free market, the salary demanded to be for example, a toilet cleaner, would have to go up. Things might get to the point where the toilet cleaner is earning close to what the office worker is earning. This is a good thing. But when mass immigration of the unskilled is allowed, this can no longer happen. The poorest people in an advanced economy are now in that race to the bottom against those who are coming over from other countries. Therefore, it should not be surprising at all that those people feel disenfranchised. It is not the elite, the highly educated who are suffering from mass immigration, in fact those people are gaining a lot. They are now able to hire servants to help them at home and do all the things that they don't like to do for a much cheaper price. They also have people to serve them in restaurants or cafes who are cheaper and therefore they pay less for their no fat, full whip, tall, caramel macchiato with sprinkles than they would have otherwise. These "elites" are also usually claiming to be "progressives" who care about immigrants and they probably even believe themselves to be exactly that, whereas they are simply in it for the short-term gains that they can obtain, and don't care about the longer-term poverty that this will present. They don't even care about things like crime because they live in their own gated communities, or areas far away from high crime neighbourhoods, and their children go to private schools where they are told all about the tolerance and goodness of the philosophy that is trotted out by their parents.

---

[47] Since 2007, there is a general agreement amongst economists that inflation is being significantly underreported in official government statistics.

And it is ironic that those who espouse socialist and communist ideas are also generally the ones for open borders. They are the ones who claim to represent the poor and the disenfranchised, but they do nothing of the sort, they just make the labour of the poor worth less and less over time. And it's not that they are lying when they claim that they think they are representing the poor, it's just that they have no idea what the problems of the impoverished masses are. They believe that they can create a utopia for everything using a tissue of loosely convoluted progressive concepts that are not able to mutually coexist without an exceptional amount of cognitive dissonance. These elites were battered on June the 23rd and less than half a year later they were to be virtually destroyed once again on the day of the US elections. A day that shall live in "infamy" unless you are rational, or a realist, or a patriot, or even just someone who believes in the US Constitution of course.

President Trump and the problem of Loss Aversion.

Whilst my birthday was a day to remember, November the 8th was yet another red-letter day. As if to mark the occasion of my father's 70th birthday, another man the same age was making history in the US. Donald Trump, billionaire property tycoon, reality tv hyper-star, opinionated, controversial, somewhat boorish, and certainly not politically correct had become President Elect. To put it into context, this was the first ever person who had neither held public office nor served in the armed forces to be elected to the most powerful position in the world. Not only is the accomplishment unprecedented, but the media almost overwhelmingly failed to see it coming: practically no newspapers were willing to publicly endorse him and even those that prided themselves on being "neutral" such as USA Today insisted that their readers did not vote for him. Hillary Clinton trotted out celebrity after celebrity who used their fan base to endorse her and spent more than a billion dollars on her campaign – more than twice that of Trump. The media were so utterly and completely biased that even little children noticed that the press "don't like Trump mommy". Nevertheless, President Trump had his hand on the pulse of the country far more soundly than either the press or his opponent. He had tapped into something that was a huge motivator and that thing is the disaffection that human beings have with things getting worse, and especially things getting worse without any clear hope for the future.

Human beings have an interesting relationship with volatility. It is said that most human beings cannot deal with volatility and simply want things not to change. This isn't correct, because people care more about things getting always better and never worse rather than how much better things get. Generally, I have found from both observation of traders in the market (particularly the weaker ones who were not able to make money consistently) and in the behaviour of my own self that human beings are simply bad at dealing with things ever getting worse. Humans can quite happily get along without any great upside events in their life but only if, every day, life gets a tiny bit better. In fact, if they own a share portfolio, they will be far happier with their stocks going up in value 1% a year for 20 years than doubling after ten years and then going down in value by a total of 25% over the next 10. Even though in aggregate, they have earned just over 1% a year more in the second scenario[48], people feel the total loss far more than they gain happiness from the gain.

Another way to look at it is that people prefer to gamble only when they didn't already process the gains they made before. Many variants of the classic experiment to show this have been conducted and a framework called Prospect theory was developed to mathematically analyse decision making of this sort[49]. The ideas in Prospect theory are that people have an aversion to losses and like certainty. There are also a few more nuances and factors which are worth investigating if you have interest but don't add

---

[48] If in the first 10 years your portfolio doubles and then over the next 10 it goes down 25% then you have 1.5 times your original portfolio. If you assume annual compounding this equates to 2.048 percent a year which you get by solving the equation: $x^{20}=1.5$ which basically means you take $1.5^{1/20}$ to get back 1.02048 the factor by which any given amount of money grows each year.

[49] Kahneman, Daniel; Tversky, Amos (1979). "Prospect Theory an analysis of Decision under Risk." *Econometrica*. **47** (2): 263. doi:10.2307/1914185. ISSN 0012-9682.

much to the argument here. Note also that the anecdotal evidence that I had seen regarding concern about things getting worse is loss aversion itself.

A typical experiment to demonstrate certainty involved giving someone 10 dollars and asking if they would like to gamble on flip of a fair coin. If they gambled, they would get 20 dollars if they won the coin toss or lose the 10 dollars they were given if they lost. If they didn't gamble, they would keep the 10 dollars of course. Now given that the expected return if they gambled was 10 dollars (because you had a 50% chance of getting 20 dollars and a 50% chance of zero hence the expected return was just $0.5 \times 20 + 0.5 \times 0 = 10$), you might think that people would equally be comfortable with gambling or not, but the result was that the overwhelming majority would prefer keeping the 10 dollars, because they wanted certainty.

A further experiment was done which focused on loss aversion. In this there were two groups of people. The first cohort were given a certain amount say 100 dollars and then told that they could either keep 60 dollars or gamble on some game with say a 40% chance of losing the whole 100 or a 60% chance of keeping the whole 100. In this case most decided to keep 60. But the second group was offered a different deal. They were given 100 dollars, and then they were told they could either lose 40 dollars or gamble with a 60% chance of keeping the whole 100 or a 40% chance of losing the whole 100. Here the game is identical not just in probabilities but in the exact thing that is going to happen. There is no difference except in the way that the question is framed. But the amazing thing was that the majority of the second group chose to gamble. They had lost some of their risk aversion because of their loss aversion. They were willing to gamble in order to preserve what they already regarded as being "theirs". This is because they had already got used to the gain they had made and now it was theirs and they were less comfortable with losing it. The time dependency mattered to them because the happiness of the gain and the pain of loss were not equal. Because utilitarianism is wrong in operational terms. The utility that someone has from an event is truly time dependent. Therefore someone who has had a life that may have been difficult but was always improving, will often have felt far happier than someone who had huge ups and downs even if the ups were far beyond what the first person might have experienced, and even if the downs were no worse than the experiences of that afore mentioned person. And this is exactly the "American Dream". As was stated in that gem of a film "The Pursuit of Happiness", the founding fathers knew that the push and the improvement ever onwards was what made people happy. They never had to have utopia, they just had to have the dream and the realisation of a better tomorrow. Tomorrow never had to be that great just better than today and better than yesterday.

And this is exactly why Trump's message resonated. The average American in the Midwest didn't care about being politically correct, having a more culturally diverse society, or making sure to be "inclusive", and this was because they felt that their life in 1996 was far better than their life 20 years later in 2016; they were the ones excluded by the modern US economy. Despite the inexorable rise in GDP in the US throughout the past decade, they hadn't participated. All they saw was jobs that paid the bills in short supply, their medical insurance premiums skyrocketing, and the country letting in more and more people who they perceived as "un-American" and who because of their lack of skills took the most menial jobs and therefore drove the pricing power of the labour of Middle America to rock bottom. And because the media in the US is so left wing, and was so biased against Trump, he became the candidate for a protest vote from a far more diverse group than anyone believed possible. Not just this, but that group as we have said included the most disenfranchised people in the demographic, those people that the Democrats in the US claimed to represent but where being used simply to buy votes in the past. To the average American cultural enrichment just meant they were less likely to be able to support themselves and their families in the style to which they were accustomed. It meant that things would get worse and even if it was just a bit worse, they would have no part of it. And so Ironically, the US elected a man who took truly enormous risks in his previous business life in part to shoulder the burden of an increasingly risk averse American public.

But many have attributed other causes to the populist uprising in the west. For example, as I was riding in a delayed ICE train in Germany at the end of February 2017 (yes that does happen even in Germany – there were as I was reliably informed in 4 languages only 3 of which I understood – trees on the track), I happened to glance at a book that the person in front of me was reading with a very interesting title. That title was "The Populist Explosion. How the great recession transformed American and European politics" I was interested in it partly because the title had exactly the same structure as I was using for my book (A three-word title beginning with the definite article, with a sentence broadly describing the overall thesis). Immediately the next day, I bought the book and read it. Overall it is a good work, but it is interesting that the book sort of takes the great recession (something I usually refer to as the global financial crisis[50]) as a given event and goes on the claim that this was the direct root cause of populism. With regards to that, I feel that the author (John B Judis) misses the point. The global financial crisis didn't in and of itself incite a change towards populism, it is just another symptom of the disease of which populism is also symptomatic. The very key to my thesis is not that the great recession was some unique crazy event, but that something like it was going to happen anyway and that the response of the central banks was the way it was because everybody was bankrupt in the first place. And the world was bankrupt somewhat because the west was spending very large amounts of money on "social programs "that they could just not afford due to the progressive agenda that has been a hive of decay and academic decadence over the last 40-50 years and more.

Who is really to blame for the Global Financial Crisis?

There already extant a myriad of tomes written on the global financial crisis. From the crazy, through the sensational, through to the downright boring, everyone seems to have a slightly different angle on the event. However, to me one of the most shocking things about the financial crisis having witnessed it first -hand as it was happening (executing several trades in Lehman bonds even at the very hour that it was filling for bankruptcy protection), was how few people in the press seemed to really understand the causes of the crisis as it unfolded and even today. Indeed, there have been many books written by people who should have known what was going on but who maybe were unable to look at the facts objectively because they held to a particular world view reinforced by an eco-chamber of those who thought in exactly the same way. There was a lot of blame placed over time, but the most vehement blame that was assigned was against the banks themselves. The most surprising thing about this is that the banks suffered most of the losses from the financial crisis. Otherwise very profitable banks had an "Anus Horibilis" from the mark to market of things called subprime mortgages.

The number of subprime loans that were effectively guaranteed by government agencies adds up to over 19 million.[51] Of these at least 60 percent were guaranteed by Freddie Mac or Fannie Mae the two major government mortgage agencies that needed to be bailed out in the midst of the crisis. These mortgage agencies were incentivised by regulation to essentially grant mortgages to those who might not be able to repay, i.e. those with a poor credit rating as part of the requirement post 1992 to provide "affordable housing" financing. This is a result of the Housing and Community Development Act which mandated that at least 30% of Fannie and Freddie loan purchases had to be related to "affordable housing". In this context, "affordable housing" meant basically those who did not have enough credit to be able to take out loans in another way. This is an example of the free market being artificially driven towards a point of destruction by regulation that was intended to do something good. And this is a key point when we think about regulation especially the ideas of the left. The reason that regulation should be reserved for

---

[50] One can argue the question is simply one of semantics, but I think there are subtle nuances that make global financial crisis more apt, simply due to things like China not actually entering a recession but certainly suffering a meltdown in its stock market for example. In any case, most authors use the terms pretty much interchangeably.
[51] https://www.theatlantic.com/business/archive/2011/12/hey-barney-frank-the-government-did-cause-the-housing-crisis/249903/

the most important things and should otherwise be very limited is that it affects the free market skewing it in a direction that is often not intended and usually meaning that the free market cannot be as efficient as it might otherwise be. We need to start thinking of the feedback loops that can be set up by otherwise innocuous, and well meaning, legislation. And the reason I single out the left here is that the left is usually far less consistent on policies which has the mathematical propensity to cause far more unforeseen consequences. You see when policies are consistent, the potential ramifications are relatively easy to anticipate, because there is no conflict in approach and thus only a first or possible second order calculation is needed to see potential effects. With the modern left, there are far too many inconsistencies; demanding green energy but rejecting Nuclear power (which causes less deaths per kilowatt hour generated than any other system of electrical generation), or pushing for High Speed Rail but complaining when certain land is used for those same purposes. The right doesn't have as many of these inconsistencies in policy, so that the results of their policies are generally more transparent, and easy to predict. So, in one very palpable sense, government regulations effectively caused the subprime crisis. But not everyone thought so.

There were a whole bunch of people who decided that what was to blame was the bugbear of the evil "derivatives market". Derivatives are the great scapegoat of finance, they have achieved a notoriety that is frankly comparable to that of the "Chupacabra" in Mexico, except that derivatives are real things. During any financial crisis there is always an outcry from journalists that derivatives have been responsible for most of the losses associated with anything at all. And strangely enough, sometimes, just sometimes, this was even true. But the point is that it wasn't true that often, and it was certainly false when it came to the financial crisis. In fact, complex derivatives were quite irrelevant to the crisis itself, and basically have never really created a crisis although they have always been quite conveniently blamed.

As usual the true picture is not so clear cut but what is certain is that a very large portion of the blame does lie with the originators of the mortgages. The arrangers who lied about the credit worthiness of their "clients" so that their clients could purchase overpriced property that they would only be able to benefit from if the price of the property continued to rise ad infinitum. This was because they would need to refinance every few years to ensure that they got a new chaser rate every time. A chaser rate was basically finance trickery predicated on something that was have talked about before; the laziness of the individual, and in particular people who are busy. Whilst human beings generally overcome their slothful nature when they are doing something interesting like their careers, they usually wallow in it aggressively when it comes to something that is not of fascination to them. And this often sadly includes things like mortgages. Given the amount of paperwork involved in getting a mortgage, many people are just comfortable to not move over mortgages, and this is how most of the banks made money on mortgages. They were expecting homeowners to continue to pay the higher rate for a while at least before they really decided to refinance. Of course, one of the problems with the whole chaser idea is that it encourages those of little means to borrow much more than they can afford, because they can afford the chaser rate at least. They hope that by the time the rate moves higher that they will be able to refinance with another chaser rate and continue thusly ad infinitum. This of course means that the banks had massively asymmetric risk because the only borrowers forced to pay the higher non-chaser rate were those who could not afford to refinance because their credit was not sufficiently high enough. The hope that the banks may have had that there were legions of upper middle-class professionals who were too busy to bother refinancing was tenuous at best. But the issue there was that the banks simply didn't check who was really the borrower in the mortgages that they were purchasing.

The press, on the other hand had a completely different idea of who the culprits were and spent rather a lot of time attacking Goldman Sachs, which I was working for at the time. This seemed very strange to me because what I was seeing on the ground as it were was something totally different. Take for example the idea that Goldman Sachs was involved in getting the then US Secretary of the Treasury Henry "Hank" Paulson to bail out AIG so that Goldman were not to lose money. Even the Financial

Crisis Enquiry Commission seemed to be of the view that Goldman had benefited directly by the bailout of AIG[52] when it presented its final report on the bailout at the start of 2011.

Publications like the Huffington Post which is politically so far to the left that in 2016 it argued that Hillary Clinton had a 98.2 percent chance of winning the election[53], and continued to post a ridiculously libellous editors note up to the day of the election[54], had a field day when the report came out bringing in supposed experts that said things like "if these allegations are correct, it appears to have been a direct transfer of wealth from the Treasury to Goldman's shareholders", and that Goldman didn't "have the fig leaf of a systemic risk argument. Normally what happens when a sophisticated institution that's doing stupid credit stuff is you let them eat it, but that didn't happen in the bailout"[55]. Ironically both these statements do apply to the financial crisis, but unfortunately for these people and the Huffington post, they do not apply to Goldman in this case. Not only that, but the two people who were interviewed were supposedly senior people at prestigious firms. However, the lack of understanding regarding derivatives that they displayed in their comments is utterly tragic for the industry and the best that I can hope for is that some way, somehow, they were taken out of context. However, my suspicion is that they were not and that even these professionals had a profound lack of capability in the way derivatives work and especially the way banks manage the positions on their books, and were card carrying beneficiaries of the Idiocracy.

We, however, are in a strong position to understand exactly what happened with Goldman and AIG and why the most senior guys there protested so strongly that they were being misrepresented in the commission's final report. The specific class of derivatives that have been accused of a myriad of awful things are known as credit derivatives. And one particular contract, the very simplest form of credit derivative called a Credit Default Swap otherwise known as CDS. CDS should not be confused with CDs which are certificates of deposit that are essentially short dated and very liquid bonds issued by almost every corporate institution. CDS is a derivative structure and takes the form of a contract for differences.

A CDS contract, is quite straightforward. It is a simple insurance agreement between two parties. Party A called the buyer of the CDS, or more colloquially the buyer of the "protection" pays Party B the seller of the protection a certain amount for a certain length of time. That time frame is usually greater than 1 year, with the canonical being 5yr, which we call 5-year protection or 5-year CDS. Each CDS contract also has a certain reference notional which is the nominal amount of insurance protection that exists. Now that notional represents the face value of a bond that has been issued by a given company or entity (which is called the "name"). This name is usually neither party A nor party B. The reason for this I will explain shortly. So, let's say that the CDS references a bond of another company that I worked for called UBS. UBS is a Swiss bank, and for various reasons is now a very strong credit (amongst the three strongest generally) in terms of the different banks in the world today. Now we have said that party A pays a certain amount to party B. Party A is obligated to pay that amount every year for the length of the contract. What does party A get in return? Well party B receives that constant amount every year, but if the name (in this case UBS) that is referenced ever defaults on their obligations, party A has the right to deliver the face amount agreed referenced UBS bond issued by that name to party B in exchange for par, another name for 100% of the referenced notional price. Now as you know, if a bond defaults, its price will plummet so that party A would have earned a hefty payday if UBS had defaulted.

---

[52] Of course, Goldman did benefit very much from the overall bailout as a whole due to the fact that TARP essentially stabilised the markets and allowed Goldman to make significant profits over the next year, but the specific bailout of AIG didn't do much for them as I will explain.

[53] https://www.huffingtonpost.com/entry/polls-hillary-clinton-win_us_5821074ce4b0e80b02cc2a94

[54] https://www.politico.com/blogs/on-media/2016/11/the-huffington-post-ending-its-editors-note-about-donald-trump-231044

[55] https://www.huffingtonpost.com/2011/01/26/goldman-sachs-aig-backdoor-bailout_n_814589.html

CDS has evolved significantly over time in order to try and improve the structure of the product. For example, in the past if there was a default all of the current coupon that the buyer was supposed to pay would no longer be owed, which would lead to pathological events where buyers of CDS were willing to pay an almost infinite coupon if they believed that the default would happen before the first coupon was due. When ISDA[56] the regulatory body governing most traded derivatives contracts changed the terms to require at least the first coupon to be paid in a contract whatever happened, and additionally required accrued interest to be paid, many of these weaknesses disappeared, but a few remained.

So, we know what CDS is and we know that Goldman had bought CDS insurance contracts from AIG in order to hedge another position that it had on its books. However, if I as a Goldman Sachs trader bought CDS from a company, I would always be worried that the company who sold the insurance to me might default. Now this is true for any derivative so, in general, banks required (and still do) anyone who had traded derivatives with them that were still live (i.e. the contract had yet to pay out either way) to post collateral to cover the expected value of the derivative. That collateral is usually either cash or government bonds or something which essentially is riskless. It works in the same way as a mortgage where the bank has your house as collateral for any loan they give. If you default on your payments the bank can simply take your house away from you and sell it. But for derivatives, the collateral is liquid assets that are easy to sell almost instantaneously such that they can immediately realise any shortfall.

Of course, the problem is that the value of the CDS can change radically from day to day, and you have to keep coming back to the banks for collateral, so there is always the chance that a company that looked healthy suddenly has some awful news that brings them on the brink of default and changes the value of the CDS that you hold to a huge extent. Now you have to scramble to collect (we use the term call) collateral and if your counterparty were to default in this process then the value of your derivatives would no longer be secure. But all is not lost because, in general, the net exposure of CDS at any given time on the books of an investment bank is often far smaller (typically at least a couple of orders of magnitude) than the sum of the notionals of all these exposures. This is because banks manage portfolios that have both long and short positions in derivatives, and the aim overall for the bank is to run as much of their position properly hedged so that their exposure is very limited.

The key here is if I have a portfolio that is hedged in CDS and there is a default, there will be a big change in the individual positions that I hold and a very small one (or none at all if I am perfectly hedged by being long one CDS derivative and short the exact same one) overall in my portfolio. This is critical to understanding what went on with Goldman Sachs, and why Goldman would not have been financially in trouble if AIG had defaulted. If AIG did default, then Goldman would keep the collateral that had already been posted and claim the balance from those who had sold Goldman the CDS. Now they could also have defaulted, but it is extremely unlikely that they would have defaulted in the exact same instant. Even if the parties that had insured Goldman had defaulted a week later, Goldman would have been okay, because those parties would have had to post the mark to market balance in cash or other collateral that Goldman would accept to Goldman. This could take place up to the same day, and even intraday, so in theory (and also in practice[57]) it would be possible for Goldman to have been okay on its AIG position even if the CDS sellers had defaulted later that same day and Goldman might even have made a little money on those events as Goldman had a little bit of over-hedge as far as I remember.

So, to be clear, Goldman did take money from the US Treasury, but if AIG had defaulted Goldman would have received money from whoever had insured it against the default of AIG. And, most importantly, money is money. Goldman didn't care per se who gave it the money back, just that someone would. So, from the perspective of Goldman shareholders, the default or not of AIG in and of

---

[56] The International Swaps and Derivatives Association.

[57] I am very confident that the team managing those positions at GS under Andy Hudis at that time would have been able to exit the AIG position without taking any sort of even medium size loss.

itself specifically was spectacularly unimportant compared to the grand scheme of things. There was a possibility that huge numbers of simultaneous defaults could have scuppered this protection, but as we have said this was incredibly unlikely and did not happen.

In fact, seeing this evidence first-hand, how the press had manipulated the account of the event simply to erroneously claim that Goldman Sachs had stolen money from the US taxpayer, led me to investigate the press further. If they could lie about something like this which wasn't really a matter of debate if you knew the facts, how much more could they lie in other things which were much bigger, more relevant and much more nuanced. Things where opinion is much more subjective were a much greater problem which is the incentive that the newspapers had. In the digital economy the business model was no longer that of people who bought the paper (and usually subscribed). Newspapers began to make money simply from the advertising that they could garner online, and this was determined not by how long someone spent on their website but by a simple visit. This in and of itself meant that so called clickbait became the new norm whereby most newspapers just wanted a sensational headline. Of course, this was important before, but now because all they need to do is get someone to just look at their website, they are no longer subject to any real quality control. If they were producing a printed newspaper, the most important thing was circulation over time, and this generally needed people to value the reporting of the newspaper to buy it. Yes, it was cheap to buy a newspaper but nowhere close to how cheap it is simply to click a link. This means that almost every news service online is having to use clickbait just to get enough traffic to earn sufficient money from advertising. The problem will get worse, far worse, before it gets better as Google and Facebook control over 50% of online advertising[58] which makes this an anti-trust type issue which will probably need to be solved by some radical changes in the regulations regarding online content.

But ultimately why did the US government serve the people who voted for Trump so badly? Well President Obama tried very hard to do some good things for the people, but the final record of the two terms of his administration will be that much was lost because of a combination of the government and the Federal Reserve. We shall see later how the issue with the Obama administration was basically that they were just too far to the left in ideology, and too weak in resolve, and that this meant that the Fed was allowed to run amok whilst the government expanded the national debt far too fast. At the same time, the country descended into a politically correct quagmire with strange mantras being invoked to indicate that there were great social injustices afoot of similar importance to those that took place in the early to middle of the 20th century. This was of course nonsense, but no amount of cold, hard, data would change the perception that these injustices existed. This was again because progressives had stopped being liberals and had become dictatorial "thought police" who could not abide humour, irony, or inequality of outcomes. In other words, busybodies! Then, of course, there was the actual policies that the Democrat government enacted.

The Obama administration's failing has been to allow, and indeed encourage, the perception that it was possible for a country to function whilst supporting a significant percentage of its population in such a way that working was, for them, no longer attractive versus the alternative. As we have said, benefits can only work (mathematically speaking) if they act like insurance: to cover those who have been unfortunate and no longer have the physical or mental ability to work or contribute through the usual channels. It cannot work in the way that the US (and almost all G7 countries) undertakes the system. When the safety net is so close to the tightrope there appears to be almost no point in staying on, and in that situation, there simply are not enough people working and contributing taxes to keep the entire economy going. The trapeze artist needs the net to be just for emergencies otherwise their performance is really nothing special, and it is entirely the same with the economy.

[58] https://www.investopedia.com/news/facebook-google-digital-ad-market-share-drops-amazon-climbs/

The Federal Reserve has failed even more palpably than the government because it did two things wrong. Firstly, it focussed all its efforts once the crisis had started on simply trying to make money cheaper to borrow than was appropriate in the context of the economy. This had the effect of raising the value of speculative assets and doing almost nothing at all for the poor who didn't have the credit worthiness for low rates to make any significant difference to them, and who had no money to buy speculative assets. Secondly, the Fed delayed raising rates for at least 5 years and therefore failed to provide even the most basic return to those who tried to save a little bit of their money for a rainy day. This of course caused extreme pressure on both savers and those living on a fixed income who lost every bit of benefit of saving. This really meant that those who were the most unfairly disadvantaged in society suffered. By this I don't mean people who were poor per se, but people who were poor through no fault of their own and who often had worked their entire lives to earn a meagre pension. If those people had been able to make a slightly better return on their savings, they would have suffered less. The sad truth is that savers are usually saving because they are responsible people; and the Federal Reserve betrayed almost everyone who really was responsible with their money to reward or come to the aid of those who either took excessive risks or who lived a life that was unaffordable in the long run.

I would argue that the Federal Reserve and other central banks have been found wanting to such an extreme extent especially in their response to the crisis that certain individuals should be prosecuted for criminal levels of negligence. I do not take this stance lightly, but I believe the evidence for this lies in the fact that none of the lessons of history have been properly taken to heart and, more importantly, there was never a plausible mechanism identified by the Fed or anyone else for how their policies would actually function. By this I mean that just printing money and buying US treasuries simply has the effect of boosting speculative assets without really doing anything to the real economy. The worst thing about this is that our measures of inflation do not take account of things like the price of stocks or the price of houses. So, whilst the Federal Reserve argues that it is trying to stoke inflation it is appropriate to ask; "what is the mechanism for this?" How could speculative assets going up improve the situation at all? Most people even in America do not own stocks directly[59] and even though a much greater proportion of people own their own houses, house prices going up really don't do any good for the world. Even worse than this, I will argue later that the central banks should have known exactly what their crazily speculative measures should have been doing and that they should have paid attention to the elephant in the room which was a global property market that was not just a bubble, but arguably a set of correlated price bubbles many of which remain to this day.

Safe as houses?

A huge proportion of the world sees real estate as being the closest thing that exists to a sure bet in terms of investments. The very name of the asset "real estate" sounds safe and reassuring. If there is one asset that has almost universally outperformed since 2009 it would have to be real estate. This is ironic given that one of the direct causes (if not necessarily the chief cause) of the global financial crisis was a real estate bubble. Across the world, it can be argued that massively over dovish monetary policies have led to real estate bubbles everywhere. Prices in Auckland NZ for example have more than doubled since the crisis, UK house prices have significantly outperformed pre-crisis highs, and NY flats are now trading at entirely unrealistic prices. This is before we talk about countries such as China and Hong Kong where even massive increases in stamp duty have done little to reduce the price of real estate that was already tremendously unaffordable.

Just to give you some numbers, a high quality (but not exceptionally well appointed by any standards) 2500 square foot apartment in one of the better (but not the best) areas in Hong Kong sells for roughly 10 million US dollars. That is a staggering amount especially when you consider two things. Firstly, in

---

[59] It is true that a very high percentage of the population own stocks through their 401k and other pension instruments. However, a large portion of the returns go into fees and the mediocrity of post fee returns of the average pension fund is utterly depressing.

Hong Kong the communal areas are divided between all the apartments in a building and applied to the square footage. So, if the building has for example, a gym and a swimming pool then there is a good chance that a 2500 square foot apartment as quoted is, in fact, an 1800 square foot or smaller apartment once you factor this in, as well as the fact that external rather than internal area is quoted. Thus, we are talking about apartments costing up to 5,000 USD per square foot or more. Just to put that further in context, you could pave the floor of such an apartment with solid 1 oz. bars of silver for approximately 1000 dollars a square foot (depending on the exact bar manufacturer)! When looked at in this way it does appear as if property in all the big cities is overvalued. Again, we will say more about this later but for the moment let us return to Hong Kong.

The second issue in Hong Kong is that when the territory was handed over to China in 1997, it was agreed that the rule of law and property that was extant at the time (corresponding very closely to British law) would be retained for 50 years. However, after 2047 the law would be dictated by Beijing. Thus, given that Hong Kong only has a sliver of freehold property (in the form of St John's cathedral in Central and parts of Hong Kong University[60]) all leases really are not functional with absolute certainty beyond 2047. Yet property continues to change hands as if everything was freehold and perfectly renovated. There is no discount at all for any property that is in poor cosmetic condition which is probably not surprising given the exceptionally high cost per square foot.

Hong Kong certainly is a unique place in terms of circumstance especially as it has an unparalleled fiscal situation[61], but we have seen already that the demographics here coupled with extreme unaffordability have directly been the cause of unrest and troubles. And now, we see signs of strained property markets across the world all with one thing in common in that rates in each respective country are at or close to all-time lows, and certainly long-term lows. Central banks all cut rates following the Fed primarily in order to weaken their currencies and remain competitive against the US. The price for any central bank going against the grain in terms of rates could be pathological. A case in point is the Icelandic financial crisis.

The forgotten precursor to the Global Financial Crisis – an Icy story.

Few people remember what happened in Iceland just before the financial crisis proper during 2007. This is perhaps not surprising given that the population of Iceland is exceptionally small. In fact, only around a quarter of a million people live in Iceland, and at the end of the 20th century the island which was heavily into fishing and tourism was rated AAA by all the major rating agencies. AAA is the highest credit rating that may be given to the bonds of a country or company. It is the highest of credit and basically says that it is inconceivable for a country rated AAA to be unable to pay back its debt. Iceland was one such a country, amongst just a handful of others. Then in the first decade of the 21st century things changed. The Bank of Iceland (situated in a small but rather modern building that looks more like the estate of someone who has just written the quintessential Scandinavian novel than a central bank) wanted to ensure ongoing financial stability for the small nation, and being quite diligent about the overall economic situation both at home and abroad it had notices something that gave it rather a lot of cause for concern.

The bank was worried about property prices. It was one of the few central banks that saw the bubbles forming and wanted to do something about it. The problem that Iceland found, however, was that nobody else in the developed world seem to care one jot about the issue. As a result, the raising of domestic rates in Iceland to 13.5 percent caused huge amounts of speculation in the markets. A country which was rated as AAA with rates in the double digits was too tempting for the funds to resist. They

---

[60] Although Hong Kong University technically cannot sell its land ever as any attempt to relieve itself from ownership would mean the property reverting to the state.

[61] In the good sense, given that the debt to GDP is essentially zero and the Hong Kong Monetary Authority (HKMA) has more foreign currency reserves than there are Hong Kong dollars in circulation.

bought and sold option after option on the Icelandic Krone speculating that it would rally. We traded options on ISK from the market with greater notional than the GDP of the entire country (though fortunately for me I was not speculating or expecting that the ISK would rally I was simply buying the options because volatility was cheap). Now of course the notional of an option is very different to the present value of that option but as a comparison I have never purchased an option on the notional of even 5 percent of the GDP of any other country in the world, but I did with ISK.

The Icelandic domestic banks became massively excessively levered taking the same bet. They would open branches across Europe and try to borrow as much GBP, EUR, CHF or any other European currency as they could, offering extremely generous yields. They would then convert that currency to ISK and invest in Icelandic government bonds or simply place money with the central bank. They would effectively therefore have a huge bet being long ISK against a basket of European currencies. They reasoned that the fact that they were getting at least 10% a year more in interest in ISK than they were paying to their account holders would allow them to absorb any reasonable losses. After all, how far could the ISK sell off against the other currencies? 5%? 10%? Maybe 20% but after 2 years they would have made back the 20% loss even in the worst case... and in the best case they could make money on both the FX and their interest rate "differential" (this being the term for the difference between the rates they were receiving from their investments and the average rate they were paying out to those who had money in their bank accounts abroad). Notice that the banks could simply have taken advantage of ISK rates by just offering their customers in Iceland a healthy 8% a year for an ISK investment and simply made a risk-free spread (another name for the rate differential) of 5.5% without ever needing to worry about the strength or otherwise of the Icelandic Krone. But they got greedy and wanted to make much more of the spread.

Of course, as the financial crisis unfolded the tiny, geared to extreme, economy of Iceland simply couldn't cope, the ISK sank against the EUR, USD and every other currency and all the domestic banks went bankrupt taking with them the deposits of millions of people who had simply opened a savings account in their own country (rather than Iceland). All of this was a direct result of the fact that yields were so high. There simply would not have been the stress in the market if such a yield differential were not available as the banks in Iceland would not have found lenders if rates were, for example, 3 or 4 percent. This is the danger of not following the Federal Reserve in a world that is so globally connected, and yet the Bank of Iceland was correct to target house price inflation as we have argued before. The problem is that even though this was a locally appropriate approach, and one that was badly needed globally, it failed to dovetail with the destabilizing global policies that were being enacted. And, as we shall see when we talk about Greece, this is hardly the first time that this sort of thing happened.

But I promised before that I would tell you why house prices going up are not good for almost everyone. Just imagine that you are a fortunate person. You managed to buy a house at the start of the 1990's in the UK where the housing market had just imploded following a bubble at the end of the 80's You now have managed to pay off the mortgage that you had at the time and now your equity is astronomical. Maybe you bought the house at around 100,000 pounds and it is now worth 5 to 10 times that. If you bought in a popular area, it may well be over 10 times what it was worth when you bought it. So now you are a millionaire. Congratulations. But here comes the rub. You can only take the profit that you have in the house and put it in your bank account if you sell it. If you sell it, in order to buy another one you will find that, on balance, all houses have gone up in value by similar amounts so the only way that you have benefited is if you sell your house and rent or you downsize to something much smaller, or possibly if you move from a high demand to a low demand area which will become up and coming in the future.

It may be suitable to downsize if you bought a 4-bedroom house, had a family, and are happy enough to move to a 2-bedroom house instead now that your children have left home. But what about them? How will they be able to afford what you could afford in 1990? Without salaries catching up with house prices, there is **no** benefit at all to your greater family in aggregate from your house going up in value.

The only situation where there is a benefit is if you owned many more houses than you needed and saw all of them go up in value. So, if for example, you had a fantastic 10-million-pound trust fund in 1990 that allowed you to buy 100 houses at 100,000 pounds each, you could now see a huge benefit from the fact that house prices have gone up. However, it really is just those who owned so many houses before prices went up that benefit. Even those people would probably, on balance, prefer that houses hadn't gone up quite as much so that they could still buy more houses now and not rely on a measly 4% yield or less from rents (very much less if you own in parts of central London).

So, to surmise, house prices going up are simply bad for everyone but the exceptionally rich or possibly those who were excessively leveraged. And those who are borrowing to extreme are irresponsible stewards of their own money. This is a fundamental concept that needs to be understood and it applies to any financial entity including individual human beings. "If you borrow money to the extent that the assets you buy have to go up simply to make your payments under reasonable (say 5%) interest rates, then you are way too leveraged, period"[62]. As we shall see this is very relevant for us in terms of the instability of the financial system and the stresses that housing puts on that system, but we must first ask ourselves a question. Is the fact that house prices seem to be inexorably going up almost everywhere in the world a function of a radically changed paradigm or is it something that is a symptom of lower interest rates? This is something that we need to investigate.

A radically changed world with drastically altered expectations

Around 100 years ago, it was very hard for ordinary people to obtain mortgages. This was true throughout the world, and this was even true in the so-called developed economies. There are many contemporary writings about life at the time, several contemporary writers have also looked at the issue. Derek Thompson writing in The Atlantic[63] for example, notes that "Owning was a rarity. In 1920 there were about four times as many renters as homeowners ... mortgages typically required a down payment of 50 percent." (sic).

What these writers note, but don't expound on however, is that houses were cheaper, adjusted for inflation, at that time compared to any time post 1980. And it is this sad simple fact that we see. Whilst mortgages in the past were much harder to obtain, the value for money of a house was far higher. As Thompson mentions, in 1920 the average house price was around 75,000 USD in today's dollars. And so, we see that as mortgages have become easier and easier, the price of houses has just expanded because now more people can afford houses without a large down-payment and therefore there are more people willing to buy property. With more buyers, sellers can shift the price up just a little bit more than they could before. This is a subtle effect but a real one. So, what really happens with mortgages is that, over time, the borrowing has changed the value of the asset to one that is now adjusted for the additional money that has become available from the increase in credit associated with the mortgage.

It is in **this** sense and only this sense that markets are efficient. If there is credit available, there generally will be credit expansion because the one thing that human beings can be counted to do is be selfish and greedy. We all would generally prefer to buy something now than must save up for it to get it later. As a society we love credit and we love to enjoy things now and deal with things later. So, we can see that even though mortgages have their uses and have helped more people get on the property ladder, they have also led to a significant and **permanent** inflation, or more correctly revaluation of the value of property such that it is no longer as much value for money as it was before. We see this most clearly in

---

[62] As quoted by, well, er... me. Bet you thought it was Adam Smith...
[63] http://www.theatlantic.com/business/archive/2016/02/america-in-1915/462360/

the UK where the argument is that not enough houses are being built to meet demand and therefore prices have gone up. That, in a sense, is true. However, it is just as true that access to cheap money such as extremely low mortgage rates in the UK, the "Right to Buy" program, and in particular the "Help to Buy" program which essentially is a government mortgage "tranche" that gives up to 40% (in London) of the value of the property in the form of a very low interest loan. Now there are probably many of you who are ahead of me here and have seen the key problem. And the problem is this. The minute any of these programs exists the people who are the first users of the programs will benefit the most, and in fact may be the **only** ones who benefit in any real sense. This is because those first adopters get help to buy property at low levels, but the very presence of the program then means sellers can sell at better levels later, and so subsequent participants of the schemes no longer benefit as much because they are buying property that is worse value for money. Overall this means that the programs by necessity need to be more and more aggressive in order to have any effect. So, once a scheme like "Help to Buy" exists, the market immediately prices in the credit expansion that has taken place to the value of the entire program (or thereabouts). So, you end up with inflated property prices and a few small winners (those who took advantage of the program at inception), and a few other big winners (property developers and those with significant excess property investments). If that sounds suspicious to you, it's because it is pretty much a con – not in terms of intended effects but in terms of actual consequences in the real world. This is entirely analogous to why Modern Monetary Theory fails. The market adjusts for the money that has been created by the massive credit expansion, except here you see something even more dangerous, because it does not matter if this credit was taken up by those who were able to bear the cost or not. It will affect the market whether that credit was created for people who were leveraging themselves 20% or folks who were leveraging their net wealth 10 times. It is key to know that the market effect is irrelevant, but it should also be noted that the relevance of the credit worthiness of those who took up the loans is in the instability that it causes. So, prices will go up by the same amount whoever the credit is generated for, but if it is created for those who are already leveraged to the hilt the stability of the system is radically compromised. This is because those with stronger credit are much more likely to keep making their payments if they experience headwinds. But those who are borrowing multiple times their net wealth, only require the existence of very small dips in the percentage of the market value of their assets to be in serious trouble. Lending to those who cannot realistically afford to repay their debt, unless there is a serious price increase in the asset they are purchasing, is a terrible thing, it is really something criminal. It is, in its effect, which is the only thing that really matters, one big Ponzi Scheme.

"A Fonzi Scheme".

One of my favourite TV shows of all time is the show "Psych" where a truly gifted (but woefully uneducated) detective Shawn Spencer and his partner Burton Guster (aka Guy Buttersnaps, or Domo arigato Mr Robato!) solve amazingly devious crimes in Santa Barbara (but somehow filmed on the south west coast of Canada just on the border with the US). However, Mr Spencer is so puissant that initially the police think he is the mastermind behind various crimes as there is no way he could have figured out the perpetrators otherwise. He can only convince them of his innocence by claiming that he is Psychic and has seen these crimes in the spirit world! In one particularly memorable episode, Shawn confuses Ponzi with Fonzi and believes that the perpetrators of one of those financial crimes are somehow connected with the series Happy Days. Whilst this makes for great comedy, few people know where the term Ponzi scheme comes from.

In fact, one Charles Ponzi lends his name to this con despite Ponzi schemes having existed (see for example Little Dorrit by Charles Dickens or consider the South Sea bubble) in both fiction and reality for at least a couple of hundred years before Ponzi enacted his idea. The real reason that Charles Ponzi lends his name to the scheme is simply the amount of money that was involved at the time. One very interesting characteristic of Ponzi's scheme was the thing that made it "great". This was that the stated strategy was, theoretically, a proper business proposition, and a smart one at that and would have been quite spectacularly successful had it been employed as was claimed. The strategy itself therefore was an actual arbitrage. An arbitrage is any trading strategy that essentially guarantees a riskless profit. For example if I can buy one share of a company on the NY stock exchange for 1USD, and that stock also trades on say the London Stock exchange at 1 pound, and if the pound is say at 1.30 GBP/USD, then I can buy the stock on the NYSE, sell it on the LSE, and pay for the purchase on the NYSE with 1 USD of the 1.3 USD that I have made from selling it on the LSE (assuming I can exchange GDP to USD at mid). In theory after this, I can buy more shares and perform the Atlantic trade again (an Atlantic trade is what one calls a trade where there is a sell in Europe and a buy in the US or vice versa). The arbitrage is a genuine one, but it is also something that is naturally only present in the short term, as when this arb is available, everyone wants to take advantage of it which shifts the markets to adjust to close out the arbitrage. Ponzi claimed that his scheme took advantage of the nature of the markets to develop arbitrage opportunities, and the funny thing is, he was indeed right.

In the case of Charles Ponzi, he did have a theoretical arbitrage, but instead of working hard to find a way to exploit it in practice, he came up with a way of enriching himself at the expense of his investors. Ponzi had a history of shady dealing which began almost as soon as he had arrived in the United States in the autumn of 1903 to seek his fortune as had many of his Italian compatriots. He had previously matriculated into the grand dame of Italian universities, the University of Rome otherwise known as Sapienza. However, due to his somewhat spendthrift nature, he was unable to graduate and came to the US with less than 3 dollars in his pocket. In the US he had initially been promoted to waiter after a stint of washing dishes, but had been fired for cheating customers, and this was sadly a pattern for the rest of his life. Having been unsuccessful in the US after 4 years or so, he moved to Montreal where, due to his language skills (he supposedly spoke fluent English, Italian and French), he got a job at a new bank which had been created for the benefit of Italian and other European immigrants, Banco Zarossi. It was here that Ponzi learned that it was possible to pay people returns using new deposits in the "Robbing Peter to pay Paul" shell game, and when the bank eventually collapsed (with its founder Zarossi escaping to Mexico with the lions share of the leftover capital), he resorted to forging a cheque from a customer of the bank, which led him to the first of a string of jail sentences. Eventually, he returned to the US, and ended up in jail there too (this time in Atlanta Prison) having been caught smuggling illegal Italian immigrants across the border. Eventually he was released, and after another set of failed start-ups and business ventures, he discovered a genuine, honest to goodness, arbitrage.

Whilst Ponzi was always willing to take the criminals way out of things, the truth is that many criminals in fact work very hard to realise their nefarious plans, so much so that it makes one wonder why they didn't just work hard on legitimate business in the first place. Ponzi was no different. Having received an International Reply Coupon from a company he was in contact with in Spain, he became curious and started investigating how such things worked. An IRC[64] was essentially a stamp but one that was universal across the world. Thus, you could send someone anywhere in the world the coupon, and the postal systems of these countries had an agreement that an IRC would be good to cover the postage back to the country that had issued the IRC. The IRC was partly a result of one of the best globalist ideas that have ever been implemented, that being the Universal Postal Union. This was created following the Treaty of Bern in 1874 and enabled countries to no longer need individual bilateral postal agreements to exchange mail. But the IRC was always sold at prices that reflected the cost of postage in the country that was issuing the coupon, although it could be redeemed in any country covering the cost of postage from that country. This meant that there was a real arbitrage opportunity if the value of the stamps in the county that the IRC was sent to are worth more than the cost of the IRC plus the postage cost to send the IRC over. Well, because of the weaker European currencies, you really could get these IRCs from Europe in bulk and swap them for US dollars that were worth more than you paid for them, there was also an arbitrage from the fact that the Postal Union had certain pre agreed transfer conventions that

---

[64] Although IRCs are no longer sold in many countries due to lack of interest and declining correspondence in general, you can still buy them where I live in Hong Kong as of this time, at a cost of around 2.7 USD.

gave certain countries a financial advantage in this beyond the optical foreign exchange advantage –
something that President Trump was railing against when he threatened to take the US out of the Postal
Union[65]. This was real and could be profitable, but as with many arbitrage opportunities, this wasn't
necessarily scalable. As an example, just to place a million dollars in that arbitrage, Ponzi would have
had to buy around 30million IRCs. Purchasing that many IRCs would simply not have been feasible
even if that number had existed (it appears that only 27,000 were, in fact, in circulation at the time), and
Ponzi had taken in a lot more than a million dollars – 30 million in fact.

From the time that Ponzi started his scheme around the autumn of 1919, less than a year passed before
the whole thing ended in tears. The comeuppance was partly a result of the sheer success of Ponzi's
advertising and word of mouth. He had actively solicited investors through agents and his own company
incorporated in January 1920, and by the start of July 1920 he was taking in a million dollars in deposits
a week, and by the end if was almost a million a day. The zenith of all this came after he received some
very favourable publicity from the Boston Post on July the 24th, which led to his office in Boston being
inundated with potential investors the next day. Barely 2 weeks later, however, the entire thing had gone
up in smoke after he received a trifecta of bad news; a series of investigative reports by the Boston Post
(as the Post's acting publisher had become suspicious of Ponzi), an audit at the behest of Daniel
Gallagher (which suggested Ponzi's company was insolvent), the US Attorney for the district of
Massachusetts, and William McMasters (who had been acting as a publicity agent for Ponzi) having his
own concerns and himself writing an expose for the Post claiming the Ponzi was bankrupt. The result of
all this bad news led to Ponzi surrendering himself to the US authorities, and he ended up with 5 years
in federal prison, and after serving that sentence, he was put in jail by the state of Massachusetts (even
though it took three trials for him to be found guilty), and even started another deceptive fraud this time
land banking in Florida including various parcels of swampland that were physically underwater.

All told, the investors in Ponzi's enterprise lost around 20million dollars which today might be worth
around 200 million dollars. These included huge swaths of the better citizens of Boston (at one point
75% of Boston policemen had money with him), and a multitude of others. But during the frenzy of
1920, no one had thought about the mechanism that Ponzi claimed to be using until the very end. No
one had considered that Ponzi didn't seem to be investing his own money in the scheme which is
incredibly suspicious given his returns. They also believed that in a time where 5% a year would be
regarded as a good return, returns up to 100 times that amount were possible. But things do not have to
be Ponzi schemes for people to lose money. In fact, most people who do lose money tend to do so on
asset bubbles rather than outright frauds. And few of those bubbles were more impressive than that of
the humble tulip in the early 17th century.

Tulip mania.

The Dutch Golden Age was the result of the so called "Dutch Miracle" as the Netherlands
transitioned from being simply a part of the old Holy Roman Empire through to becoming the most
significant economic and naval power in the world. Now as the name implies the Dutch Golden Age
was a time of exceptional prosperity and in such a time, it is perhaps not surprising that this was the
place that the first well documented price bubble occurred. Now there were probably other times
before this which involved bubbles but the difference here is that the documentation of what happened
is so comparatively strong.

Essentially this was almost the purest possible bubble that there could be. Tulips had only come to
Europe and certainly western Europe in the middle of the 16th century at the earliest. The first noted
example in the literature (mentioned by Mackay also) was in an Augsburg garden in 1559. By all
accounts, tulips had become very sought after in Holland within a decade from that time, and by the

---

[65] https://time.com/5687134/trump-universal-postal-union-deal/

turn of the 17th century these rather humble flowers were considered a truly desirable plant by the rich and wealthy across central Europe. As with all things, however, some specific types of tulips were far more sought after than others. Those of a single colour were considered common, but those with multiple colour staining and other effects were deemed to be far more valuable.

Varieties such as the famous Semper Augustus (now sadly lost to time) became seen as symbols of status, and this variety was the most expensive. What was slightly ironic however was that these varieties with cycling colours and beautiful staining stripes were, in fact, simply diseased tulips suffering from the Tulip Breaking Virus (TBV) which caused this exceptional beauty as a biproduct. But obviously at that time there was no understanding that this was the case and therefore these were regarded as just another natural variety. Now because these more beautiful varieties were diseased, they were also much weaker and survived less easily, and therefore they were also rarer. This was a partial explanation for why tulip prices were so high for so long, as they were indeed relatively scarce during this time.

Throughout the early 17th century, the fame of tulips spread and their cost outside Holland also exploded higher. So much so, that by 1636 tulips became tradeable on the exchanges of several different Dutch cities. Records exist of a tulip of the Admiral Liefken variety trading at 4400 florins, and the aforementioned Semper Augustus was said to be considered "cheap" at 5500 florins. Roughly speaking florins at the time (which were synonymous with the Dutch guilder) would be worth around 15 USD in todays money, and therefore this single bulb traded at over 80,000 USD in terms of equivalent prices today. An interesting anecdote is that the famous painter Rembrandt purchased a huge townhouse in the middle of Amsterdam for 13,000 florins just two years after the bursting of the bubble in 1837[66]. This could easily have been paid for by just 4 or less of the rarest bulbs.

Still, everything has its end, and the best evidence is that the prices collapsed quickly at some time in early February of 1637. Supposedly, an auction in Haarlem found no buyers at a regular auction. After that, the bubble collapsed very quickly and by May of that same year, tulip prices were around 5 percent at most of their previous bubble values. Not much is known of what sort of pattern the collapse saw, but in all probability, there would have been a halving of prices within just a couple of days, and then a slower collapse further. The pattern is quite similar in all bubbles, and there may have been very brief periods of recovery that added more fuel to the fire of the selloff. There is some argument to be made that the bursting of the bubble was accelerated by the presence of bubonic plague in Holland at the time (and particularly in Haarlem). Again, it does seem that every bubble that has burst has a rationalised catalyst, but much of this attribution being after the fact, it is very unclear that there was any real catalyst at all.

The information available is partly contemporary, and partly comes from analyses that were done significantly later. More recently, some have argued that Tulip mania was not as a significant a bubble as some had described it. The biggest attack from such people has centred on the arguments that were generated by Scottish journalist Charles Mackay who wrote his book 'Extraordinary Popular Delusions and the Madness of Crowds"[67] and referenced Tulip mania as one of the main case studies (the South Sea Bubble being another one of them). It should be noted however, that whilst this is one of the best extant records, it was still written only in 1841 more than 200 years after the events of the Tulip Mania. It is like someone today writing about the Revolutionary War but without the benefits of modern

[66] http://vanosnabrugge.org/docs/dutchmoney.htm

[67] https://en.wikipedia.org/wiki/Extraordinary_Popular_Delusions_and_the_Madness_of_Crowds

technology and internet, nor even extensive libraries to consult. Thus, some of this should be taken with a grain of salt vs the contemporary literature. However, when reading the account of the Tulip mania there is no doubt in my mind that Mackay felt this was a genuine bubble. He specifically notes the discontent of those who had effectively bought at the height of the bubble, and who were left with contracts that obligated them to purchase tulips at 20 or 30 times the price they were currently worth. He also notes that "Nobles, citizens, farmers, mechanics, seamen, footmen, maidservants, even chimney-sweeps and old clothes women dabbled in tulips. People of all grades converted their property into cash and invested it in flowers. Houses and lands were offered for sale at ruinously low prices or assigned in payment of bargains made at the tulip-mart." Just this statement alone makes it clear that Mackay regards the behaviour of the Dutch at the time as delusionary. These are not the normal goings on of a market of rare goods. The key to seeing that this was a bubble is the same as the diagnostic for any other bubble. Goods were being churned a lot (many buys and sells), other assets were being sold at fire-sale prices in order to speculate on tulips. People who were not expert botanists were involved in the buying and selling of tulips and this became endemic throughout the entire societal structure, and the demand for speculation was so high that the exchanges began to trade futures and forwards on tulips. And, of course the biggest indicator that this was a bubble was just the fact that these tulips with almost no utility except for some beauty (comparable to other flowers) and scarcity became as expensive as houses or significant plots of land.

And this perhaps is one of the enduring lessons of the Tulip Mania. That when people don't consider the basic mathematics of value, they are apt to fall from a very great height. People at the time thought they had come across an easy scheme to get rich quick. Very few wanted these tulip bulbs for their beauty or any other substantive reason. They just wanted them because they thought they would double in value over a few months. This is something that even today, with our computers and modern technology, many people are apt to fall into. The very purpose that we have discussed bubbles and Ponzi schemes as well as putting the housing market in context, is to make it clear that there are many stupid people who will invest in pipe dreams, and that the markets are far from efficient as standard economic textbooks might tell you even with supercomputers and the internet. In fact, I would argue that it is our modern technology that has made it possible for mathematical illiterates to become "movers and shakers" in the financial markets ushering in the age of Financial Idiocracy.

Financial Idiocracy.

There is a new reality in finance which I like to call financial Idiocracy. Idiocracy is the title of a 2006 film which postulated an argument under the following two premises; that it is now easy for any human to survive and breed regardless of their IQ, and those who are less well educated tend to spend less time thinking of the consequences of their actions and they are more likely to reproduce in greater numbers. Combining these two things together as well as the (somewhat dubious) assumption that those with low IQ beget progeny with low IQ, the film postulated that several generations later, human beings will have on average become stupider leading to a situation where the world functions as an Idiocracy, and where an average man of today would be seen as the biggest genius of the day. Technology would still exist because much of the maintenance of it is now automated, but some of it would no longer be serviceable. The entire dystopian society there has become utterly anti-intellectual, and everything is purely commercial in the crassest possible way.

Whilst the film was comedy there is a parallel here in finance and many areas in the world today that has nothing to do with the false idea that stupid people procreating are guaranteed stupid progeny. The decade that started around 30 years ago from 1988 to 1998 was what I would term as the golden age of mathematical financial derivatives. During this decade, to be able to trade complex derivatives effectively, you had to understand mathematics well and deal with the mathematical nuances very carefully. And when I say trade here, I mean risk manage the trades not sell them; sales people very rarely if at all had to understand the derivatives that they were selling from any modelling or mathematical point of view, and this hasn't changed much over time.

Scroll forward 30 years and mathematical finance has become something extremely easy. Trading systems have progressed to the extent that you are required to have almost no mathematical knowledge to trade and risk manage even the most complex derivative products This applies even more so to basic financial products. Humans no longer need to understand very much to look at the consequences of anything financial. There are spreadsheets to look at this without any need to model or check or confirm. In wealth management, this is typically now "hard" coded on websites in a "user friendly" way, where the pricing engine is just a black box.

We are going even further in finance whereby AI is beginning to make even the most complex financial things look trivial. But the problem with all of this is that there is no systematic guide to finance nor will there ever be. That means that no matter how good AI gets in terms of the machine learning approach, there will never be this kind of AI that beats a very capable human who has access to a very powerful computer and appropriate market data. This may seem counterintuitive as I am arguing that humans are getting worse at finance, but my point is that unless we achieve AI with the same qualitative reasoning skills that humans have, the AI will always make a lot of mistakes, and people on average will do worse over time in the financial industry. To be clear, I don't mean mistakes in the same sense that a human would make mistakes, by say forgetting some sort of past experience. Machines do not make those kinds of mistakes. This is why once chess computers could look further than say 8 moves ahead (roughly the maximum a player looks ahead), they could never be defeated tactically because chess is a deterministic game and a computer would see all the possible tactics available up to however many moves ahead it could look. But when it comes to the markets, there is no deterministic approach to defining where the markets will trade. And that means that for AI to beat humans it needs to be able to think like a human and create its own heuristic approaches to determining where the markets would go. And as we have discussed, true AI is quite a bit away. However, the basic rules of finance that most portfolio managers in asset management employ can easily be programmed into some kind of "expert system" and therefore computers can already beat the financier of "Idiocracy".

But financial Idiocracy has consequences and many of those consequences are already beginning to manifest themselves. Those consequences appear in generally poor results by the banks in terms of trading. Although it is true that trading as a business has been weathering many headwinds such as the Volcker rule (which effectively bans taking proprietary trading positions i.e. those on behalf of the account of the bank itself), the performance of banks in the last fiver years compared to the potential growth that existed has been laughable. The number of managers and other support staff in banking versus those who are generally described as producers has exploded both due to increased compliance and regulatory requirements, and because much of the business has become E-trading. E-trading is genuinely boring and many of us quants hate the entire discipline. Unfortunately, that boring quality means that the entire field has been infected by the Idiocracy with poor execution algorithms and a lack of ability to attract top mathematical talent which, quite understandably is either more interested in working for the best quant funds or finds other industries more useful. The draw of Wall Street was always big deals and the ability to trade, if you cannot be part of it why should you be involved when your skills could earn you much more (both in terms of money and prestige) somewhere else.

What is much more worrying than this is that there is some evidence extant that demonstrates that we might really be seeing true Idiocracy in action. There have been two different papers published that seem to identify that human IQ is dropping from generation to generation. The exact amount of deterioration in human cognition is unclear, but what is clear is that the Flynn effect seems to be in full reverse. The Flynn effect[68] is coined after the New Zealand researcher James Flynn[69] who found through several studies that over the 20th Century, IQ across the Western World increased significantly and constantly. But sadly, there is now evidence that starting in the early 1990's the Flynn effect has been

---

[68] https://en.wikipedia.org/wiki/Flynn_effect
[69] https://en.wikipedia.org/wiki/James_Flynn_(academic)

running in reverse. There have been various speculations as to why this is the case, but even the most optimistic diagnosis is that this will probably continue. The indication is that the causes are environmental[70] but there have not been sufficient numbers of studies undertaken to identify a specific issue or trigger for certain. Whatever the cause, this does not bode well for the future. My personal view, and this is just a view rather than some deep insight, is that just like in the case of Finance, human beings have basically grown up in a world where they don't have to have a strong fundamental understanding of the basic concepts that underpin that world. It is far easier for a human to learn to operate an Iphone than to understand the technology on which it is based thoroughly. In the same way, very few computer programmers these days know how to program in machine code because they spend all their time coding in high level languages. And through the vast abundance of libraries to perform various mathematical procedures, computer programmers also understand algorithmics less and less too. And financial Idiocracy has therefore parallels in all sorts of other areas. The most palpable area of financial Idiocracy has been the advent of something that can only be described as a phenomenon; that of the cryptocurrency.

Cryptos.

The rise of Cryptocurrencies has been one of the most spectacular events ever to be seen in the financial world. Essentially back in 2008 someone using the name Satoshi Nakamoto (a not altogether atypical name for a Japanese man) wrote a paper describing a method to create a distributed ledger that was secure and allowed essentially every transaction described in the database to be executed peer to peer without reliance on a centralised middle man. The way this was envisaged was through a socialised networking system whereby the network participants themselves all had interest in the services provided by the network itself. The idea therefore was that it would be impossible to hack the network unless 50% or more of the network participants (in terms of computational power) were involved directly in the attack – something which intuitively is extraordinarily unlikely to happen in a widely enough distributed network.

I would advise anyone to read the paper itself[71]. You don't really have to be a computer scientist or a mathematician to understand it, and it will give you a very good understanding of what blockchain really does and what cryptocurrencies are. But the key here is that the focus of the paper is not on ascribing any sort of value to bitcoin, but in describing how a network could be created which would be able to be used to deliver financial transactions but where there was a very high likelihood that the network could not be hacked. The way it did this is by essentially building a huge number of redundancies in the system. Redundancies are very common in things like airplanes and any other mission critical constructions either physical or virtual. For those of you who have a fear of flying, it might hearten you somewhat to know that advanced planes such as the Boeing 777 have multiple redundancies in the flight critical systems[72]. The 777 for example has 4 flight management computers located at different places throughout its fuselage so that even a collision in mid-air is unlikely to shut everything down. In the same way, if you want to ensure the integrity of a network, it is useful to have a bunch of redundancies. The internet generally has an incredible number of these with cross connectivity between different servers such that if one major server goes down, there are a myriad of others that can take its place and users notice nothing at all. This is all very well and useful, but the problem came in the first implementation of such a network and the creation of the first bitcoins.

What's in a bitcoin?

---

[70] http://www.pnas.org/content/115/26/6674
[71] https://bitcoin.org/bitcoin.pdf

[72] And no that is not true for the entertainment systems so don't be surprised if the video on demand crashes, but the plane carries on its merry way.

This is a very good question. A bitcoin is really a receipt that says that a certain amount of work has been done to solve a certain set of mathematical puzzles (extremely mundane mathematics from the purely theoretical point of view) through number crunching. More specifically, the algorithm that is used is a specific example of what we call a hash. There isn't very much more to it than that, and anyone who argues there is has never coded a cryptocurrency (I have by the way). With bitcoin itself, though there are several rather severe misconceptions that people have, partly encouraged by rhetoric from the crypto investment community, regarding what it gives you recourse to. More on that very soon, but first we have to discuss one modern-day Ponzi scheme that is analogous to cryptocurrencies.

A sure sign of a Ponzi scheme is one where there is no logical reason for the supposed business than is being invested in to be able to make money. The premise might initially seem reasonable but there seems to be no mechanism by which the scheme could really work that way. You can see that illustrated perfectly with Bernie Madoff's approach to the Ponzi scheme.

Just as the Global Financial Crisis looked as if it might have turned the corner, with the implementation of TARP and various other measures, a rather nasty aftershock occurred. Bernie Madoff, who was a well-known New York philanthropist, and had been non-executive chairman of the NASDAQ stock exchange, fell from grace at the beginning of December 2008 when his sons reported him to the SEC for running a giant Ponzi scheme since the early 90's. He had claimed to be able to give his clients regular above market returns with little to no variation or volatility, and it turned out that he was just making up the results after the fact.

Madoff argued that his "secret" to constant returns was a so-called split strike option strategy. This in trading terms is a very basic beginner strategy where you essentially just invest in the market but sell off your upside by shorting call options on each stock you buy (so that your gains are capped) but use the premium you obtain from shorting to buy puts on your stocks also. This limits your downside of course, but you get very little upside too due to the calls you sold, and due to market costs you are unlikely to make a lot of money unless your call and put strikes are significantly away from the current market level. However, in that situation, there is very little difference between this "strategy" and just buying stocks except for the cost in bid offer to sell calls and buy puts. A junior trader in a bank may be told to use such a strategy in order to learn how calls and puts function (in terms of the mechanics of exercising an option etc.), but this genuinely is not a useful strategy at all for a trader who wants to generate significant returns, and certainly not if said trader wants to outperform others. Of course, people who understood this generally assumed that Madoff was lying and had some much deeper way of making money instead.[73] Madoff was someone that I was interested in from the start. Not just because he ran the largest Ponzi scheme in history, but because he was an alumnus of the Far Rockaway High School. This was the same school that one of my childhood heroes Richard Feynman went to.

Madoff ran his scheme by compartmentalising everything so that almost no one realised what his deal was not real. Even some of his closest confidants such as his wife and his sons had no idea what he was doing. Some have argued that these people knew that there was something wrong but simply chose to ignore it because they were personally making a lot of money. If that were true then both their behaviour after they found out the scheme (his sons reported him themselves), as well as before (his family were not squirreling away money in hidden accounts for the inevitable time when Bernie would see his demise) was very strange. The most likely truth of it in my opinion is that they simply did believe that Bernie was an excellent trader and managed his accounts carefully and safely. There are unfortunately many people in finance today who have very little idea of what it takes to consistently make money in the markets. I know this from personal experience; even in places like Goldman and UBS there were many charlatans who didn't really know how to make money but worked instead to ensure that they could either take credit for the work done by others, or that they could promote their brand to such an extent that they were never in a particular job long enough to be assessed as

---

[73] Perhaps they thought he was using AI.

incompetent and continue to be overpromoted to infinity (and beyond). So, Madoff wasn't really anything special or a complete outlier in terms of people in finance, he simply was willing to take this to a criminal level for reasons that we may never be fully certain of. There is something important to notice here which is an axiom of our thinking when it comes to these sorts of cheating schemes. Whilst the amount of possible investments in the world are finite, the number of possible Ponzi schemes is not. This means that if you find yourself with an investment that looks too good to be true, it almost certainly is simply because the number of instances where your investment is a good one are dwarfed by the plethora of schemes that range from being small falsehoods to demonstrating outright lies.

Now back to bitcoin and the cryptocurrencies.

One of the metrics that people claimed was an indication of a "cheap" cryptocurrency was something which was known as the crypto price earnings ratio. But to discuss this crypto Price earnings ratio (or P/E ratio) we need to know what this looks like in the real world, so back to the world of stocks and businesses. The price earnings ratio is a good metric for a quick measure of the value of a company. Basically, it is simply the price of a stock divided by the earnings per share. This gives you a number which is a quick snapshot of the financial health of the company. The reason that this represents a good general indicator of the value of a stock is that the earnings of a company in a mature market generally are relatively stable whilst the stock price can be volatile. So, for example if a company has earnings per share of 1 dollar and a price of 5 dollars this is a P/E ratio of 5. This represents a potentially good investment because in theory this implies that the company would earn its entire market capitalisation after 5 years of operation if the earnings remained the same each year. Therefore, one would reasonably expect that the stock is cheap because essentially the yield of the stock internally is 20% of the market cap. However, if the P/E ratio is 50, this means that if earnings stay the same you would need 50 years of earnings to make back the investment in the stock from an earnings perspective. This implies the stock is very expensive.

Of course, as always, low P/E ratios are not a guarantee of a cheap stock nor are high P/E ratios a guarantee of an overvalued stock. This is because companies that reinvest their earnings into new businesses and R&D might well not show particularly good earnings even if their business is very profitable. Equally speaking if a company is highly leveraged and is on the verge of being unable to support its debt, the P/E ratio may still look very good if the company is by some miracle still able to claw out an accounting profit even if they are in danger of imploding. In addition, companies in markets that are growing very substantially often look very expensive with this measure because the P/E ratio assumes that earnings are constant by construction, and if a market is growing rapidly, the earnings of the company are likely to grow rapidly with it, therefore a P/E ratio of 50 might not be so bad (because if earnings are doubling each year and the price of the stock stays the same, in 5 years' time the P/E ratio will have collapsed to below 2 due to an earnings growth of 3200 percent. But despite these weaknesses, flaws, and foibles, in a market of reasonable stability with a relatively healthy company the P/E ratio provides a good snapshot of the relative cheapness of a stock. Now we understand what a P/E ratio is and why it works let's go back to the crypto version.

Well initially you can see that a P/E ratio does not seem to exist with crypto currencies. Cryptos do not make any money in any absolute sense and therefore there are no tangible earnings. The price of a crypto does exist but how can one find a P/E ratio? Well they did find one, but it is very suspicious. What the crypto guys did was take the market capitalisation in dollars (or any other currency) of a given crypto currency (this is analogous to the price of a stock) and divide it by the dollar price of the turnover in that crypto currency. This gives a number that looks a bit like a P/E ratio. But whereas the earnings number is a good number to use, this turnover number is utterly pointless. How can we tell? We do the same thing that we always do to identify reasonableness; we look at the limits of the situation. The argument for this P/E ratio is that a low number indicates a cheap crypto because if the turnover of the crypto daily is 50 percent of the market cap this should mean that lots of people want it and therefore the price should go up[74]. Alternatively, some people look at this in the context of an assumption that turnover in a stock or a crypto should be constant to the first order, and therefore this should tell us something about the value of the crypto.

But in the limit of a situation where the turnover is greater than the market cap, this could mean quite the opposite. If huge amounts of a currency was being bought and sold that it was turning over more than the market cap, (hence every single bitcoin in circulation is changing hands more than once on average) this should imply that there is too much speculation rather than demand. Why? Because if there was simply demand all that would happen is that the currency would go up and there would be little turnover (as everyone wanted the currency). But huge turnover implies a lot of churning. Equally the idea is that if the P/T ratio is very high this currency is overvalued but again this makes no sense as if for example there was a huge demand in the currency it might not be surprising that there are very few transactions because everyone wants to buy. You can see confirmation that the P/T ratio makes no sense because you can generate this number for real stocks and there you see absolutely no value to it. Some stocks have a very high P/T ratio, others have very low ones with no clearly obvious pattern. The P/T ratio as a level of value idea is clearly wrong. P/T ratio simply represents an indicator of the level of turnover in a stock. This may be a good diagnostic for identifying potential fraud in a finance situation of course [75] but for valuation purposes it is entirely irrelevant at best, and at worst should instead be a negative indicator rather than an indicator of value.

There would be some merit to the idea if cryptos transactions were primarily used to pay for something real, but in a world where almost no crypto is used to buy something tangible, it becomes a meaningless churn measure. In fact, it is almost a negative indicator of value because an asset that is churned a great deal is likely to be one which is either in heavy distress or massively overvalued and in a rising market only the second is a realistic option (for obvious reasons). Even during the 2018 bear market, we didn't see people spending cryptos as the currencies fell which tells you that the holders never really saw these as currencies in the first place. Now the fact that practitioners in crypto are entirely unable to identify the pathological nature of this indicator, is itself indicative of the fact that crypto "experts" are part of the Idiocracy. So, when you hear the claim that people who don't think cryptocurrencies are valuable really don't understand them, see if the person who is making that assertion believes or used to believe in the P/T ratio for valuation. If they did, then they are in no position to claim either authority or the ability to value these assets. And even if they don't what is their method of valuation?

Other people have tried to run simulations to predict the price of cryptos or force crypto pricing to standard derivative models, but in doing so they often make ridiculous assumptions and mistakes that a derivatives trader at a bank would consider "schoolboy errors". These models often end up having an "implied" crypto forward rate that is multiple times the rate that it is trading today. Again, without any clear argument, other than the fact that this needs to be the case to fit into some of the mathematical models for these currencies. But these models assume that the underlying asset has some genuine value, they are simply not built to assess something that is so utterly speculative and takes its entire worth from the consensus of its buyers. The crypto "bulls" simply don't have a single diagnostic indicator of value because there isn't a good one. Or to be more precise, there are some good ones but all of them would imply that the price of any extant cryptocurrency should be far smaller than the market currently implies. These include things like comparing the transaction speed of the network vs that of real-world transaction networks and implying a valuation of the network from that etc. We should note that the behaviour of the market of cryptocurrency is entirely analogous to that of the previously mentioned

---

[74] https://medium.com/@matthewfinestone/nvt-ratio-cryptos-p-e-cousin-c6b264b4fea8
[75] For example, fund managers who have full discretion in their investments might be tempted to do lots of trades in return for a kickback. The practice of trading many times pointlessly is called churning and it is a crime.

Tulip Mania. Just as with tulips, cryptos are being used primarily for speculation. As with tulips, cryptos are being churned thoroughly with sometimes 20 or 30 percent of the entire market cap traded in 24 hours. And all sorts of people who are not experts in financial assets are buying bitcoin like there is no tomorrow. And although people don't seem to be selling their assets at discounts to buy cryptos, there are many who are willing to borrow money on credit cards to buy these things. All is eerily like the time of the Tulip Mania.

So why is bitcoin a Ponzi scheme?

The answer to that comes from answering the question; what can I do with a bitcoin? And by this I specifically mean what recourse does a bit coin allow an owner? If you stick this question into google you will of course get a bunch of articles on which merchants accept bitcoin for payment. The number of merchants who do is, unfortunately, a tiny fraction of the vendors who accept any other sort of payment online. Worse than this, those that do accept some form of cryptocurrency charge a very hefty spread versus the exchange tradable bitcoin price. None of the bitcoin bull websites will tell you this of course because it damages the argument that bitcoin makes financial transactions much easier. Now credit card companies also charge such fees, but they do so to the merchant rather than the user for the most part[76]. Then there are the fees charged in doing a bitcoin transaction in the first place which at the height of the last bitcoin mania (at the end of 2017) got to above 30$ per transaction. This does not bode well for a cheap system of buying things, even if suddenly many more merchants began to accept bitcoin.

But this is not really that relevant when it comes to actual recourse. Yes of course if a bitcoin is worth 15,000$ then you can buy 15,000$ worth of stuff with one bitcoin (minus the spreads and costs of course). But then you need to ask yourself what does 1 bitcoin at 15,000 mean in the real world. What can you do with the bitcoin in terms of a contractual right that you might have other than sell the thing? If you own a share of stock in a company, then you own a fraction (very tiny of course) of that company lock stock and barrel. That usually means that you can vote at the AGM of the company for this and that measure. Of course, it does not mean that you have a significant say in what the company does, but you can group with other investors and you can always ask questions at the AGM which is pretty fun; if you have never tried it I highly recommend it given that the cost of this is often just the price of one share of stock of whatever local company interests you. With one USD you don't have a recourse to a company, but you do own USD which allows you to buy natural US assets. Houses in the US will always be houses in the US and they will always be available in US dollars unless the US experiences hyperinflation and some other currency is used as the de facto standard. This, of course, is highly unlikely. With bitcoin you have absolutely no recourse to anything except other cryptocurrencies. If there is no recourse at all to anything that has intrinsic value, then bitcoin also has no intrinsic value. Put simply, owning a bitcoin gives you no ownership of anything that has any guaranteed value.

But what about transaction fees you might say? Well the transaction fees go to whoever mined the bitcoin that is being transacted on. They still have recourse to every single bitcoin transaction that the bitcoin which they mined makes. They have this right in perpetuity which **is** worth something. But the point is that unless you mined your bitcoin in the first place you don't have the right to those fees. So, you don't have the right to any fees at all which again means no recourse. So, what about the argument that you can notarise transactions with bitcoin and that notary services cost money. Well yes this is true in theory, but the point is that with things like bitcoin the cost of notarisation in basically infinitely low and therefore the value ascribed to this is still basically zero. A distributed and decentralised blockchain

---

[76] Especially in some of the more niche areas such as with bullion dealers, a wire transfer will usually get you a cheaper price than charging through a credit card at least in the US. In the UK there is specific legislation requiring the price to the customer to be identical regardless of payment accepted.

is the culprit here because it can be created for almost no cost and can be used to notarise anything either through existing protocols or through newly innovated ones.

And whilst it is true that bitcoin is limited in terms of the number of possible bitcoins in existence at 21 million, what is not limited is how many different bitcoins can be created. I can literally create a coin right now just by copying the bitcoin code (which is public) or even writing my own (I did this, it took me around 3 days and I am not amongst the best coders in the world by any stretch of the imagination). So, these coins are far worse than fiat. They are ultra-fiat as an unlimited number of types of coins can be issued not just an unlimited number of coins! Whichever way that you look at it, a bitcoin buys you nothing. It simply exists as a memento that some miner somewhere solved a difficult mathematical problem by brute force. Now I don't know about you, but my maths competition mementos are not worth anything at all.

We are all simultaneously Ponzi and his victims.

The fact is that you can do very little with a bitcoin. It is of no value at all and yet because a huge number of people have no understanding of value they race in and buy it at any cost. Others have argued that bitcoin cannot be a Ponzi scheme because it wasn't created to steal money from people[77], there are no guaranteed returns, and that there is no Charles Ponzi here masterminding the whole thing. But this is where, in an example of infinite irony, we see people unable to really understand what a modern Ponzi scheme looks like. Yes, there are no promised returns in this Ponzi scheme, but the returns are clearly expected by everyone who invests. How do we know? Because virtually no one at all (except at the very start of the entire thing[78]) uses or used bitcoin to buy stuff as they are simply holding it in expectation that it would go up in value. Now even someone not particularly well versed in finance can understand that an investment going up in value is entirely equivalent to paying returns (as you can obviously sell some fraction of your holding to generate those income returns yourself), but for some reason the bitcoin community refuse to see this obvious notion. And the fact that there is no dark Machiavellian mastermind controlling the levers behind the curtain simply shows that the Ponzi scheme is decentralised. The crypto converts fail to see the decentralised aspects of their own totem of worship. With technology, the Ponzi scheme has been decentralised between the early adopters. In fact, every single person who buys cryptocurrencies (except those who buy at the very top or the first ever miners) is in some sense partly Charles Ponzi, and in some sense somewhat of a victim. They are a blend of both with the first purchasers mostly representing the role of Ponzi, and later buyers mostly victims. The same is true in a traditional Ponzi scheme because some people who early adopt do get returns, but it is even more the case when the returns are in terms of capital appreciation as everyone except the people purchasing before the bubble collapse generally make some return on their investment. But the fact that the mastermind is distributed rather than embodied in a single person doesn't change the truth that bitcoin only has value through consensus and that consensus is simply a function of the number of people that can be convinced to own bitcoin or any other cryptocurrency. What bitcoin is, in fact, is a truly decentralised Ponzi scheme where there is no one to go after when this all ends in tears.

Does this mean that cryptocurrencies are pointless? Of course, it does not. In fact, currencies will be digital rather than physical for certain in the future. It might be argued that they already are basically digital as pretty much every bank creates money through the ledger that they record deposits on. They will also probably use some kind of distributed ledger technology or at least the base of it but it won't be

---

[77] Several early adopters have indeed given much of their gains to charity.
[78] Where in 2010 someone paid 10,000 bitcoins (which would be worth almost 200 million at the peak of the bitcoin bubble) for a couple of large Papa John's pizzas.
https://qz.com/1285209/bitcoin-pizza-day-2018-eight-years-ago-someone-bought-two-pizzas-with-bitcoins-now-worth-82-million/

anything like bitcoin, and the coin that is generated will have full recourse to the network and will be a stable coin with a value that does fluctuate, but only in the same way that other currencies do. Also, the governments will take full control of the crypto markets because they are basically obliged to do this. They are just too poor and beleaguered financially to be able to do otherwise. And this is where Cryptocurrencies are very dangerous. Let's say that all the current financial currencies have now morphed to online currencies. What is to stop a government who has no money to impose a tax on your wealth through direct taxation of your bank accounts? They can do so stunningly easily without any concern whatsoever. They can just state that the interest rate is now minus 2percent, or minus 20 percent, or even minus 50 percent meaning that just about everyone in the country is unable to remain rich by staying in cash. They can cut out the middleman and impose taxes directly through the buying power of the currency far more than ever before. Before, if a government just printed money like in Weimar, they would eventually generate runaway inflation that would devalue the currency they could print so much that the very printing of currency becomes an unprofitable endeavour. Now, if the government chooses to tax more, they just need to cut it out at the bank accounts. And this should scare pretty much everyone who believes in any form of freedom.

Ultimately, networks like that of Ethereum will emerge that offer the features of things like smart contracts together with a stability in value that allows them to become proper currencies probably by offering a more standard method of valuation such as a synthetic currency board, or a network guarantee pricing for verification, or something we have yet to consider. These will require a network that can transact around 100,000 times a second as a minimum to be viable[79] and this will take some time. But for the moment, every single crypto remains a genuine crock at the point of writing. And it is worthwhile remembering that even this will not necessarily mean that valuations are reasonable because, of course, there needs to be adoption and confidence that the network will remain in place and do what it needs to do forever. This on its own is something that can be problematic. If the US government were to disappear overnight somehow, there would undoubtedly be a successor. It may be that your dollars lose money, and certainly you would lose more than if the USD was backed by gold or silver, but you would certainly fare better than if you held cryptocurrency authorised by some random network with no guarantee.

And so, the evolution of speculative manias is complete. We went from the middle ages with essentially no financial tools at all, through to the 19th century where companies were evaluated fairly simply on the basis of their revenues (current revenues that is) and not much else, to the 20th century where companies were evaluated based on their revenues and some calculation of what their future revenues might be, to the point at the end of the 20th century which was the height of the dot come bubble where companies no longer needed revenues and certainly not profits. Thus, we have the bubbles of Tesla where the company in 2017 traded as if it had already become a top player in a massively well-established marketplace the size of the current market for the petrol car. Finally, however, the "coup de gras" came in the form of cryptocurrencies, where value was ascribed to something which cannot ever lead to revenues simply because of scarcity of a specific digital issue, even though the code used could be replicated again and again. Even Mr Ponzi would certainly blush crimson at what we have become. But to those who have studied this area this should not be surprising. In fact, it should be regarded as the natural result of a morally bankrupt central bank system. The central bankers created the mania for cryptocurrencies by taking the volatility out of the market that should have existed in the first place. You see, the volatility of an asset and its potential return are generally two sides of the same coin as the volatility is there because of the inherent risk of the particular investment. And the risk of the investment is very much linked to its potential return simply because no one would buy a risky security without expecting a big potential return. Without assets that could provide a significant amount of

---

[79] This would put such a currency at roughly 1.5 times the capacity of Visa and Mastercard combined.

market return available, investors turned to cryptos as the new thing that could provide them with very strong returns.

But the central banks did more than this. The ECB for example was responsible for a financial crisis that took place right after the Global Financial Crisis as the developed nations were struggling to recover and grow. The crisis that followed was the crisis of one of the smaller countries in Europe, with a population of barely 12million people; that of Greece.

Greece with its immortal glories.

Winston Churchill was arguably the greatest orator of the 20th century, in my mind narrowly squeezing out the likes of Martin Luther King, and John Fitzgerald Kennedy. Although it is not his most famous speech, the address entitled "The sinews of peace" delivered at Westminster College in Fulton, Missouri on the 5th of March of 1946 was certainly the most important in terms of visions of the future. This speech is best known for coining both the phrase "iron curtain" as well as the term "special relationship" regarding the US and the UK. It is something well worth listening to and I thoroughly recommend it being available both in transcript[80] and as a recording in the BBC archives[81]. It was delivered in front of President Truman[82] as well as the Governor of Missouri and several other notable persons.

In the speech, Churchill delivers a veritable polemic defending the west and effectively arguing that it is only the west that can prevent the two great evils of war and tyranny. He described an iron curtain having descended across the continent of Europe. He lamented that all the great capitals of central and eastern Europe have all been subsumed by the "Soviet sphere" (of influence). He pointed out however that "Athens alone – Greece with its immortal glories – is free to decide its future....". And he was indeed right. Greece was lucky to escape, and only just, the horrors of Communism. I say only just, because not even a month after Churchill delivered this speech, Civil War[83] erupted in Greece, and even though Democracy eventually won the day, by the end of the war in 1949, Greece was left in tatters. For the next three decades, the aftershocks of this event were still being felt, and Greece took a very long time to reach first world levels of GDP per capita compared to any country in Western Europe. But from joining the EU in 1981, Greece began to develop into an advanced economy. Especially in the 1990s, inflation began to collapse to levels comparable with the rest of the EU. In addition, the government managed to control its deficit somewhat and became able to borrow at better and better levels through that decade. 10-year government bonds which were yielding over 25% in the early 90s, appreciated so much that by the time that Greece gave up the drachma for the Euro in 2002, the same government bonds were now yielding just 5%.

But all was not well with Greece. In order to qualify for the use of the Euro under the Maastricht criteria[84], Greece was obligated to reduce its deficits below 3% of GDP. They had done so, but in order to achieve this they had used some exceptional creative accounting processes which failed to demonstrate the true nature of the deficits. But Greece appeared to be the canonical story of success in terms of a developed European economy. The economy itself grew almost 50 percent in the decade between the middle of the 90s and the 2000s.

---

[80] http://www.historyguide.org/europe/churchill.html
[81] https://1d4vws37vmp124vlehygoxxd-wpengine.netdna-ssl.com/wp-content/uploads/1946/03/1946-03-05_BBC_Winston_Churchill_The_Sinews_Of_Peace.mp3
[82] Who specifically states that he had become fond of both Churchill and Stalin. Make of that what you will.
[83] Richard Clogg, *Greece, 1940–1949: Occupation, Resistance, Civil War: a Documentary History*, New York, 2003 (ISBN 0-333-52369-5)
[84] http://ec.europa.eu/economy_finance/economic_governance/sgp/pdf/coc/2012-01-24.pdf

And then the Global Financial Crisis hit, and Greece was not left out which, was strange, as Greece by itself should have been largely unaffected by a bond crisis involving US low quality property bonds. The Greek banks had not invested in any shady subprime derivatives. They hadn't bought any low-grade bonds, or anything that would have been regarded as toxic. They had simply done what would have been considered the most conservative possible investment; they bought the government bonds of their country. Standard economic theory would say that this was effectively AAA at least in the local currency of Greece. The idea being, as we have seen with Modern Monetary Theory, that a government can just print money. The Central Bank of Greece should have been able to step in and support the bonds of the country. But of course, we all know the flaw with this; Greece was using the Euro and only the ECB was able to print Euros. The Central Bank of Greece could not at all do this and therefore simply stood helpless and impotent to do anything at all to save either the economy or the various actors involved.

So, the banks, which had basically only bought government bonds also essentially collapsed and aggravated the situation. Furthermore, the banks in Cyprus (which is independent from Greece and where my parents are both from) had also invested in Greek Government Bonds which led to the banking crisis in Cyprus in 2013. This domino effect of owning government debt that wasn't really backed by a central bank that could print that money, hit Cyprus badly, so much so that it only managed to recover in 2019 and even that involved a significant loss of assets for many Cypriots that had cash on deposit with the local banks, who had to be nationalised and combined. Any deposit above the EU insured limits (and there were plans in Cyprus to not even honour that) was subject to significant haircuts up to 40 percent. Greece, however, never really recovered at all and up until August of 2019 unemployment in Greece was still at 16.7% down from the highs of 27.8% in July of 2013. So, Greece could represent the future for the US perhaps, but we don't even have to look as far afield as "the old country" to see the telos of all this, it has already begun on the west coast of the United States.

The Golden State.

The California coastline presents a stark beauty all its own[85], with some magical contrasts. It is the most populous state in the Union and is also exceptionally endowed with natural resources. It was the state that epitomised the gold rush bringing prosperity to a huge number of people in the 19th and early 20th century. It has a fantastic climate which allows for exceptional yields in crop growth. California soil produces a cornucopia of vegetables including over 90% of the crop of US walnuts, broccoli, artichokes, garlic, plums and celery. So much fruits and vegetables are produced in California, that Snopes the fact checking website was able to deceive their readership that the bear in the flag of California was originally intended to be a pear, but the handwriting of the designer was misread by the artist who was to draw it[86]. California also has forests, and huge numbers of rivers. It is also the home of Hollywood and Silicon Valley, two exceptionally profitable institutions (if you could call them such things). So, California would seem to have it all when it came to resources.

It also taxes the people who live there very aggressively compared to most other states in the union. There are high levels of state income tax (with a maximum of 12.3 percent) as well as high ancillary taxes such as a 9% sales tax which is one of the highest in the US. All these things should mean that there are plenty of resources for California to protect its poor as well as to provide all necessary services, and, should also mean that the state is very well capitalised. And yet somehow, California is failing. It is failing in several ways. Firstly, the state is completely bankrupt. The average net debt of California is 33,000 USD per resident of the State. This is a staggering amount especially when you look at it per

---

[85] Just like the moon as described by the crew of the Eagle on Apollo 11.
[86] To me it is monumentally ridiculous for a fact checking website to put stories that it knows is untrue as facts that have been checked. The site supposedly did so in order to demonstrate that there is no such thing as a golden source. However, given the fact that Snopes is notorious for basically lying about a number of its supposed checks, I guess they were just saying "caveat emptor" in preparation for numerous lawsuits.

taxpayer where it is 74,000$[87]. This doesn't really compare favourably with the debt of most countries to GDP, but there is more. The debt load of CalPERS which is the California Public Employees Retirement Scheme has a debt such that it is 11,000$ per household[88]. When all these are stacked up, it becomes clear that the State has significant problems in terms of its debts.

California also has massive disparity between the rich and the poor. Property prices are extremely high all over the coast and even further inland it is very difficult to find a reasonably priced place to lay your head. The Democrats who have controlled California for at least the last 20 years will say that California is the growth engine of the United States and that if it were a country it would be the 5th largest economy in the world. But then you must compare it to what it would have looked like if California had simply been a little more fiscally responsible. The reason that California is doing badly is because whilst it exists within a very capitalist country, it is heading closer to a socialist system. It has far more government overreach than the average state and simply is unwilling to deal with the many problems that exist in its environs with anything approaching a reasonable procedure.

California is also suffering from a large homeless and illegal immigration problem. These are significant headwinds to the ability of California to properly support the people of the state and citizens particularly. The problem here is that California has become essentially a sanctuary state for illegals which has massively increased income inequality with a race to the bottom in terms of employment. California issues driving licences to illegal immigrants at will, and essentially provides for Medicare and several benefits. The idea of this was ostensibly to ensure that everyone who is driving in California is properly insured, but it has done little to achieve this. In fact, California is chock full of well-meaning laws that just serve to cause chaos. For example, after it became no longer a felony to defecate on the street in San Francisco, the entire city became virtually inundated in faeces. The idea to decriminalise this was to help the homeless, but it had the effect of just making things more disgusting for everyone. In Los Angeles, the homeless problem is so bad that medieval diseases have been able to get a foothold again such as Typhus, and there is even the possibility that bubonic plague might resurface. Petty theft in California has been decriminalised, whereby any theft of value less than 950 dollars is effectively ignored. This has basically made shoplifting utterly commonplace and gangs of shop-lifters ravage stores with each person stealing a few hundred dollars of merchandise, an amount that is lower than these limits so that the police don't bother to arrest them. There are countless of these laws in California that just make everything worse, and yet the people still elect the very same politicians who never do anything to change this.

California should be an example to the rest of the United States in terms of what happens when you move your economy from a capitalist structure to a socialist structure. What occurs when you allow illegal immigration to flourish, and things that happen when your rules and regulations become so restrictive that businesses can no longer function. The Golden state has lost its shine and the United States would do well to learn from the mistakes that the progressive left has made in California. And yet time and time again, the response to failed socialist approaches is to have more socialism. The entire practice of California has been to scramble desperately to fix problems that may not be there (such as Climate Change), and those that California cannot possible do anything about by itself (Climate Change also). All the while it has been ignoring the gaping hole in its finances. This is monumentally problematic for the progressives that manage California, and we have already seen an exodus of people on a relatively large scale. It is almost impossible in California to start a business in comparison with states like Texas because of all the health and safety issues, the building code and the bureaucracy.

[87] https://www.forbes.com/sites/patrickgleason/2019/04/16/no-californias-finances-are-not-back-in-black/#7d97583e37b5
[88] https://www.mercurynews.com/2019/02/13/borenstein-calpers-piling-more-pension-debt-on-california-taxpayers/

These things all mean that businesses that can are leaving in droves which will further weaken both the economy and the tax base.

So, California is the potential future in the US if the left essentially ever retains power again and this is a very sobering thought, because although there appears to have been a minor postponement in the issues that are extant from the election of President Trump, California continues on its merry way, and even the people fleeing to other states seem to bring their California politics with them. But there is one other cause of the current destabilisation which we have not talked about yet, mostly because it has been a factor for a very long time indeed, centuries even. We will do so now as we talk about the issue of fractional banking.

Fractional banking.

On the 10th of June 2018, there was a plebiscite in Switzerland. Amid a "spat" between Prime Minister Trudeau and President Trump at the G7 summit[89], as well as President Trump's summit with Kim Jong Un in Singapore, nobody paid it much of a mind because it did not seem that important, but it was. In that little referendum the Swiss public had to decide whether to reverse the system of fractional banking that is basically the cornerstone of fiat and banking as it exists today.

Fractional banking simply means that a bank can take on leverage. Let me explain what this means. If you and I decided that we wanted to go into the banking business and create "Bank Zebedee – the bank of brothers" or some such entity, we would first need some depositors to open accounts. We might begin with say 10 million dollars in deposits from various people. So, given that we have those deposits we have to do two things. Firstly, we must provide some interest for our depositors. That interest rate needs to be attractive versus other banks that exist and so we might give 1.5% interest on deposits.

So, this is a good start; we have borrowed money at 1.5% a year. Now we need to be able to invest that money to make a profit. Of course, we could invest it in the stock market but that is an extremely dangerous thing as we would be very easily bankrupted on even a relatively small stock move lower. Remember when someone deposits money with us, they generally can get access to it at almost any time, so we always must have sufficient funds to return their money. So, a stock market investment is dangerous indeed.

We could instead lend money to people who need mortgages. This of course is much less dangerous. This is because although we would be receiving a relatively low interest rates from those who we provide a mortgage to, we would also own the title deed to the house that we have lent money against. Therefore, if the customer were to default on their obligations, we could take ownership of the house and sell it to recoup our investment. If we are careful with the amount of capital we lend against the value of the house, we can ensure that we are very unlikely to lose money against it. So if we lend say 70% of the market value of a given house against the title deed, we will only be in trouble if the borrower is both unable to pay the mortgage interest, and also the house becomes worth 30% less than it was when we lent the money. Obviously, this gives us a very good cushion against market moves because a 30% drop in house prices is quite unlikely. Not impossible at all, but unlikely. So, we might be happy with an interest rate of say 4 percent a year.

But let us look at our returns. We have taken in 10million in deposits and we can assume that we lent it all out at 3.5% against housing collateral. That's wonderful isn't it? Well this is before we consider costs. If we had no costs, we would take in 350,000 dollars in income, and pay out 150,000 dollars a year. This would make us 200,000 dollars in profit. But then of course we would have to pay for our costs.

_____

To start, we would have to pay an FDIC insurance premium[90]. This is the premium banks pay for the US government to insure any deposits they have at any time to the tune of 200,000 USD. For a new bank this could be up to 0.4% depending on risk category. So now we are looking at 160,000 dollars. But of course, we would now need to account for our costs. In order to receive 10 million dollars in deposits we would need to have advertised significantly. We also would need to have at least one bank branch with the usual paraphernalia that a bank has. For example, we might need a vault or at least safety deposit boxes, we would need to pay for security, and pay for bank tellers, and pay for the rent of the branch.

So, let's say the rent is at a very good price; 5,000 dollars a month. So that will cost us 60,000 dollars. A security guard might cost us 25,000 dollars (that would be good value). And say we had 2 bank tellers at 25,000 each also. That's a total of 135,000 dollars a year. And finally let's assume low costs for utilities, cleaning, and maintenance of 15,000 dollars, along with a cost of 15,000 for all the benefits of the employees.

We can therefore see the grand total of 165,000$ in costs. But we only made 160,000 dollars of profit. So, we have lost money in starting our bank. The losses are even larger when we consider that our assets and liabilities don't have the same tenors. The mortgages we have provided generally cannot be cancelled by us unless the customer is not paying their interest. The deposits however can indeed be redeemed generally with very little notice. If around 20% of the money on deposit needs to be available to pay immediate redemptions at any time, we really only had 8 million dollars to deposit and therefore we would only have earnt 280,000 in mortgage interest.

Thus, we would have ended our first year with 75,000 dollars in losses from having achieved 10million in deposits and successfully lent out the majority to mortgages. And this is assuming that everyone who took out a mortgage with us paid everything they were obligated to that year. So therefore, we should ask. How can we run a bank? Do we need therefore just huge amounts of deposits to ensure that our fixed costs are diluted? Well that is one way to do it but a long time ago the predecessors of the bankers of today figured out a better way to do it.

Let's go back to when we talked about money in China and those merchants that invented the promissory note. Now at some point, some enterprising person whose name has been lost to the ravages of time realised that the promissory notes had one additional advantage to just being easy to handle (or better in terms of security). That advantage was that you could in theory issue many more of these promissory notes than you had in your inventory. This would give you a benefit by effectively allowing you to borrow the inventory of others.

This crystalized and formalised later in Europe as the first banks began to be created. These banks typically began life as deposit keepers of gold with depository receipts matching their gold in a cellar one for one. They would receive a small fee for the safe keeping of the gold and therefore would be fulfilling a custodian function. Over time just as in China, it became clear that because most customers did not redeem their gold very often, some of the gold inventory could be invested by the custodian to gain a return. At this point the question was how much of a reserve was needed in case the customers suddenly decided to come back.

And this then became what is known as Fractional banking. This is a situation where a bank makes investments of a much bigger size than there are deposits in their reserves through the issuance of promissory notes. And this is the solution to our problem with Bank Zebedee ®. We would give much larger loans than we could really afford to, and we would do this by essentially borrowing from the Federal Reserve. This could work well, so that we now might be able to have a profitable banking

[90] https://www.fdic.gov/deposit/insurance/assessments/risk.html

enterprise. But and this is the key point here, we would be entirely reliant on the fractional banking regime for us to be able to maintain our businesses. This means that any business like a bank has leverage that is implicit in its day to day running. And that also implies that when there is a crisis there is always a danger that any given bank will fail. And, of course, the Fed exacerbates this. When the rate the Fed pays on balances is very low, it means that banks of necessity are forced to lend to individuals in order to get enough interest to essentially make payroll. And this is yet another cause of inherent instability in our highly intrinsically leveraged system.

In the end, back in Switzerland, the vote failed and fractional banking in lived to fight another day, but it does bring up a good question. Should fractional banking even be allowed? I would argue that it should but what cannot be allowed is a laissez faire attitude to fractional banking without a similar attitude towards the concept of too big to fail. There is nothing wrong with fractional banking as something to help facilitate transactions and general trade in the markets. In that sense it is useful for price discovery, but when fractional banking is coupled with too big to fail concepts fractional banking become deleterious to price discovery. This is because the true risk of a bank conducting operations under a laissez faire economic scheme is artificially lowered with the too big to fail mechanism and thus prices (in this case the value of the risk associated with investing in the bank or placing money on deposit with them) are again made more opaque.

And this, finally explains why inflation is not symmetrical. Negative inflation is just that, prices go down. It isn't particularly bad other than it does make investment less likely and tends to keep economies in the doldrums for a while but generally this is only marginally problematic as investment is natural and inflation has almost never been significantly negative for any length of time. This is natural, of course, as however bath things are, there will always been entrepreneurs that wish to start businesses and invest, and also because governments will always be tempted to increase the money supply if they see that there is no upward pressure on inflation which tends to stop deflation in its tracks. However, positive price inflation at the high end is truly a disaster, and this is because, as a hidden tax on savings, it makes price discovery much harder. The Soviet Union failed partly because it had no mechanism for price discovery, but Weimar also effectively didn't have one because the rate of increase of the money supply was just too high for real price discovery to be effective. Oh, prices did exist, but they were just numbers that changed by the minute. In such a scenario where you go into a café look at the price on the board and then find by the time you finished your coffee that the price has changed and you didn't bring enough money (as happened to a number of people in Weimar[91]), there is no true price discovery and this is why inflation and a vast increase in the money supply must be avoided at all costs. One overarching principle for a healthy market must be is this good for price discovery? This is required for capitalism to work properly. And those who are the best and working out price discovery under capitalism have a chance to become exceedingly rich over the course of time, even having a chance of becoming Billionaires.

Billionaires.

When the Forbes List of Billionaires came out on the 20th of March 2017 there was a new milestone. The number of Billionaires (and Forbes measures dollar Billionaires) in the world was now over 2000 for the first time. To put this in context, in 2009 Forbes estimated there were less than 800 Billionaires in the world. In addition, the total net worth of the Billionaires list was around 7.4 trillion USD. That's 7400 Billion meaning that 200 Billionaires taken at random from the list could have facilitated the TARP program with just their own money. Even more mind boggling is the statistic that in 2009 around 1000 Billionaires would have been needed to have the same amount of total wealth as the poorest half of the entire world. But amazingly, that number is down to around 50 - you could fit that group in a chinook helicopter! By any measure that is amazing. The reason of course is the fact that we have had

---

[91] https://www.pbs.org/wgbh/commandingheights/shared/minitext/ess_germanhyperinflation.html

protracted low interest rates, coupled with the nature of something called the Pareto distribution which sounds mysterious but isn't; we will talk about that soon.

 The interest rate factor is just the same phenomenon that we mentioned when we talked about house prices. Just as we said that the only ones who benefit from house price rises were the super-rich (because they have vast inventory to spare), the ultra-rich as a whole always benefit from low interest rates because they are able to borrow the most money and find the best investments to place that money (through economies of scale and also pricing power). So low interest rates are a rigged game where the already rich get richer and the poor cannot begin to grow wealth because they are too poor to be able to borrow in the first place. And, of course, interest rates are low partly because the governments need to perpetuate the Prosperity Mirage that is the solvency of the West.

Rich people – and by that, I mean ultra-rich people – generally those with 100mm USD in assets or more – were able over the last decade to borrow money at extremely attractive levels. At the same time asset values exploded, as cash was readily available to invest which of course ultimately came from the central banks. Therefore, we are now seeing extreme levels of asset inequality. And if we continue at this rate, we would end up with a situation where the richest person in the world in 2033 will have more wealth than the poorest half of the world just on their own. That would mean if that person were to forgo their fortune and redistribute it to the 4 billion poorest people in the world each of them would become twice as rich as they were before. And, of course there will eventually be a push for this to happen. Already there are those such as Alexandria Ocasio Cortez that claim that a moral world would not allow for Billionaires[92]. It has become extremely gauche to be wealthy, and this is wrong because having wealth is a great blessing, in and of itself. It's just that with great wealth comes great power, and with great power comes great responsibility as all Spiderman fans completely understand.

Despite the simple realisation that billionaires are not at all the cause of our current woes, rather something of a symptom of the issues, there have been significant calls already for a drastic change to the way society works. A Business Insider article recently detailed[93] a five-part formula that would supposedly save the world and end inequality advocated by an ecologist Johan Rockström. His plan is quite simple. All that needs to happen is that emissions are halved every decade starting in 2020, increase the "food to table" efficiency by 1 percent every year, invest more in family planning (aka depopulation) etc., and two other things, that positively scream socialism. The first is an insistence that the richest 10 percent own less than 40% of the world's wealth. This is basically saying wealth inequality should go to very close to zero[94] given that currently the world's 1% own more than 50% of the world's wealth. The second, sounds epic. He expects no less than a dramatic redistribution (the article says reshuffling) of cash including even more taxation on those with the highest incomes, as well as supposedly significant increases in salary for the middle classes.

Now mathematically it has always been the case that a small percentage of the population owns a disproportionate percentage of the population and we shall see that soon when we discuss the Pareto distribution, but there is a phenomenon in the west which should concern everyone and this is that the middle class which historically has been the engine of spending growth in the western economies seems to be somewhat of an endangered species.

The disappearing "middle class"

Throughout the countries of the G7 we are witnessing the phenomenon of the middle class seemingly dwindling. Economists appear surprised, seemingly baffled by the idea what it could be possible that in growing and sophisticated economies, the middle class is not thriving. In the US, the middle class is

[92] https://www.businessinsider.com/alexandria-ocasio-cortez-thinks-billionaires-shouldnt-exist-2019-1
[93] https://www.businessinsider.com/climate-change-plan-billionaires-share-money-2018-10
[94] If you don't see this quickly mathematically, you will do quite easily once we discuss Pareto.

hovering at very close to 50%, a level that represents an 80-year low[95]. Yes, the upper class is getting more populous, but so is the lower class and this should not be the case in a country where real GDP per capita over the last 100 years has grown around 700 percent inflation adjusted.

But mathematically speaking it should be obvious that current policies with regards to two things have obliterated the middle class. Those two things have been interest rates which we have talked about already and, especially taxes. More specifically, it is not the fact that taxes are high but that income taxes are in almost every jurisdiction in the developed world are far higher than capital gains taxes. I myself wrote a paper demonstrating mathematically that income tax being higher than capital gains tax is one of the factors that shifts families out of the middle class (in both directions admittedly), along with low interest rates. Why is this important? Because a healthy middle class is a critical part of any well-functioning economy. It represents something that someone can aspire to reach in their lifetimes even if they start from poverty. A healthy middle class is something very attractive because it represents a wholesome and enjoyable lifestyle and because in a capitalist democratic society it is seen as something of a realistic achievement in, and of, itself. In particular, a burgeoning middle class is seen as the true engine of growth in capitalism and represents the transition class between the rich and the poor. So, when the percentage of the population that is middle class is reduced (regardless of how you choose to define the term middle class) there is general dissent and a country begins to enter a crisis state. This is because the **hope** of a better future is always far more attractive than to have that hope kindled and dashed again and again, or even worse to never have it. To believe that you will always live your life in abject poverty is extremely soul destroying. Again, the American dream is seen to fall by the wayside when the middle-class falls. Once there is no transition group between the rich and poor, your country cannot fail to disappoint the masses.

In order to test how capital gains taxes and income taxes affected individual families, we simulated typical families and calculated over time the value of their total assets under certain conditions. Whilst simulating the exact actions of a family unit over time is relatively hard to do exactly, it is quite easy to simulate after making some general and reasonable assumptions. This paper shows very simply that, as a rule of thumb, income tax is currently too high in most developed countries and capital gains tax is far too low. In particular, the spread between capital gains and income tax rates for the highest earners is far too high and should be essentially reversed. So typically, if the highest level of marginal income tax is 50%, capital gains taxes might be 30%, but in order to ensure that middle class families in general can prosper, something more like 30% income tax and 50% capital gains is far more effective. This is also partly because it is far easier for those with a billion dollars to find attractive returns for capital gain than those who have say a million dollars. The reason for that is simply the purchasing power of more capital be it in terms of financial relevance or even just in terms of access to projects through contacts obtained through this financial relevance (e.g. the average billionaire can easily afford to go to Davos for the forum each year, the typical millionaire certainly could not as just the fees would represent 5% of their portfolio not to mention accommodation etc). When you have a billion dollars, the world comes to you with their best ideas, if you only have a million very few geniuses care, it's just that simple.

Now what I am advocating here is something that I will summarise later, but really what I am saying is that the tax systems currently tax the true middle class far more than they tax the very and extremely rich. This has the effect of making it almost impossible to maintain at least upper-middle class status without having what would be regarded as an extremely high salaried income. This should not be the case in general, and it should not be the case that someone with a given income as valued in mark to market terms should be taxed at a significantly lower rate simply because their income comes from stock dividends or from capital gains. This is wrong from every possible perspective and serves to destabilise the markets themselves as less people are willing to work on a salaried basis and more want

95 https://www.pewresearch.org/fact-tank/2018/09/06/the-american-middle-class-is-stable-in-size-but-losing-ground-financially-to-upper-income-families/

to start their own companies sometimes without a very significant amount of experience or financial sense. They have simply identified the fact that there is an arbitrage here between money earnt due to investment and money earnt for services rendered. They are valued differently by the taxation system, and so, lo and behold, people flock to the one that is "cheaper" all else being equal.

Eric Weinstein who is an excellent writer and someone with whom I often (but certainly not always) agree with, talks about the issue that wealth has moved from US workers to US capital. I fully agree with this, and I also go further and see income tax as being relevant to US workers, and capital gains tax being most relevant to US capital. Therefore, to ensure that value and worth does move back to the worker from capital, it is best to tax capital gains and not income. This is the other side of the immigration coin which favours populist leaders like President Trump. When the value of the most menial labour is both crushed by immigration, and you add to that an inability to grow even the little bit that a worker could manage by some miracle to save, they become disenfranchised exceedingly quickly. So, when you hear people especially the central banks say that interest rates were kept low and this helped the economies of the west, you can read from that that interest rates basically cemented and grew wealth inequality everywhere and transferred wealth from those who generally have jobs to those who generally invest.

And again, I contend that the last generation of central bankers deserve as a group to be prosecuted, and indeed, some of them at least belong in jail. Either that or they were too stupid to be central bankers in the first place. What the central bankers ultimately have achieved is to rig the casino in favour of those with capital to begin with. With the "Bernanke Put"[96] in place, the world is now set up entirely in favour of those with assets and overpriced assets to boot. And when the game is this rigged, mathematics comes into play and explains why you will always end up with a few extremely rich people who win the game whatever world we are living on.

The Pareto distribution – or why there is almost no chance that one of your children will win Wimbledon.

Suppose that you have a young daughter. As with all good parents you probably did your best to engage her in as many activities as possible. You might have taken her to ballet for example, or you might have encouraged her to take up Chess. But one day maybe you introduce her to tennis. Perhaps you play a little yourself and you begin by showing her the basics. She seems to take to it and enjoy it a lot. After just a few days she became capable of having a rally with you, and she seems to have a natural talent at it. Well as a conscientious father or mother, you decide to encourage her as much as possible. Perhaps you take her to various classes and even engage a trainer. You see her improve dramatically, and now not only is she enjoying tennis, but she is even beginning to improve to the extent that she is able to play and beat children one, two, or even three years ahead of her in the club. At some point, the tennis pro might take notice and he might even suggest that she could go pro with the right amount of training. You suddenly have visions of being there at Centre Court in Wimbledon, eating strawberries, having drunk just a little too much Champagne in the public bar before the game. You might even imagine a "Pat Cash" moment where your little girl climbs into the stands to hug you having just won the entire tournament. All very beautiful things. But then, if you are realistic, you begin to think about what would become of her if by some chance she was not the next Sabrina Williams... and then you begin to worry. Well, you should worry and here's why.

---

[96] This is not to direct anything specifically at the Chairman himself, simply this is the phrase coined for the idea that the Fed and other central banks will essentially defend asset prices a manifest change from central banking policy in the past as well as central bank mandates in general – this is not true for every central bank of course.

It is certainly true that you don't have to win Wimbledon to make a decent living at tennis but a 2013 article from Forbes[97] showed how players even in the top 100 in either the men's or the women's tour are likely to struggle. In the article it talks about how expensive the tour is. The subject of the article was ranked 92nd in the world and won around 2.1 million in prize money over 15 years. On a yearly basis that comes out to around 140,000 USD per year and once you consider expenses (the player in question estimated that he had to spend around 75,000 USD per year on expenses including 9,000 just to string his rackets), you are left with a reasonable living but nothing exceptional. And this was for a player in the top 100 in the world. For those below the top 100, the amount they can earn collapses very quickly. Those that are just about in the top 200 cannot support themselves on the tour through their winnings and again let's consider what this means. You cannot earn a living playing competitive tennis unless you are better than the top 200 in your field amongst everyone in the entire world. And to be honest, I knew this to be true even before I read anything about it, because unfortunately this is dictated by mathematics and we shall explain it all soon.

Now let's compare that to a professional job such as being a doctor or a lawyer. If you are in the top 200 lawyers, doctors, hedge fund managers, accountants in the world etc you are earning a very large amount of money with all sorts of perks. Even if you are in the top 10,000 of any given one of these professions you are doing very well indeed. You also don't have to worry too much about whether you will have a career in 10 years because if anything your additional experience will make you more employable not less. However, if you are a tennis player you have maybe 20 years at most in your career so if you never make the top ten ever you are unlikely to do better financially than even someone in the bottom 10% of investment bankers in terms of pay. The situation is even more exacerbated by things like sponsorship. Whilst the top 5 players at any time (such as Murray, Federer, Nadal, etc.) can expect to receive many millions in sponsorship, players below the top 100 effectively get far less than their prize money (the top 5 get far more than their prize money in sponsorship).So, if your daughter doesn't make the top 100 she is likely to need a whole new career if she is to succeed and given the commitment that is required to play tennis at even the top regional levels, she is unlikely to be well prepared to change. Of course, she could go on to be the "tennis pro" at the local club, but that doesn't make for a particularly well-paid career and may make her more bitter than anything else.

The curious situation of professional tennis players is common in anything where it is competitive or creative. This occurs in areas like art where Gerhard Richter (who probably few have heard of) has sold upwards of a billion dollars of his own art between 2011 and 2016. However, if you look at the 100th placed person they have sold only 22million, and the vast majority of artists cannot make a living from their creations. You see it with music; there are huge numbers of songs available online for purchase and 99% of them are utter flops with a very small handful being massive hits. We can go on giving example after example but what is curious in all these examples is that the distribution of the success of participants in a specific area of creative or competitive endeavour (usually as measured by money but not always) generally appears very similar. It's a bit like a lottery. Almost all the entrants get nothing, but a few do so very well that they explode out of the ballpark. This distribution and, more generally, this class of distributions is called Pareto and was first generally used the man who lends his name to this class of functions Vilfredo Pareto[98]. Pareto was, in the tradition of many scientists in the middle of the

[97] https://www.forbes.com/sites/miguelmorales/2013/08/26/aces-into-assets-how-michael-russell-has-made-a-profitable-career-in-the-demanding-world-of-pro-tennis/#335fbb9e4754

[98] His formal name was Wilfried Fritz Pareto (15 July 1848 – 18 August 1923) as, although he was half Italian and half French, his parents were sufficiently enamoured with the German revolution of 1848 to bestow Prussian names on him. When he came to live in Italy however, his names reverted to Vilfredo Federico. The equivalent today would, I suppose, be the naming of your son as Boris or Donald.

19th century, somewhat of a polymath. He made seminal contributions to economics, but he was made significant contributions to the fields of Philosophy and came up with the Pareto Principle[99] sometimes known as the 80:20 rule. This rule generally expresses a Pareto distribution in words. This rule occurs a lot in human situations (because Pareto distributions do also), and a typical example is that in a corporation 80% of the value of the brand of that corporation was created by the work of 20% of the people. The point being that much of the work of a company is very mundane, but the thing that makes it distinct is being conducted by relatively few people. And the idea is that this type of rule applies to many things in a rough fashion. For example, in the US (and this is generally true in every developed nation) around 80% of the wealth is owned by the wealthiest 20% of the population in terms of very long-term averages. When interest rates are low and the difference between income tax and capital gains tax rates are high, this population is shifted towards the richer. Thus, right now, the richest 20% in the US own quite a bit more than this 80%, but the number does tend to average around that 80% over the very long term.

Now the 80:20 rule describes the aggregate mathematics of a specific Pareto distribution. The fact that it is generally seen in several different contexts indicates that there are many Pareto distributions of this specific structure present in the world. But the Pareto distribution of Tennis players seems to be far more steeply shaped, such that if you look at the net income of tennis players you see a much worse picture. Right now, there are just over 1800 men playing on the ATP tour[100], and essentially no one below the top 100 can do anything better than breaking even. So, for tennis players we have more of a 1% (the top 20) earning maybe 90-95% adjusted for costs and sponsorship. And we see this in almost any distribution in areas where it is possible to definitively assess the number one person. You see in areas like banking or law, it is simply impossible to properly identify "the best". There is no global tournament for the best banker or best lawyer or doctor. Yes, there are some very famous ones but even the not so famous ones do well. It is also understood that the most senior people in banking succeed through their juniors and therefore it isn't possible to properly identify the top person. But with sports this is completely different and hence the Pareto distribution for sports is much steeper. Any field where there are clear quantitative metrics for the number one in that field will generally sport a much worse Pareto distribution. Another way of looking at it, is that if there are many niches in a particular area or where there is no present good way to automate a process (such as the law or medicine) then there will be the opportunity for many mini-Pareto distributions to exist within the main one, making the overall distribution flatter and less peaked hence with more potential winners extant.

But let's go back to those billionaires with their 7.4 trillion dollars. Supposed they decided to suddenly give their entire wealth in cash to "humanity". Then everyone in the whole world would receive a grand total of, well, not that much. They would receive pretty much 1000 USD, every man woman, and child. Whilst that is genuinely a lot of money, it also barely buys anything of value. With that you couldn't even purchase a decent used car. So, we need to realise that the problem is not actually the rich, or even income inequality (although this is a bad thing in itself because it means that there is less and less incentive for people to work hard and better their situation), but poverty itself. And poverty is an extremely bad thing. Poverty leads to much destruction, anguish, and misery.

Paradoxically though, to curb poverty, removing income inequality at all costs is probably one of if not the worst possible thing to do. This will be made obvious when we dissect socialism and communism, but for now let's just note that even if everyone in the world were to take the money of the billionaires and use it for themselves, it will barely have an effect on poverty in and of itself – for those living on a dollar a day it would give them a little under three years more of their current earnings. Something else needs to be done, and just the basic mathematics we have done has been enough to tell us this. And

[99] Although he was not so arrogant as to name it himself.
[100] https://www.onlinetennisinstruction.com/professionaltennisplayers/

here is another paradox, we need to create more Pareto distributions to reduce poverty, and I will explain why later on.

And so, we can see why the Pareto distribution that describes the wealth of billionaires came into being. It is the result of thousands of other Pareto distributions where the most successful handful of people in each different Pareto distribution (e.g. finance, e-commerce etc.) appear as the winners in something which can be regarded as a Super-Pareto distribution[101] describing the net wealth of every human being in existence. The Pareto distribution demonstrates that there will always be those who are rich beyond the dreams of avarice, but this is not the problem. The problem is what happens to those who have done the worst, those who are most impoverished, and the goal must always be to remove that group from existence in the only morally reasonable way, by helping them save and find a measure of prosperity so that the station of the impoverished becomes as minimal as it ever can be. Unfortunately, however, there is a barrier to this goal that is in the form of a disease that is prevalent throughout almost the world and this illness is not a physical one but a mental one in the form of mathematical Idiocracy.

The idiocy of not understanding mathematics.

The lack of mathematical knowledge in the world has spread far beyond finance. It has now thoroughly infested areas such as politics and budgeting. This is partly a function of weaker standards, and partly a result of easily available calculating devices that require no mathematical insight at all to operate. Whilst it is true that simply knowing how to do arithmetic does not give one a quick advantage any more, the fact remains that a rich understanding of mathematics totally changes your ability to analyse data (and really to find the flaws in the presentation of said data), to approximate real world problems closely, and to think logically or scientifically. This is particularly important when it comes to statistics where the exact details of the data can change a potential conclusion almost entirely, as can small errors in said data. One might not think that those who are politicians should have anything to do with numbers. After all their abilities need to be those of demagoguery as well as looking suitably serious and conscientious. You would be tempted to imagine that maths isn't necessary. And we all know that, in the past, certain professors of the arts would consider their "utter ineptitude in mathematics" somewhat of a badge of honour.

However, over 2400 years ago there are many would have disagreed with you, and one particular man would have had a significant problem with the idea that you would not need to understand mathematics to function in a civilised world. That man was Plato. He was a mentored pupil of the great Socrates and is now regarded as the greatest philosopher possibly ever (at least in the western tradition). In fact, Alfred North Whitehead, in a truly gripping polemic writing about cosmology of all things, stated that "The safest general characterization of the European philosophical tradition is that it consists of a series of footnotes to Plato."[102] Plato in book VII of the Republic made it clear that those most suited to government were to have extensive training in and knowledge of Mathematics in order to understand logic and be able to fully assess the various arguments of their advisors. However, in this supposedly more enlightened age it is even more important for leaders and especially politicians to understand mathematics. This is because budgets and funding methods have become increasingly more complex and now do not compare at all to those in the ancient world. This is not only just because of just the sheer size of human populations, but also because of the number of different things that budgets can be applied to has ballooned. The fact is that the human experience at this time is orders of magnitude richer than it was in the ancient world (due to both our increased lifespans and exceptional levels of technology), and this means that that budgets become far more complex as there are so many different

---

[101] To be clear this is not a statement of mathematics rather one of taxonomy. This super-Pareto distribution is mathematically the same form of distribution as any other one.

[102] Alfred North Whitehead, *Process and Reality; An Essay in Cosmology (1929)*, Pt. II, ch.1, sec.1

things that we need to be concerned with to budget effectively. Simply stated, choice itself has changed things and made them far more complicated. Now there are trillions of algorithms that run our lives (present in everything from traffic lights, to the doctors surgery, to the way we look for information on the web), and people who don't understand mathematics deeply simply have no ability to comprehend how all these algorithms might be manipulating them and changing their daily lives and even loves.

Scientific Idiocracy.

At this point please permit me to go back to something that I worked on in the past. It's a diversion to our major narrative, but I hope you will bear with me. If you choose not to then that's fine just skip the discussion as it shouldn't affect your overall understanding very much. But for the moment I want to talk about the Scientific Method which really represents the very eyes that we use to view the workings of the world.

The Greeks are often regarded as the founders of many aspects of scientific thinking and with good reason. Their mathematics was much more abstract, formalised and systematic than the mathematics of those who had gone before. This is partly to do with the use that was made of the subject. The Chinese and the Egyptians for example clearly saw their exceptionally strong mathematical techniques as tools to produce their great wonders, and therefore took an engineering approach to the subject. Whilst the practical geometric capabilities of the Egyptians and Mesopotamians is undeniable, only the Ancient Greeks looked at mathematics as its own reward. Something to strive for because it was there rather than because it was practical. Probably because of their ability to think of mathematics as an abstract thing, the Greeks were able to begin thinking in terms of logic and in terms of axioms. An axiom is something irreducible which we take as a given. We cannot prove any axiom by itself logically (any attempt will lead to a circular argument), it is simply the place we start and is meant to be a self-evident truth. The Greeks essentially looked for basic axioms to allow them to create a mathematical foundation that could be used to develop whole "metropolises" of mathematical constructs. And like it or not, their mathematics had many applications. One of those applications was the beginning of everything that our technology is based on today, that of the Scientific Method.

The Scientific Method was developed with one major premise in mind; that of reproducibility. For example if I were on a farm in the middle of Kansas and I climbed to the top of the tallest water tower with an apple or tennis ball, or some object like that in my hand, and if I dropped that apple and a companion of mine on the ground used a stopwatch to time how long it would take, I would expect that number in seconds to be the same no matter how many times I do this. Of course, the number wouldn't be exactly the same every time. My companion might not start and stop the stopwatch exactly perfectly, a gust of wind might slow down the ball on one occasion, I might not drop the ball from the exact same height each time. All these things would affect the time recorded. But here is the thing. If we were to tabulate those times, we would see that they would cluster around one area with very minor variations. Furthermore, if we were more careful, we could narrow down the variation drastically. For example, we could use motion sensitive cameras to record the times. We could also have a specific drop off point and an automatic system to release the ball. We could also use weathervanes or even more sophisticated tech to ensure that the ball was only dropped during periods of calm. As we did more and more of these things, we would see the times come closer and closer to being identical. This is exactly how a scientific experiment works. It is based on the idea that if we conduct an experiment with a certain set of starting conditions, we will always see the exact same result happen. The ball will always take the exact same time to reach the ground as long as there was no wind and it was dropped from the same place.

So, the axiom of Reproducibility is a requirement for scientific thinking. This is what makes the experimental method possible. The other part of the experimental method requires logic. Logic is just the idea that if we have certain premises, we can make increase the scope of what these premises mean by a process that is independent of other information. So, for example if I was to take the premise that

Anna was in the kitchen of my house, and that Mike was in the bathroom, I could logically infer that Anna and Mike were not in the same room. Furthermore, I could also infer that if I wanted to talk to both Anna and Mike, I would have to enter two different rooms etc, etc. The only situation where this was not true would be if I lived in the potential apartment that Ross of Friends was looking at (after he noted that Joey and Chandler were getting annoyed with his presence in their abode) which featured a "kitchen slash bathroom"

Logic is used by those who undertake the scientific method as follows. They first make hypotheses or premises about how the world works. Then they use logic to infer a consequence that would be the case if all their hypothesis were true, one that can be measured by an experiment. They then undertake that experiment and see if that is indeed the consequence that happens in the real world. If it is so, then they have some evidence for their initial hypotheses or assumptions. They typically then spend more time coming up with things that their assumptions would predict to test experimentally. Over time, if their assumptions pass all sorts of different tests that the scientist might think about, they can then say that they have a theory of a certain physical principle that is useful in predicting the behaviour of the Natural World. Eventually, once these theories have been developed more systematically, and many of the possible logical inferences of these assumptions have been investigated under a broad range of different conditions, and the results of the experiments have been replicated by many different people in the scientific community, these premises now become so called Laws of Nature. That means that these are now the best principles that we currently can employ to describe how the world works. The whole idea is to create a model of the universe that is increasingly close to the real thing in the same way that computer game simulations have begun to approach photorealism as computer technology has improved. The better it gets, the better our predictions about the world become and the closer we are to reflecting reality.

Notice here that the scientific method is firstly, a continuous process. Meaning that we are continually doing more and more experiments both to verify old ones (under better conditions), and to get better and better Laws over time. So, this process is never envisaged to finish at all. Secondly, the scientific method does involve this idea that there do exist these Laws that will manifest themselves over time that describe all the workings of the world. This is still an assumption, but one that seems to work very well indeed in the real world. For example, all our technology has been delivered to us through the scientific method. It would be a very strange world if your laptop one day decided that it would stop working not because it was broken but because the way the natural world behaves now would mean it could never work. The natural world seems to have laws that are invariant, unchanging. And the scientific method assumes that this is the case axiomatically so.

Of course, that might not be true, and in fact there are some hints from observations of cosmic rays that some laws of nature have changed very slightly over time. This may or may not be true, but if it is indeed correct, it means that the scientific method now needs to be modified to no longer have this assumption, or at least the weaken the assumption somewhat. We can still do science particularly if it is the case that these laws change extremely slowly over time, but it does mean that the scientific method is indeed slightly compromised that way. There exist far more nuances and richness to science than what I have described above, and maybe one day I will write more down although there are already some excellent books on the subject from minds far more learned than mine. However, the point here is that science is far deeper and more miraculous than most people are taught in school.

In high school particularly, little is taught about how the scientific method was created after much sweat and toil. In fact, it took millennia for a systematic scientific method to be created, which is why the term itself was not coined until the 19th century, for before this there wasn't quite an established approach. Logic itself emerged quite early in the first millennium BC and grew quite naturally from the mathematical wonderings of the ancient Greeks. Whilst the Qin dynasty (221-206BC) destroyed much of Chinese learning with book burnings, and the mathematicians of India didn't quite get there (or maybe they did, and the documents are lost to the sands of time), the Ancient Greek Philosopher

Aristotle did codify a system of Logic that is similar to Logic as we understand it today. This was further developed into very formal systems much later by the likes of Boole, Frege and several others. However other aspects of the scientific method took even longer to develop. In fact, Reproducibility was only really pushed aggressively from the 17th century onwards. In some sense, the requirement of Reproducibility came about due to improving communications at that time.

During the Middle Ages and before the industrial revolution, it was difficult to make long journeys and the only fast mode of transport was the horse which could at the very best cover perhaps 60 miles per day when required by soldiers or some emergency. At any rate the best that could be managed at a comfortable pace for the horse was really 20 miles per day. This means that in the middle ages travelling between the great university cities of Oxford and Cambridge both in the middle of England being a relatively small island would still take up to 4 days (the best current roads imply a distance of 83 miles versus the flying distance of 66 miles). Then there was the fact that the various nascent postal systems that had began to function starting in the 11th century (the Chinese had a very extensive postal system more than a millennium and possibly two before that), were not particularly reliable and certainly not universal. Also, in the days before the printing press, there was just very little individual ownership of books and even the largest libraries did not contain such huge collections. But starting in the middle of the 15th Century, we have printing, and furthermore we begin to see some of the early mailing systems working more efficiently. More and more universities began to be created at this time, and even the extant Universities saw very large growth. For example, in Cambridge University 8 new colleges were founded between the mid-15th century and the end of the 16th century, which doubled the number of colleges in existence. There was a similar picture all over Europe which became by the end of the 17th century AD, the centre of scholarly learning for the entire world far outpacing anywhere else.

And just as the Universities were growing, other academic institutions sprung up and began to grow and so did the exchange of knowledge between academics. With the creation of institutions such as the Royal Society, philosophical investigation came into its own with another characteristic of the scientific method being created. That of collaboration. Before this time, much of European science was shrouded in mystery with many scientists hiding their findings and not really publishing them. At that time, many scientists were reliant on the patronage of the various kings and Queens of Europe and this meant some secrecy would exist. But the Royal Society was different. Members were expected not just to work on various projects, but to present their findings to everyone at the society. And whilst some such as the very distrustful Robert Hooke the first "Curator of Experiments" still remained quite secretive about their endeavours (Hooke famously hid the formula for the Law that bears his name in a Latin anagram and only published the solution to it 1678 2 years after the anagram itself), the focus was now on academics researching in the open, publishing their results and each academic building on that progress to allow for an accelerated system of gathering of scholarly knowledge.

Obviously, this meant finally that Reproducibility was invoked as an axiom because for everyone to do science together there had to be some ability for others to verify the results of the endeavours presented. It wasn't quite that no one had understood that Reproducibility was required for science before, but more the case that it was implicitly assumed but not talked about. After all what would be the point in a scientific theory that could not be tested at all? What would be the point in a prediction that could not be reproduced? The truth is that everyone over time had always believed in Reproducibility; every stone mason that taught their apprentices how to cut a boulder into a Corinthian Column had to, by definition, implicitly understand that if you do certain specific things you will get a deterministic result. That stone could be quarried and chiselled in a predictable manner. Farmers planted at certain times of the year because they knew that nature worked in a predictable way.

The person who advocated most aggressively for Reproducibility initially was Robert Boyle who interestingly had Robert Hooke as his assistant. The reason that Boyle had to advocate strongly for Reproducibility was because there was a disagreement about what his most famous invention could do. That was the air pump. When we talk about air pumps now, they are an almost trivial thing. Even a 10-

year old child will most likely understand the principle and even the practice of how they work, and it is quite easy to build one at home if you want to. However, in the 17ᵗʰ century this was advanced technology and both Boyle and Hooke (who physically constructed the one for the use of Boyle) were rightly proud of the invention. Well there was another scientist in Amsterdam named Christiaan Huygens who built his own version of the pump and experimented. And when he did so he saw a curious thing. He noted that he could essentially get water to levitate in the glass jar that was inside his air pump. This was something that Boyle and Hooke could not replicate at all, and therefore they would not believe that it was the case. It was through the insistence of Reproducibility that the phenomenon was better understood and later replicated by Hooke when Huygens travelled to see him in 1663. The consequences of being able to replicate this meant both that Huygens became a member of the Royal Society, and that the idea of Reproducibility was codified by the society and became one of the tenants of the scientific method.

There is one other thing that we need to talk about with regards to the scientific method. This is the idea of the "null hypothesis". This is fundamentally important to test the viability of experiments that we undertake, and it is basically a requirement to correctly frame a scientific problem. What I mean by this is that the real world is highly complex. It is not generally digital or binary. For example, if we believe that a certain drug will cure the common cold, we need to test this in carefully controlled conditions. Now we know that almost everyone does not die from the common cold, so we know that people are likely to recover from colds anyway and therefore just giving them the drug we are testing and seeing that they get better is not a good confirmation of the efficacy of the medication. The way to make sure that this is a cure for a cold is to formulate a "null hypothesis" and test statistically against this. The null hypothesis basically identifies what is to be expected if the drug is not effective against the cold and gives us a scenario for that in terms of how long people will take to get better. In medical trials like these, the best way to identify the null hypothesis is to have what we call a "control group" of subjects who also have colds that are not treated with the drug (they may be treated with a placebo or nothing at all), and to compare the rate of recovery between these two. We then use mathematics to identify the statistical significance of the effectiveness of the medicine to determine if we can reject the null hypothesis. This approach is common to all branches of scientific experimentation and is another great pillar of the scientific method.

The Replication Crisis

However, there is a problem with reproducibility particularly in the life and social sciences, which has become known as the Replication Crisis or reproducibility crisis. This is something that is present in experimental rather than theoretical work in general because theoretical work can usually be replicated simply by following the mathematics and also because most theoretical journals will ask for mathematical proofs for any models that are created. What the Replication Crisis represents is the failure of a large number of experiments mostly in what we might call the "soft" sciences to be reproduced. That is, researchers conduct a study and come up with a certain conclusion, and then other academics who try to verify the results seem to be unable to do so. There have been various different explanations for why this is not the case articulated, but as usual with many of these kinds of issues the problem is highly nuanced, and there may be many different reasons for the crisis occurring. One of the most concerning is that scientists may have been falsifying their data. A 2009 study revealed that almost 2% of the scientists who were polled admitted to having falsified data[103], and furthermore 14% admitted that they had observed falsification or manipulation of data, with an overwhelming majority (72%) saying that they had seen some kind of questionable behaviour. Given that this was self-reporting, this data is likely to be significantly underestimated, and this can certainly be one of the reasons for the Replication Crisis. Other possibilities include human error in conducting various experiments, and external factors that affected the results. The likelihood of a specific type of error

---

[103] https://www.ncbi.nlm.nih.gov/pmc/articles/PMC2685008/

depends of course on the details of the situation. If, for example, we are looking at a hugely complex experiment in say the CERN Large Hadron Collider, the chances of human error are very high indeed due to the sheer complexity of the equipment involved. This was the case in one very famous experiment at CERN where a group working on the OPERA detector at the laboratory initially reported in 2011 that they had observed particles called neutrinos travel faster than the speed of light[104]. If this was verified, it would have turned much of theoretical physics on its head as one of the basic axioms of the subject is that the speed of light is the limiting speed to any elementary particle. Even though the detector had only seen these neutrinos travel 0.002% faster than light, this discovery would have led to a string of awards and prizes including the Nobel prize for the leaders of the team. However, it was not to be. The 0.002% should have been the thing to scare them because as it turns out, when you are measuring something as fast as the speed of light which is roughly 300,000 kilometres per second, or about 1.08 billion kilometres per hour, it really does matter how well your systems are calibrated. Anything including very slightly sub-standard equipment, or even failing to properly screw in a lead can end up with these errors appearing. And, in fact, it was indeed a lead that wasn't properly screwed in that caused the apparent anomaly. Within 6 months, several other research labs had failed to produce the same result[105] (finding that neutrinos moved at exactly the speed of light as current Physics theory predicts) and thus Reproducibility was restored.

And of course, the reason that the Replication Crisis is more evident in the social sciences, is that the framework for those disciplines is far more ephemeral. There are many different inputs that may or may not have an effect on the outcome of the study. Even in medicine, because each human being is a different person with slightly different responses to chemicals, enough risk of error is introduced that it is possible for Replication to fail even if all other things such as conditions are very carefully controlled for. This should not be a reason to doubt the scientific method however, simply that we should note that in fields which involve significant uncertainty from the get-go we should take individual studies with a pinch of salt until they have been properly replicated. The efficacy of Penicillin for example was demonstrated through test after test and is very well reproduced, but the claim that say eating a specific food has health benefits is something that is much harder to demonstrate mostly because it is far harder to formulate this into a proper null hypothesis vs what we are looking for (the alternative hypothesis) than with a drug where it either cures someone of a disease or it fails to do so. Now why have I spent such a long time talking about Reproducibility, and the "null hypothesis"? Well because many people don't understand the scientific method at all. Many people think that science is just a set of laws that must be true because its science, and not something that is a living thing and is evolving through time. Furthermore, few really understand the importance of being able to reproduce the results of an experiment. And this brings us neatly to Global Warming, or Climate Change as its now called.

The Global Warming debate heats up.

Sorry for that rather obvious pun, but in all seriousness, Global Warming or Climate Change is one of the biggest scientific misunderstandings in history. To be clear the specific thing I am calling a misunderstanding or even a fraud is the premise that the earth is heating up entirely because of increasing levels of carbon dioxide that human beings are emitting into the atmosphere, and that the heating caused will be catastrophic to life as we know it today in some kind of runaway event, along with sea levels rising uncontrollably. That essentially, continuing to burn fossil fuels will lead us to a disaster equivalent to the event that killed off the dinosaurs or the Ice Age.

It is important that we note the entirety of the previous paragraph. Firstly, the premise is that the heating is due to carbon dioxide and only that, and secondly that it will be catastrophic unless we can get the carbon back out of the atmosphere. And it turns out, that neither of these premises is backed up with

[104] https://scienceblogs.com/startswithabang/2011/11/18/the-new-opera-faster-than-ligh
[105] https://www.sciencemag.org/news/2012/06/once-again-physicists-debunk-faster-light-neutrinos

significant evidentiary support in scientific terms, and the last one is certainly not true at all in any meaningful sense for the world.

Now when I was a young scientist before I entered banking, I was pretty much a wreck. During almost my entire PhD years, I flitted around doing almost nothing on my actual thesis and spending time on one of three things. Playing Table Tennis[106], looking for a girlfriend, and trying to get invited to as many scientific conferences that I did not have to pay for as I could. The fact that was that as a lowly graduate student, I didn't have much personal money. However, there was always funding available to go to some international conference on condition you were able to present a paper, or at least a poster at the conference in return. Of course, this was very exiting because for a scientist the only way to travel especially towards the end of the 20th century in the UK was through these conferences. You just weren't paid enough to go to interesting places on your own dime. So, when I joined banking, I was expecting the same thing but of course bankers especially during the golden era of derivatives, didn't care about location and generally preferred to attend conferences in (relatively) boring Finance places like New York, London, or Hong Kong – the difference of course being the money that bankers made which allowed them to go to exotic places with just their family and spend no time working at all. But by doing various researches in areas that were not exactly my field but close enough to it, I was able to go on nice vacations and see some of the world.

Well as a result, I ended up doing small amounts of research in many different mathematical areas that were not related to Astrophysics or Cosmology (my main scientific interests). And one such interest was Climate Change. Now again because science was science, I didn't always have to have a great paper or board to present at a conference, but I would go if I could afford to pay for it myself[107], and I did once end up at a conference where climate Change was discussed. It wasn't specifically on climate change, I forget what this was about, but it was in the middle of Japan and one thing that I did work on was a model for climate change given known physics.

The known physics that determined climate change is extremely hard but it didn't initially seem that bad. You had to know about the Sun and its energy output. I already had that covered because much of the work that was to by my PhD thesis was indeed in how the Sun radiates heat. You had to also be able to simulate the atmosphere of the earth which I could do reasonably well. And finally, you had to be able to add in the effects of things like calderas and volcanoes which have a surprisingly large input on the temperature of the earth[108]. It turns out there was significantly more to it, but at the time these were the factors regarded as important.

Well I calculated and calculated and solved various equations. Much of the work I did was a rehash of various things that I could have found already in the literature, however I was not that big on building of the work of others. This wasn't through some moral choice but basically because I was quite lazy and preferred to do things by myself rather than replicate the results of others. It didn't make me a good scientist, but it did mean that when I worked at something, I built up a strong foundational understanding.

Anyway, I ended up building a nifty little simulation of the earth and its heating on my laptop. I wrote this in FORTRAN which shows how old I am even though I would have preferred python which I liked a lot more. I did this mostly because the scientific add-in libraries (open source code that basically

---

[106] I was extremely fortunate that the top player at the Cambridge University Table Tennis club was one Deng Yaping, who is almost certainly the greatest female Table Tennis player of all time but had just retired and came to Cambridge to study for a degree and then later a PhD. To say that she trounced me when we played is quite un understatement unfortunately.

[107] Usually if I happened to be presenting at a different conference in a given country I would try to see if there was another scientific conference that I could attend to get the most benefit of my time there.

[108] This is due to the potential for a major eruption to replicate something like a "nuclear winter" if it is able to spew sufficient particulates into the air.

implemented various standard physics formulas) were much bigger than for python which was a very new language at the time having been invented in the early 90's. I was very happy having finished the code, and I waited with anticipation as the code was compiled down to machine code. Then I ran the software and looked at the first runs. Well I got absolutely nothing. The forward predictions for the earth's temperature 20 years from the present, 50 years forward, 100 years ahead were not even close to the "scientific consensus" or what the press had indicated was the scientific consensus at the time (and still now).

I looked through the code scanning for errors. In this I followed the scientific method as applied to simulations. With simulations the scientific method is even easier to follow as all your conditions are exactly predefined. So, what I did was vary just one condition and see if there was a difference. If I made different assumptions about the sun, well everything changed. If I changed the sun's power output even by a percent there were significant changes. But I knew this already and it wasn't useful. We are unlikely to have technology even in 100 years that can affect the sun so there is no point at all in worrying about this. We can do nothing about it. So, I played around with other things. Sure, if you changed the amount of expected volcanic eruptions etc., you could get some relatively small changes in average temperature over the medium to long term, and rather large ones in the short term. But again, there is little anyone can do about volcanoes even with current tech and probably there will be nothing even in the next 50 years.

Thus, I focussed on CO_2 and found to my surprise that there was next to nothing going on here. I should have been able to tell from the start because there just wasn't a good mechanism for the tiny amount of CO_2 trapped in the atmosphere to properly heat up the planet. Not just because the CO_2 was a small amount but also because there were correcting mechanisms such as ocean expansion and enhanced forestation (assuming we humans did nothing about that – this is a different story of course) and a more verdant earth. Also, the biggest effect in the atmosphere by far was that of water vapour.

After about 2 months trying to see what I did wrong with my simulation, I came to the simple conclusion that I just didn't understand the fundamental physics and that I was wrong. I therefore spent most of that conference in the doghouse because I didn't have time to write any paper on other topics either and so I ended up going with nothing. Of course, scientists understand that sometimes you don't really achieve anything even through a lot of research and work. But this was the interesting thing. After that conference as well as during it I did study a lot of the literature therein and it was far different to what I understood it to be before I researched it for myself. I had been incorrect about being wrong.

I realised one thing that the papers that predicted some huge climate change event were not based on the best Physics and were mathematically weak. The papers that were the most rigorous either predicted a very small (and manageable) amount of warming due to humans or they predicted nothing pointing out, as my model showed, that the Sun and Calderas/Volcanoes were more important than what we were doing with CO_2. What was worse than this however was that the scientific evidence was flimsy at best. From looking at the available papers, most simulations were laughably trivial in their approach and didn't take many different considerations into account particularly in terms of the heating coming out of the Sun. In addition, much of the Physics that they were applying to estimate the change in mean temperature of the earth was inappropriate. In fact, it wasn't clear that it worked when it came to an atmosphere like that of the earth at all.

I realised that from a scientific perspective my calculations were not wrong and that I should have published my findings. Despite my findings being unable to validate Global Warming, this didn't mean that the earth couldn't heat up. What it did mean though was that **if** the earth was going to heat up it would not be from carbon dioxide in the atmosphere but would most likely be from heating by the Sun. Even a fraction of a percent change in the output of the Sun would seriously affect the temperature of the earth far more than would carbon emissions at current levels. Furthermore, even things like a huge explosion from a volcano would have a far bigger effect at least in the short term than any CO_2

emissions would at current levels. Of course, the biggest problem with applying the Scientific method was the fact that we could not do any experiment other than through a mathematical simulation. We could basically do a whole bunch of things mathematically but no real experiment.

A very good comparison for simulating global warming is simulating weather.

But weather and temperature predictions are shockingly difficult for one simple reason that wasn't discovered until (relatively) recently. That even the most straight forward and apparently benign equations can end up with utterly unpredictable results which are intractable to brute force simulation solutions. By this I mean the following. At the turn of the 20th Century, mathematicians had some sense that, given the amazing strides that the great thinkers like Gauss, Riemann and others had made in some of the deepest problems in the field, that the 20th century might make mathematics essentially complete in terms of the fundamentals. How very wrong they were. In fact, something very strange, and extremely ugly was lurking just around the corner. That thing was, quite literally, chaos.

What they found was that there were various equations that were very simple to describe, and mathematically deterministic, but where solutions to those equations had such a high sensitivity to the initial starting conditions of the system described that it was impossible to determine what state that system will be at over any reasonable length of time. This was shocking because it meant that there were a huge number of real-world problems that could be well described by mathematics but were essentially intractable to any known brute force method of attack in terms of the generation of useful results. One of these mathematicians was Edward Lorenz who was essentially the father both of modern chaos theory and properly mathematical and computer aided meteorology. In 1961, he had been trying to use a computer to predict weather patterns using some simple equations and solving them numerically in a simulation and found that the results of his simulations differed massively when the initial conditions were almost identical which was expected by no one at all. It is no exaggeration that this caused a shock in the world of mathematics, and the maths of chaos theory as it became known (for obvious reasons) has been something the very best mathematicians have wrestled with ever since with relatively little progress. This chaotic behaviour in such relatively simple systems has demonstrated a mathematical richness that is so far beyond what anyone had expected, and it was there all along in some of the simplest sequences and equations.

The upshot of this is that weather is chaotic in nature, and it is very hard to predict the weather precisely because the results of a simulation are so dependent on the initial conditions that we feed into the equations. As we cannot know the weather outside right now to perfection, we will find that over a relatively short period of time (around a week) our forecasting will completely diverge from reality. The same is true for the assessment of the climate over time but on a different scale. Because we only need to know average temperatures to have an assessment of climate change, we don't have to make predictions over weeks or even months but over years. But there again, chaos rears its ugly head. It is no easier to determine the average climate of the earth than it is to predict the weather over useful time horizons respectively. In fact, now we don't really have adequate modelling in any of the simulations of climate change even to consider of changes over a couple of years let along 20 or 30 years. The actual changes in mean temperature are too small, and the starting conditions are just too poorly known, for proper modelling to be sufficiently predictive.

And yet we have the UN, and apologists for the great "Climate Change" religion – and it is a religious dogma as I shall explain - practically screaming at us that Global Warming or Climate Change is the greatest threat to the life of the planet that has ever existed. This is despite evidence that the earth has changed significantly in temperature and in terms of sea levels previously without clear deleterious effect; certainly not one that was insurmountable to humans at the time with their technology; technology which was so far behind ours that people living even 300 years ago would think that we were using witchcraft on a daily basis. The point is very clear, whatever changes in Climate we are going to see in the future, humanity is quite capable of adapting to deal with it. And if you don't believe it let me add some context. Sea levels have, according to NASA, risen by around 230mm since 1880. That is less than a quarter of a meter in one hundred and forty years. In the first 70 years they rose around 100mm and in the last 70 years they have risen 130mm. The increase in the rise is something but it is a change in 30 percent on a very slow level of growth, with some significant error bars also present. When you put it in this context, if things are really bad, we will probably see a further rise from today by 2100 of sea levels of maybe 200mm again. This is 20 centimetres by the end of the century which is not something to be concerned about as an existential threat. Even 2 meters, which is 10 times this is by no means unmanageable over an 80-year period compared to the cost of reducing enough carbon-dioxide to theoretically stop this sea level rise if the current crop of models is to be believed. And as we shall see, the most sophisticated models seem to have been almost entirely wrong over time.

When we turn an unscientific axiom into a religion.

I am a Christian. I freely discuss it, and I really believe that Jesus Christ is the Son of God and that the way to the Father, Yahweh is only through Him. I came to believe in Jesus through a logical process which I will happily talk about at some other point in time. However, the key thing here is this. After I came to belief, I also came to faith through personal experiences that are certainly unscientific. In a sense my head came to believe through evidence but my heart through something more personal. So, here is the obvious truth. It would be quite hard indeed for someone to convince me that Christianity was not true. Whatever you did, I would find it very hard to change my mind. Later, when we mention and consider Bayes theorem, I will discuss why it is almost impossible to change the mind of a true believer. It is because evidence will always move you towards the direction of the evidence in terms of your attribution of the probability that it is true. However, if your initial view is that something can never be true, no amount of evidence will cause you to change your mind. When it comes to Christianity, no amount of proof could convince me that it was not true. Now some of this is because I believe the proof is extremely large in its favour, but part of this is because I really attribute almost no chance at this point that Christianity is not true.

When it comes to religion this should be fine in general. Under the simple condition that you obey the laws of the country that you live in, and you are believing in a religion not an ideology, you can always function lawfully with very few exceptions. Sadly, not all religions work that way, but the point is that most religions do not require the world to be in a certain state. Christianity accepts the world is as it is and requires a Christian to be a light of good behaviour in the darkness that is the world. Judaism is exactly like that too which should not be surprising as they share the Old Testament in common and given that Christians believe that Jesus is the promised Messiah, they still retain almost everything morally speaking that is in Judaism. Judaism and Christianity have certainly shaped the view of the world, but usually exactly in the way that I have described – as a light to the nations. Not always, but often, Christianity and Judaism demonstrated the best that humans can be. Also, the followers of Christ were given strict instructions to accept the laws of the world and those who have authority on earth. The idea being that God gave authority to those who have it on earth and that those in authority are there to protect the weak and ensure that people are able to live their lives in peace. Jesus at no time advocated any kind of physical revolution against those in authority even if they were being oppressive and persecuted Christians.

The mantra of the Global Warming adherents is very much like a religion. They will never accept that accelerated Global Warming isn't happening despite the data which show that the best models currently are indicating nothing like the disaster that they are expecting. They believe that mankind is sinning simply by being on the planet, and that the very earth has become diseased from the presence of human beings on it. These activists see the planet as an organism and humans as just a bacterium that is plaguing an otherwise healthy organism Such acolytes see the value of a human being as irrelevant compared to the planet, and wish us all to repent by removing the sin of carbon from the atmosphere.

Even some scientific journals are beginning to accept op-ed style arguments that are no longer bothering with evidence but simply argue from an axiomatic perspective such as the following from the blog of Scientific American[109]. The arguments are always ad hominem as this one is for complaining about the fact that Bill Nye "the science guy" was coming to the State of the Union address as the guest of Republican Representative Jim Bridenstine, who was President Trump's nominee for NASA administrator. The authors are supposedly "500 women scientists" which isn't a very helpful or professional designation as any reasonable scientific article would at least state the name of the lead author, but in any case, any semblance of scientific objectivity dissolves in a matter of three paragraphs to blatant hysteria decrying the supposed fact that the Trump administration is "expressly xenophobic, homophobic, racist, ableist, and anti-science." Whilst this list is disgustingly comprehensive, there is one slight problem in that none of those accusations are remotely true, and in fact if the administration was any of those things members of the administration would already be in jail. The whole article again smacks of religious fervour and propaganda. To some, Global Warming as a concept seems more important than life itself. And when I say concept, I mean it because it sure doesn't seem as if anybody who has this belief is behaving as though it is, in fact, true.

Does anyone really believe in catastrophic Global Warming?

If I believed that Global Warming was going to lead to a big change in the worlds environment **such that it would seriously affect the survivability of the entire human race,** I would at an absolute minimum follow a few basic rules. Firstly, I would never buy property on the coast or at an elevation of less than 50, and ideally 200 feet. Secondly, I would buy a lot of property in the far north of the world where it is currently extremely cheap and where the climate will improve significantly over time, and more specifically my lifetime or at least the lifetime of my first line of descendants. Finally, I would make sure that the house I lived in was not even close to a stream let alone a river or lake of any kind.

I don't see any of those things happening. Miami where there are always flooding issues, and generally the whole of Florida, is not suffering from any precipitous drop in prices due to belief in catastrophic Global Warming, despite most people who have purchased in Miami being supposedly ardent believers in the phenomenon. The same is true throughout the East and West coasts. In fact, one of the greatest political advocates for climate change, President Obama himself, recently closed escrow on a 14.8mm USD house[110] in Martha's Vineyard[111]. Given that his net wealth when he left the Whitehouse was at 12.2[112]mm USD, this is a very big investment for President Obama, and happens to be at an elevation of just one meter if we are being generous[113] and barely even a couple of feet if we are being more realistic. If you don't believe me, it is quite easy to check with some basic elevation finder tools that I have referenced. Now, no one who is remotely worried about climate change and sea levels rising should ever purchase something that low on the coast, and yet here is a former President of the United States, signatory to the Paris Climate Accord, willing to invest a good chunk of his net wealth of a property that, by his own thesis supposedly, should be underwater in a couple of decades at best. And unfortunately for those who claim that everyone believes in climate change as an existential threat, the free market does not seem to have assessed this. If for example you want to buy a house on the coast of Connecticut, you can expect to pay multiples of what that house would cost you 3 or 4 miles inland. It is even more if you purchase an island on the Long Island Sound. If there were significant concerns that

[109] https://blogs.scientificamerican.com/observations/bill-nye-does-not-speak-for-us-and-he-does-not-speak-for-science/

[110] https://www.realtor.com/realestateandhomes-detail/79-Turkeyland-Cove-Rd_Edgartown_MA_02539_M46762-74498#photo0

[111] https://www.realtor.com/news/celebrity-real-estate/barack-and-michelle-obama-marthas-vineyard-home/

[112] https://www.aol.com/article/finance/2017/01/11/barack-obama-s-net-worth-as-he-leaves-the-white-house/21652889/

[113] https://www.freemaptools.com/elevation-finder.htm

sea levels would rise this simply would not be the case. That doesn't mean sea levels won't rise of course but it does mean that whether subconsciously or not, many of the very same people that are so adamant that Global Warming is the biggest threat to the human race in our time (liberal, "well-educated", and left leaning) do not behave, economically speaking, as if this is really the case. Some of the mainstream media have tried to argue otherwise making some rather poor correlation arguments to suggest that some coastal properties are losing value versus others further inland gaining value. However, there is still a huge imbalance in the wrong direction even in the examples that they cite with changes in property values showing no statistical differences from regular market moves. In Miami beach, median property values have, according to Zillow, gone from around 250k to 365k in the last decade (May 2009 through May 2019), and oceanfront property has gone from 268k to 416k, which has in fact, out-performed Miami Beach itself. Of course, the increase in prices has been even greater as a percentage for the ultra-luxury market – exactly the reverse of what you would expect given how left wing most of the ultra-rich seem to be[114]. The return just for median ocean front property is a healthy 4.4% per annum, which is certainly not indicative of a market where people are sure that disastrous climate change is, or even could be, taking place.

It is even worse in California. Beachfront property even when there is no protection at all against sea level rises is many times more expensive than property in the hills still within walking distance to the beach itself. This makes no sense at all from any perspective other than one that maintains that sea levels will not rise even a foot within the next 100 years. Oh, there are stories of those who have had trouble selling their properties due to such fears, but what is not mentioned is that these are almost exclusively houses built on marsh type lands where these sorts of changes have taken place quite often even prior to the industrial age. What there isn't is this vast stampede to get out of anything on the coast.

And of course, the pundits always do get this disaster prediction wrong. The only reason that Climate Change is on the agenda now is that the "big freeze" predicted 50 years ago didn't happen, and neither did a great deal of Global Warming (we are now 5 years after the predicted time when the Arctic ice was meant to be all gone and it is still here pretty much unchanged from when Al Gore made that prediction). This happened also when people were concerned that we had reached "peak oil" and that the reserves of the earth were nearly depleted in 1960. Today we are still as far from peak oil as we ever were simply because our technology is constantly improving, and we therefore have access to reserves that we could not have done anything about even 20 years ago. This should serve as a lesson for the Global Warming die hard acolytes, but I fear that it will not do so in any way. Such is the nature of a true believer, or a true con artist.

Tellingly, this is also very evident in both India and China who are some of the biggest proponents of the current Paris Agreement on climate change and who under that agreement have committed to nothing at all, and to stop increasing emissions by 2030 respectively. Both these countries intend to continue to pollute and emit carbon whilst decrying the fact that President Trump has exited the US from the agreement. If they were genuinely concerned about this to the extent that politicians particularly from the left would have us believe, then there would be an agreement to take carbon emissions to very low levels indeed and not just put the onus on the US. This all comes even though the US is arguably ahead of everybody in reducing CO_2 pollution having done better than anyone else recently at dealing with their footprint. [115]

Then there is the problem with the "null hypothesis". Whenever temperatures are higher, Climate Change is touted as the cause. Whenever winters are colder, Climate Change is again trotted out. When there are hurricanes, Climate Change is invoked once more. And the political left through the

114 https://www.zillow.com/homedetails/3651-Collins-Ave-Miami-Beach-FL-33140/2137119331_zpid/

115 https://www.hollandsentinel.com/entertainmentlife/20181202/con-us-already-leads-world-in-reducing-emissions

newspapers always focuses on the heatwaves but interestingly, in the summer never the coldest points (such as the coldest May in 4 decades in LA in 2019[116], or central England having its 17th coldest June in 360 years of records[117]).

Regardless of whatever seems to happen, proof of Climate Change is cited. But of course, this is utterly unscientific, because no one at all has been able to provide the "null hypothesis" against the Climate Change theory. And this is because, as we have seen, the mathematics is so complicated that no one can simulate the heating of the Earth adequately well and therefore no one can properly define a "null hypothesis". And if you cannot define even the null hypothesis for a given situation, then you can't even properly state the problem and you certainly cannot come close to solving it.

Then there are all the things that we haven't thought about which I briefly alluded to before. One of things I failed to look at all in my modelling two decades ago, was the role that the earth's magnetic field or the recent weakening[118] of it might play in climate change. I guess I can be forgiven for not looking at this because 20 years ago the magnetic field was not changing as fast as it is now. Right now, the position of magnetic north is moving by roughly 40 miles a year, and this is of great significance. There is also some evidence that the earth might be undergoing what is called a pole reversal something that will take potentially thousands of years to fully manifest itself, but during that time the strength of the magnetic field will fluctuate. Now there is evidence that as the field strength changes, cloud cover will be affected. And as we have mentioned water vapour is the best greenhouse gas. I had assumed, reasonably so, that cloud coverage over time was likely to be constant, but there is now good evidence that cloud cover has changed and may be a major cause of climate change[119].

Another thing that I didn't think much about was localised heating and basis measurements. Localised heating is indeed a human effect in that we are heating up areas close to weather stations artificially though use of air-conditioning (that cools us but heats up the area around it). This is not as insignificant as it might seem. For example, in my country of Cyprus, air conditioning was almost unheard of when I was a child, although it is standard everywhere now. The same is due for central heating which again pumps out a lot of heat into the environment. These effects are not negligible when we are talking about very small changes in overall detected temperature, and they are compounded by employing weather stations that may have originally been well positioned but through development are now in places where the climate in the environs is highly affected by artificial heating. Case in point would be a weather station initially in the countryside outside a big city like Paris or Hong Kong. The data coming from that station is virtually useless in helping to ascertain the temperature of the general environs of Paris or Hong Kong (and therefore a point of data for the earth) in totality over time, as the temperature can shift by a several degrees just because these weather stations used to be in the countryside and have essentially moved into the city as the city has grown around them. This is nothing to do with the climate in aggregate as it is an entirely localised effect.

It should also be noted that until we had satellite imaging, we relied on weather stations that were on land and had virtually none at sea (even now there are few at sea). And even worse, 50 years or so ago, many weather stations still used mercury thermometers for measurements, and therefore the entire calibration to data back in time is problematic as the accuracy of those readings were probably limited to 0.2 degrees or so, close to the size of the effect that we are measuring.

All this is to show that when you are dealing with an exceptionally complex and multidisciplinary problem such as the mean temperature of the earth (required to exceptional accuracy), there are so many ways that you can overestimate or underestimate your modelling, that you need vast amounts of

---

[116] https://la.curbed.com/2019/5/31/18647460/los-angeles-may-weather-temperature-rain
[117] https://electroverse.net/central-england-on-course-for-its-17th-coldest-june-in-360-years-of-records-crop-concerns-grand-solar-minimum/
[118] Or rather, instability more technically speaking.
[119] https://journals.plos.org/plosone/article?id=10.1371/journal.pone.0207270

data to prove the truth of a given hypothesis – data that we still don't possess because at the minimum we need 100 years of satellite monitoring data and we have around 40 years (and less of good holistic data).

The final thing to note on the benighted story of Climate Change[120] is that reducing particulate pollutants is something that can be done and would indeed save many people from really dying today and not in some mythical ever on the horizon scenario of 10,20,30,40, or even 100 years. It would give millions a far longer lifespan and would generally benefit everyone in the world. The problem is, of course, the people who would be saved are the destitute, the disenfranchised, and the poor and have no special interest funds to pay for their case. They have no one to advocate for them and no money to pay for someone to do so, and they are not "educated" elite leftists. And that is why instead of agreeing to work on creating and distributing technology that removes particulate pollutants from the atmosphere, the only thing the world is willing to agree to is to limit Carbon Dioxide which has only really caused one thing thus far that is supported by concrete evidence; a greening[121] of our verdant planet as a direct consequence of an increased abundance of plant food in the form of CO_2.

The age of Sophistry.

My father was a theoretical Physicist, and I initially followed in his footsteps. He studied at Oxford being the Senior Scholar of St John's college, I studied at Cambridge – enough said about that! But I didn't stay on in Physics as a career because there was no money in it[122] and, being the son of a physicist, I had no inherited wealth to use. My father, however, being a man of much more noble character did have a career in Physics and wrote many academic papers. In one paper from 1987 whilst working at CERN, he began with a deadpan quote as follows: "It is well known that in four dimensions a spinor field of positive chirality can be associated with a massless fermion of helicity -½ but not with one of helicity ½." I didn't understand what this meant till I went to university myself, but the point is not its complexity, just that this is a statement that is empirically correct, based on a mathematical construct of theoretical physics to be sure, but a factual statement none the less. If you disagree with this, you can work through the mathematics of 4 dimensional spinor systems[123] (I would advise you to work hard at university maths if you intend to do this) and you will find that you are wrong. It is something you can verify for yourself using some admittedly reasonably advanced, mathematics. In the same way if you disagree with the famous and often quoted equation of Einstein stating mass-energy equivalence which is written as: $E=mc^2$, you can conduct experiments to verify this. You will find that every experiment you do agrees with this formula very well.

Statements like the above are factual because they make specific claims regarding a situation which can be verified. The physical conditions of that situation are something others can replicate and check either mathematically in the case of my fathers claim, or experimentally in the case of mass-energy equivalence.

However, let's look at an optically similar statement in form that the UN has made[124]. "Limiting global warming to 1.5 degrees C would require rapid, far-reaching and unprecedented changes in all aspects of society." Now this does seem like a scientific statement until you begin to peel the onion as it were. Firstly, there is no specific claim as to what would be needed to limit this global warming. Secondly, it presumes from the start that any natural events that might change the amount of warming are irrelevant

---

[120] The reason that Climate Change has replaced Global Warming as the term in general is precisely because Global Warming hasn't occurred as expected.
[121] https://www.nasa.gov/feature/goddard/2016/carbon-dioxide-fertilization-greening-earth
[122] By this I mean no money at all. At the very end of the 20th century science with no direct application had almost no funding available for it whatsoever.
[123] https://en.wikipedia.org/wiki/Spinor
[124] https://www.un.org/sustainabledevelopment/climate-change-2/

which we know is not the case. When you cannot control the big factors, tweaking things here and there achieves pretty much nothing when adjusted for the cost of this. Thirdly, it also presumes that global warming of 1.5 degrees is both evenly distributed across the world and that essentially for the world in aggregate the warming is truly a bad thing. This is utterly unclear. And fourthly, of course, it presumes that there is any control at all from simply changing the amount of carbon dioxide in the atmosphere in the first place. The statement sounds scientific, seems specific and even precise, but isn't anything more than a kind of religious mantra. It is also audacious in its claim that human beings genuinely could have such control of their global environment so easily.

And the reason that the UN allowed such a statement to be made, and indeed even considers it something good is precisely because we are now living in an age that is not one of reason but of Sophistry. Sophistry is simply the use of arguments that are clever, sound authoritative but that fail because the logic is flawed, or because they assume the premise they are trying to prove, or simply are deliberately deceptive. An example of an argument that is Sophistry is to say something like "there have been studies which show x leads to y" when the truth is that there was one study out of 20 which indicated that this was the case, that this test was conducted with poor mitigation against the existence of data artefacts, and all the other studies demonstrated that the causality was false. Notice that the Sophistry in this case is a true statement technically speaking, but it is misleading because a reasonable person would have assumed that someone saying this meant that the entirety (or at the very least a large proportion) of the research that was conducted under laboratory conditions to investigate the possibility that x leads to y would have confirmed the theory.

Other examples of sophistry are things like saying "It is well known that gender is purely a construct of society" when almost the exact opposite is true. In this case compare that with the quote from my father's paper. The part of the quote saying "it is well known that" is pretty much irrelevant to my father's statement. It doesn't matter. In fact, it may well not be true if you are considering the entire population of the world in its totality, but if you are only thinking about subscribers to the journal it was published in, or experts in particle physics, it is undoubtably correct. However, it makes no difference to what my father is trying to say. Even if he was the only one who previously had known it to be true, it remains irrelevant to the discussion. However, for the gender idea, it is the whole crux of the false argument, and it is designed to condition you to just accept the rest of the statement as a fact. If the "It is well known" was removed, a reader of my father's paper might be tempted to perform a bunch of mathematics and see if it was true. If someone read the line about social constructs in a gender studies paper, they would just think it was ridiculous and might dismiss the rest of the paper out of hand. And they would be quite right too.

On the subject of Climate Change, the UN trots out children (I will not mention any as I feel that children should always be protected and should generally never be in the public eye if possible but you can find video of this even from as far back as 1992 – the events in 2019 are certainly not without precedent), who are quite understandably terrified by the idea that catastrophic climate change cannot be stopped unless something radical is done in the next 12 years. Such children are being abused by their parents who allow them to be treated in this way without disabusing them of the concept, and they are being even more manipulated by the politicians who enable this. The hysteria of the climate panic is such that a recent poll by Rasmussen found that 67% of Democrats believe this nonsense[125]. I expect that in 100 years the idea of catastrophic global warming will be regarded as the biggest con of the 20th and early 21st centuries (along with cryptocurrencies), but for the moment the gospel holds sway over the sophists. There are many scientists that have already debunked all the aggressive global warming theories but it doesn't matter to the sophists because they have an agenda, and they are only willing to look at science when it agrees with their particular narrative de choix.

---

[125]http://www.rasmussenreports.com/public_content/politics/general_politics/may_2019/67_of_democrats_think_u_s_has_12_years_to_fight_global_warming_or_else

But this should hardly be considered surprising as sophistry is prevalent all over the world now. The media is riddled with these kinds of straw man arguments, and as usual, this is beginning to infiltrate into other areas. This is now happening in arenas that you would have never expected it such as serious academic research. I am not the only scientist who has noticed this happening, and in fact a trio of scientists set out to demonstrate just that. The three researchers self-identified as 'left leaning but hating the current paradigm of political correctness' sought to cast light on the problems of sophistry in modern day research journals[126]. So, they submitted a few hoax papers to various highly regarded journals in the liberal arts such as the *Journal of Poetry Therapy; Fat Studies; Gender, Place and Culture,* or *Affilia* which is a journal that focuses on women and social work. In all, they managed to get seven different papers published in several of these highly regarded periodicals.

The crown jewel of their work was a paper that was published in the journal *Gender, Place and Culture* entitled "Human reactions to rape culture and queer performativity at urban dog parks in Portland, Oregon." The paper claimed to present a study that in the words of the 'author' Helen Wilson (a pseudonym) was seeking to find the answers to key and important questions such as "What issues surround queer performativity and human reaction to homosexual sex between and among dogs?" and "Do dogs suffer oppression based upon (perceived) gender". Now whilst these questions are clearly patently ridiculous, the fact that a supposedly peer reviewed journal was willing to publish it was clearly (as argued by the authors) evidence that there was a systemic crisis in the peer review system for liberal arts publications. Their penetration into several journals was not limited to this. All told, they managed to gain acceptance of one of their papers from seven different academic publications. The eclectic mix of sophistry extended all the way from claiming that bodybuilding was "fat-exclusionary" (this published in the journal *Fat Studies*) through to descriptions of "womb rooms" at a monthly feminist spirituality meeting. The fact that, as these researchers demonstrated, sophistry is alive and well in the ranks of academia makes the palpability of this as an explanation of the Replication Crisis very clear. When peer review is clearly perfunctory, it is not surprising that Replication is very hard to do, as research papers making false claims fail to be challenged and become part of the accepted cannon of science. And once something is accepted as a given, it becomes an axiom that is assumed and not something that is verified again and again, thus it can be very hard to make fundamental progress when one of your axioms is wrong.

Another bit of sophistry that is often cited is the idea that there is a "gender pay gap". This makes no sense at all in, and of, itself because the claimed gap exists in countries where often it is illegal to discriminate based on gender. The fact that this is the case then is cited as evidence that these countries (the west particularly as the west is where most of these laws exist) are somehow set up in such a way as to create such a pay gap. And yet, even though this gap is declared to be true, it is in fact as false as can be at least in terms of anything structural and is mathematically non-existent when any factors unrelated to sexism are taken into consideration. When factors such as area of work, hours worked, and personal preference in terms of career are accounted for, the gender pay gap simply vanishes into nothing at all, and even inverts if anything. Men work more hours, they are much more likely to want to work in areas that either pay very well and have specific skill requirements (such as STEM areas), or are willing to take work that seriously endangers their lives (men make up more than 90% of all workplace related deaths[127]), or are simply more aggressive in demanding pay increases. In fact, it turns out that in the younger demographics generally women seem to be doing even slightly better than men. As a recent Google investigation found out (supposedly to the surprise of everyone – which makes me very concerned as to the mathematical expertise of those in Google management), men at Google were

---

[126] https://nationalpost.com/news/world/dog-parks-are-petri-dishes-for-canine-rape-culture-and-more-of-the-ridiculous-studies-a-team-of-hoaxsters-got-published-in-academic-journals
[127] https://www.investors.com/politics/commentary/how-come-nobody-talks-about-the-gender-workplace-death-gap/

generally being underpaid for doing similar work as an equivalent woman at the company[128]. And yet, you still hear sophistic arguments that the pay gap exists. The fact that the press in the west still brings out these sorts of talking points should be an indication that the Idiocracy is alive and well and living rent free in the 4th estate. But because we all live in the Idiocracy, there are many people who don't even have the simple mathematical skills to consider the difference between the median, the mode, and the mean and realise that the gender pay gap metric is truly irrelevant.

Please permit me to talk about Global warming briefly just once more – I promise this will be the last time! If we are this worried about something that has yet to be properly scientifically proven, and if we really are poisoning the lives of our children and our grandchildren, then why do those who care so much about this and particularly the left, not care about budget deficits. Why does the left insist that Climate Change needs to be addressed when a burgeoning debt to GDP is just something that we will deal with further down the line? What I hope I have demonstrated, is that in terms of quality of life and in terms of potential deaths, the debt to GDP of the US is far more dangerous than climate change is, but the question remains as to why no one sees it as existential. Of course, as we shall discuss the reason is simple; because dealing with debt to GDP gives them less control, in fact it takes away dependency on the government or state, and therefore removes control from the left, and insisting on economically crippling and inane things in a desperate attempt to reduce the temperature of the earth by a fraction of a degree necessitates that they have more power and control. They want to force you to believe in their religion, and if they cannot, then they will die trying. But of course, this is the entire stratagem. Climate Change is not something anyone who properly understands Physics and Mathematics should be worried about as the most important consideration of our times. Or perhaps it is. Not because of the problem in and of itself, but because the only solution that has been offered is the very thing that we should be most concerned about. Global control of what individual human beings do regarding their day to day business. Those who espouse radical change on the Climate Change side have only one mechanism. That mechanism is full control of what people do. And there is another word for this. It is called Socialism, or Marxism if you want to use that word. It also requires an authoritarian dictatorship, but then again Marxism or Socialism always require this even though they claim that is not the case. We will discuss this more very soon, but for now let's go to another of the great drivers of fear that we have in our current world that of technology taking over.

Rage against the machines?

In his book "The Rise of the Robots", Martin Ford argues quite coherently that the world's economies are due to suffer some extreme shocks from robots replacing human workers in almost every possible way. The argument is that almost every job that is in any sense predicable can and will be replaced by robots eventually. Ford and other authors with similar views disagree somewhat over the time scale that this will take place, but most agree that the next 100 years will bring unprecedented dangers to world employment from the development of robotic substitutes for any job that can be described in any way in terms of a "procedure". So that we no longer simply have robots taking over from humans in a factory, but in finance (computer programs can already trade effectively for short periods as capably as any but the very best traders in the market), in medicine (expert systems development etc.), in education (robot teachers and cloud learning); basically, in just about every sphere of human endeavour. Such thinkers believe we will soon see a time where robots can effectively maintain and program themselves so even high-level jobs like robot maintenance and programming will soon be superseded. Worse still is the claim that true AI is just around the corner which will make basically all human beings entirely redundant as there will never be anything that any human could contribute that a robot could not do better. In fact, some predict that with the rise of the "singularity" either the robots will decide that humans are pointless and simply eradicate us, or humans themselves will program their own existence

---

[128] https://www.nytimes.com/2019/03/04/technology/google-gender-pay-gap.html

into a computer and function entirely in a cyber reality. Some of those who are looking at these predictions even make some more aggressive speculations that all organic species who develop a certain level of technology will eventually find that it is far more attractive to exit their organic bodies that are, by necessity, prone to failure, and become a consciousness in cyberspace able to survive forever. This implies that what it means to be human will have to be radically revised in the coming decades and centuries. But I think they are utterly wrong at least when it comes to the singularity.

Whilst many of the arguments regarding automation do make sense, there is a problem with the general perception of being able to achieve the singularity. Whilst computing power is far ahead of what the de factor founder of computing Alan Turing had hoped would be achieved by the turn of the century, the distance to AI is almost as far as it was in his day at least conceptually. Even though we hear about programs that can pass the famous "Turing Test", they only pass the test using a ridiculously naïve brute force method. What Turing had envisaged was a general processing machine that was at such a level of thinking that it would essentially have a human type intelligence and therefore it would be able to learn languages and communicate just like a human. What we have with computers that can pass the Turing test is just a set of algorithms that mimic a human response based on huge amounts of data stored in the machine or the cloud, and the gestalt of these algorithms essentially tries to fool an operator into thinking they are talking to a human. There is no pretence that such computers are thinking even at the most basic level, nor can these "Turing replicators" do very much that is useful other than beat the Turing test. The same applies to chess computers – it was thought that taking a computer to the level of being able to beat humans at chess would require some form of genuine conscious intelligence. Unfortunately, a mid-range PC (heck my phone with a chess app) equipped with free software can now beat every single human player in the world and yet, this program is not thinking at all, it is simply doing a lot of calculations assisted with some heuristics that have been developed by chess players regarding what good positions should look like.

Even AI specialists admit that we are not close to a true AI[129], with the majority saying we are around 10% of the way to an AI. Unfortunately, however, this essentially means that we are not anywhere close, and we may never even get there. We cannot see right now over the horizon and the only thing that indicates to us that we might eventually get to an AI is that we see that human beings can think and therefore there is a device in existence that could, in theory, be replicated. I myself worked on a lot of AI development in the context of creating trading predictors that could decide whether an asset was going up or down and various algorithms that generated advanced trading strategies. Whilst my strategies are very powerful and excellent predictors of the markets, the algorithms are not thinking at all, they simply reflect things about the market that I know to be true from experience and they use the power of computers to crunch incredibly large amounts of data to implement those heuristics and ideas so that it seems as if these trading strategies are the product of an advance intelligence. But they are not. They are simply the result of a bunch of rules that govern the markets that have been expressed mathematically (just like the heuristics in the chess engine) and those rules have been applied to a huge amount of market data. This is not unimpressive, but it is certainly a far cry from a thinking machine displaying superhuman intelligence as envisaged in any number of dystopian works of science fiction.

The internet joins the Idiocracy and becomes the Library of Babel.

The Library of Babel is a rather beautiful short story written in 1941 by Jorge Luis Borges an author who was also a librarian from Argentina. The entire story is essentially about one physical structure which is huge and is believed by all who dwell within to house every single 410-page book that can be written with 25 different characters (including a comma and a space) regardless of whether such books have any meaning at all. Thus, if we assume that there are 400 words per page with an average word length of 5, then each 410-page book contains 820,000 characters so the number of possible unique

---

[129] In terms of AI development, I have myself worked on it quite extensively in order to attempt to predict changes in the financial markets.

books is approximately 25 raised to the power of 820,000. This is an unimaginable number of books given that there are around 10 to the power of 80 atoms estimated to exist in our entire observable universe. Now clearly we can see from this that almost every book that is in the library is likely to be entirely meaningless just a jumble of letters, however because every single possible combination of characters exists, every book that anyone could ever envisage of 410 pages must also exist in the library. Thus, in theory, almost all useful knowledge would exist. This book you are reading now would also exist in the library, because even though it isn't 820,000 characters long, it would exist just as it is with a whole bunch of spaces after the end. Not only this, but a huge number of copies of this book will also exist (around 200,000 of them basically identical, and exponentially more that are almost the same in meaning). That is, they will be this book but with a bunch of spaces scattered around the words of the book. Even more copies of this book will exist with essentially the same information but with one additional character or one less character, and so on. But of course, the number of meaningless books will swamp by far any books that contain actual information, and as in the story, any person trying to get useful information from the library in any finite time will probably fail to do so. In the story all sorts of philosophical implications are investigated, for example because every book is contained there is the view that there must exist in the library a list of all meaningful books in the library (this is of course quite a spurious assertion[130] as the number of meaningful books in the library will certainly be greater than the number of words available to a book of 410 words.

But why am I suddenly talking about the Library of Babel? This is because, aside from the issues associated with the moral aspects of creating an AI that works just like a human, there is no evidence at all that such an AI would be superior to a human in the way that its intelligence is expressed. I.e. it may be that human levels of intelligence are the highest possible physically speaking and the idea that somehow an AI could program itself to be smarter doesn't necessarily work. After all – a human being with access to a computer has themselves plugged in to an almost infinite amount of data, but there is little evidence that human thought processes have dramatically improved in their quality with the advent of the internet. On the contrary, the internet has led to huge amounts of disinformation filling websites and even things like the search engines are failing to keep up. For example, anecdotally speaking, it was much easier to find good reliable information 20 years ago on say a holiday destination than today. This is because there are now so many more websites and so many of them are geared towards making money rather than to inform as was the case 20 years ago. The internet has become just like the Library of Babel from the story – maybe a bit more useful but is rapidly reaching a state of decay. The algorithms for sites such as Google haven't kept up because companies know the general keyword process that Google uses and tailor their websites to get the most hits. Also, companies pay to be the first in line on searches which means that many searches must be trawled through before you can find what you really need. In addition, companies like Google have started to basically virtue signal by modifying their algorithm to favour more left leaning websites. This is something that is critically problematic given that Google essentially has the monopoly on search.

In fact, the only thing that has kept the idea that we are getting much closer to AI alive has been the equivalent of Moore's law (which basically says that every 2 years or so the computing power of the average computer doubles) applied to the number of computers in existence. This law (although it is technically a heuristic rather than a law) – I don't happen to know its name - basically notes that since the 1960's the number of computers (here you have to count cell phones etc as computers) basically multiplies by 10 every decade. This vast increase in computing devices as well as their absolute computing power has led to the illusion that we were always at the very edge of developing AI because our computers could do more and more complex things so quickly.

---

[130] Because of course, although every 410-page book exists in the library, this does not imply that every possible book is contained in the library which would require the book lengths to be infinite.

The reality is that, far from AI being just around the corner, the problem of Artificial intelligence is far harder than anyone might have thought and, even if solved, might not take intelligence any further than it currently is. But even if AI is never achieved, there is no doubt that a huge percentage of jobs currently being done by humans are likely to be replaced by robots and the only jobs that will remain will be those that involve advanced and dynamic thinking that involves many different paradigm shifts over the course of a number of years.

But most futurists are forgetting the two biggest issues with automation and the rise of tech. The first issue is that automation turns industries into things that people who are less qualified, and less intelligent, are capable of functioning in, at least in the short term. It is this point that is most pertinent, because if someone is able to generate even a facsimile of competence for even a short time, they can have a real (negative) impact on how things are conducted that will potentially have ramifications that significantly outlast that person themselves. Some of these consequences may never be in a situation that they can be reversed. In short, technology enables the Idiocracy even amongst people who are otherwise extremely intelligent. Take myself for example[131]. As a boy, having been inspired by "Surely you're joking Mr Feynman"[132], I got very involved in electronics and at the height of my powers I was even able to fix basic solid-state radios with ease, even creating my own tuning coils by hand. However, now that I am older and radios are pure digital devices with just a few electronic chips, I am simply unable to do it. I have joined the ranks of the growing Idiocracy in this area, and even worse, it is now virtually impossible for anyone to do this without computer assistance and some hugely high tech and expensive machinery.

So, let us go back to our example of financial Idiocracy from before. As we have already said, around 25 years ago saw the advent of a golden age of derivatives in finance. The trades that were being executed became so complex that Wall street had to hire people with PhD's in Physics or Mathematics in order to price those trades and know what the value of those trades should be. It was at the height of this golden decade that I was hired straight out of University to trade derivatives. At that time, I had no idea what a derivative was (other than, of course, in the purely mathematical sense) but I found that, due to my mathematical background, I became an expert in pricing derivatives within a year of starting at Goldman Sachs. At that time, the world appeared to be far less complex in one area in finance that people don't think about very much, this was the area of funding.

Funding.

But now, because technology has improved greatly, and because most products have been moved on exchanges, the financial literacy that is required to trade even the most complex products is much less. You see that everywhere in finance. The average graduate has a learning curve that is much less steep than it was 20 years ago or even 10 years ago.

I remember interviewing someone even ten years ago and asking them to solve a relatively easy problem in finance (involving the construction of something called a yield curve) and getting the answer that the person (he was a senior trader at an American bank not just someone applying for a graduate program) would just "use my spreadsheet to do the calculation". To me it was a crazy idea that anyone who was supposed to be making money from the financial markets could even begin to try and do so if they could not understand the basic processes of finance. It is like an engineer who simply uses their CAD software to build blueprints but does not head-check of whether this will work or not.

It was appealing to believe that this was confined only to those who were working in the slightly weaker banking institutions, but I found this at the very top institutions such as Goldman where a structurer

---

[131] And yes, I am arrogant enough to consider myself extremely intelligent.
[132] The proto biography of my childhood hero Richard P Feynman who I did meet once (even though I was too young to properly remember) and who had possibly the best intuition in Physics excepting the legendary Albert Einstein.

asked me to explain how a specific financial product worked but only wanted to know how to put this in the system in order to allow them to generate a price for the structure. They didn't really want to understand the product at all – simply to be able to generate a value for the product with the firm's system. That might sound okay but here is the problem. If you don't understand the trade how do you make sure that the price the system gives you is the correct one? How do you know if the program that generates that price is working correctly, and how can you possibly decide that the price is the right one for the risk that is being generated? If you understood the mathematical processes below you could do what any good structurer or trader does which is perform back of the envelope calculations to sanity check each step of the pricing so that you could be confident that the price you got from the system was an appropriate one.

Those two were examples that at the start of my career were fortunately somewhat atypical of those in trading or even structuring in finance. However, within around 12 years of the start of my time in finance, systems had become so sophisticated at every bank that you really could manage your career without ever really understanding these products, and therefore people like these two individuals became the norm and not outliers. This has an important consequence and it is this. People are no longer succeeding in their careers in finance based on their superior capability in the practice of finance and financial engineering, because this is no longer needed. There is no longer a need to be a trader that can properly assess risk for the most part, at least from the short-term point of view as we have discussed. People are therefore expanding their careers on their political savviness and other areas that mean very little in terms of the capability of advising others as to trades that will make them money. Suddenly you no longer needed even a good understanding of the concepts that you were supposed to be an expert on at all.

But this has a knock-on effect on the hedge funds. Hedge fund performances have decayed significantly over the last decade and it is somewhat difficult to see why given that over the last decade the central banks have been keeping a very tight leash on the markets. In theory, a predictable but moving market should be ideal for the hedge funds to make money from. And yet, somehow, the funds have failed here. The reason this is the case is that they no longer have the skill sets coming from the "sell side" (the banks) that allow them to replenish their benches and therefore people who are hired by the funds are progressively less capable. And all this has happened because computers and their programs and the environments that those programs have generated have become simpler and simpler to follow without any understanding of what those programs are doing.

This would all be well if we were reaching a plateau of computer capabilities that dwarfed the quality as well as the quality of human analysis, but the cold hard facts are that computers still don't think. As we have discussed AI isn't a real thing in the sense of true strong AI that thinks for itself. Whilst those who run the "quant" hedge funds would argue that even the traders in those funds don't understand the full capabilities of whatever algorithms they are putting to use it is not true that these algorithms are thinking for themselves. Rather it is that people who build financial algorithms no longer need to have such a deep knowledge of the markets and how they work. And as algorithms get better and more powerful, they become far superior to the human trader in terms of short-term analysis and behaviour, but they also become too tied to the data. One the greatest problems in creating predictive algorithms is to avoid so called data mining. Data mining is where you create an algorithm that overuses the data to modify its behaviour which has the tendency to make the algorithm look spectacularly good on past data (because it has been fitted to that data in the first place), but that algorithm doesn't do very well on new data and fails to be highly predictive. This data mining has generally happened because there is a huge amount of data available and as we have mentioned before, computers are now spectacularly more powerful in terms of operations per second and data storage than anyone ever would have expected in their wildest dreams. We have way more data, the ability to retain that data, and the ability to process it for our own good. The NSA has so much data that it gets far too many false positives and therefore finds it difficult to identify threats and give them the appropriate priority despite having awesome processing power and unbelievably powerful engines to analyse it.

Predicting the market

When it comes to predicting the market, the algorithms that even the top quant funds use are very unstable indeed. They look almost unbeatable during normal trading sessions, but when the market changes in the form of what we call a "paradigm shift" due to events such as the QE waves that the Federal Reserve and the ECB initiated in the past, the algorithms are often singularly incapable of dealing with this. This is both because the data mining that is often used to "train" even the so-called deep learning algorithms has set the algorithm to expect a certain specific market behaviour and it is difficult for the algorithm to switch its trading approach to accommodate something new in a way that a human might be able to, because we can change our views based on information that is extremely unexpected but that has a logical implication for the market. When QE2 happened in the US, the clear implication was that volatility in the markets would begin to collapse as the Federal Reserve essentially gave full direction to the stock market. This was obvious to a human, but not clear at all to the algorithm. There is a useful example about the failure of algorithms from the game of Chess, a game that we have already said computers have taken over entirely with an I-phone running an app now able to beat pretty much every human player, to the extent that even the best humans rarely play the computer because the computer is just too good and when they do they usually get odds[133]. There are a number of studies that have been created by humans where a human who is a reasonable chess player (at say my level which is around 1800 on the FIDE rating scale versus the top Grandmasters who are all above 2600) can easily see that the position is a draw, but where a computer which follows an algorithm that doesn't really think (it just analyses the position in terms of a number of moves ahead with some additional heuristic enhancements). I will put a link to a cool YouTube video in the footnotes[134] which will show you just such an example. The example that was shown which is a situation where the way that you draw is to lock up the position by using your pawns to form a chain that cannot be broken without the aggressor losing far too much material. The key point here is that most chess engines have no heuristic algorithms programmed in to deal with these sorts of positions because the engines are generally made to win the game and rarely look for draws unless they are behind in material or they are suffering from an aggressive attack which is about to checkmate them. Because the chess engine is not thinking, it cannot see something that is (relatively) obvious. And in the same way, the algorithms that predict the market are not able to properly adapt to market moves that happen because of an "unseen hand"; something like the Federal Reserve during QE, or if suddenly income taxes were to go to zero. The algorithms simply cannot see the consequences of these events because they haven't been programmed to do so and because they haven't seen the behaviour in the data that they have been fed. It truly is the case that for learning algorithms that they "are what they eat".

But as the algorithms get better at predicting ordinary events, humans get worse at identifying and responding to the paradigm shifts. They are not able to because they have become trained to look at the algorithms and they have also been trained that the pathological events will only happen perhaps once in their careers and that therefore the best short-term strategy is just to behave as if the intractable things will never happen at all. They must behave as if the Global Financial Crisis was a genuine aberration across the eons of time and that such a thing can never happen again. And that leads to market instabilities which mean that the seeds of the demise of the financial system are at least partially sown in the algorithms that were developed to predict the market moves that would occur over time. And as the Idiocracy in finance continues to grow and prosper we will see more of these algorithms take over and make coming crises less and less easily dealt with.

---

[133] https://en.wikipedia.org/wiki/Human–computer_chess_matches
[134] https://www.youtube.com/watch?v=N0k-VGrOuX8

What is even more of a concern is that there is some good evidence that people are giving up on active management altogether. There has been a significant trend towards passive funds. These would be pools of capital that are not invested by an algorithm or a human trader, but simply are invested in an index or some basket of stocks or bonds and is not changed whatever happens to the market. The reason for this has been the poor returns of the actively managed money. That money has failed to perform strongly both due to the financial Idiocracy – that money is being managed by humans who have little understanding of fundamental value, and the inherent instability caused by the Central Banks adding liquidity where they should not. This paradigm shift has made algorithms fail too. So, the result has been just to invest and close one's eyes. The attraction of passive money is a result of the returns that basically doing nothing but going limit long has generated since the Financial Crisis and this is simply an artefact caused by the Federal Reserve and other central banks. They have taken the natural volatility of the market away by creating too much money and investing it into the equity market indirectly by buying other securities (mostly government bonds and mortgage bonds). When there is a multi-trillion dollar balance sheet buyer who is always on the bid in related securities, the market tends to shy away from volatility. In the process, of course, because the Fed has destroyed volatility, the ever enterprising free market has created other "assets" to generate that volatility and therefore the Fed was really one of the creators of the rise of crypto currencies as an "asset class".

One of the very deepest comments of Jordan Peterson is that "In times of radical uncertainty, what was once common becomes profound". During this time of Financial Idiocracy when things like Modern Monetary Theory can influence (dominate!) Monetary Policy, the basic mathematics that to us by now is self-evident suddenly becomes profound and something that Economists cannot see, or more accurately, are unwilling to because of their preconceptions that stem out of political ideology rather than truth. Sometimes we need to look at something through the eyes of the naïve in order to see the obvious truth which has been obfuscated. The question that we will ask very soon is, why has this been obfuscated, by whom, and to what end.

But what is the second critical thing that the futurists have missed? Well, this is that we really should not be worried about AI taking over the world in a Skynet type incident, because there are already malevolent intelligences that will have the power to do that. These evil and insidious creatures are, in fact, human beings. Yes, you and I in the form of big government have already begun to restrict freedom and take the world in the direction of totalitarianism. Because a human intelligence, or groups of humans, in control of the technology of the future could have the power to control the thoughts of people and make them behave in the way that they want them to. And we will see that this is already here, in primitive form to be sure, but certainly it is here and is already manifest. This we shall observe when we talk about the Sesame Credit system. For now, let's go back to the premise that in the future robots and AI will take over every part of our economy and essentially make humans superfluous. I don't believe that this will be the case. Throughout history we have seen waves of innovation change the world economy, and yet employment has still been available. This is to be expected, as there exist probably an infinite number of possible endeavours that humans can undertake. What simply happens is that innovation tends to take the more tedious jobs away, and unless we had real AI, we certainly would need humans to do many different things like directing and conducting scientific, moral, artistic, philosophical, and religious thought and many other things. However, let us grant the premise that somehow, jobs will generally disappear through these technological breakthroughs and look at what people who do think this way are doing to deal with the supposed issue.

If you do grant the premise, it is, of course, a major concern. The economic nuclear Armageddon that would seem to be heading our way (assuming, of course, that you subscribe to this point of view) from there no longer being the industrial worker jobs and the fear of this is leading to more and more outlandish solutions. These solutions include a so called "living stipend" which is being mulled over by the EU and has actually already completed testing in Finland[135], or something like the "Freedom dividend" proposed by current Democratic candidate for President Andrew Yang[136] who wants to give everyone over 18 in the US 1000 dollars a month. The idea of this is simple. The state pays a certain amount of money a month to everyone simply for being alive. In this way the argument is that the pain of jobs no longer existing will be mitigated at least somewhat. The idea of universal basic income is not new at all and is basically something that has been proposed historically by many thinkers. Even from ancient times such things were considered, and an argument was articulated by Thomas More in his book Utopia published in 1516, although given the name of the book, it could be argued that this was not quite in support of the idea. However, it was further developed and enhanced by various luminaries such as the Marquis de Condorcet, and even Thomas Paine the writer of the book "Common Sense". In the 20th century there were huge numbers of attempts and proposals for such things. In fact, one can argue that the currently extant Alaska dividends, whereby citizens of Alaska are given dividend payments paid for by the revenues from Oil and gas operations that take place there. It is a real UBI and is paid to everyone who has lived in the state for more than 6months, although as the population is less than 750,000 this is something that affects less than a quarter of a percent of Americans. Some of the most learned people who advocated for this include James Tobin, Joseph Pechman, and Peter Mieszkowski in their famous Yale Law Journal Paper in 1967 who provided a (highly spurious) mathematical analysis to back it up. What amazes me about this is that the concepts are coming from people who supposedly have been educated and, presumably at least, the politicians that are advocating this had investigated the consequences at least superficially.

Anyone who has been following the arguments espoused in this book and can do some basic mathematics will be able to see some serious difficulties with this and not just conceptually and we are going to do this "back of the envelope" now to see what those problems are. Let's take the example of Finland and the proposed amounts that they are considering providing in the form of monthly stipend[137].The number is just over 600 USD (560 EUR) so let's take that number. That equates to 7200 USD a year. Let us also take a hypothetical country of 100 million people (so just about 30% of the population of the united states). Let us call this country Progressia. Then the total cost of this would have to be 720 Billion USD on the basis that this is paid to every man, woman, and child. Where would this number have to come from? Assuming Progressia is a country with a balanced budget this would have to come from tax revenues.

Now let's assume that this country has a GDP per capita equal to that of the US. This is around 57,000 USD. Now the US has a total tax revenue of 7 Trillion USD. So, scaling by the population means Progressia has around 2.1Trillion in Tax revenues. Therefore, Progressia needs to pay 35% of their budget to provide this income. This is a lot, but it is doable right? Well, yes and no. And I think that you can see the big flaw in this. This assumes that the GDP per capita of Progressia remains at 57,000 per capita. But if people receive this living wage then a large percentage of people, and young people especially so, will no longer wish to go for a career. Some who have a sufficiently strong education and are from the top Ivy League or Oxbridge schools could well start off on a salary that pays them a large enough amount that they are willing to work rather than just live off the basic wage that they are given, but what of those with just a high school education?

---

[135] http://www.msn.com/en-us/money/markets/as-robots-take-jobs-europeans-mull-free-money-for-all/ar-AAlUWnE?li=BBmkt5R&ocid=spartanntp

[136] https://www.yang2020.com/policies/the-freedom-dividend/

[137] https://www.yahoo.com/news/m/52555cd1-f6fa-37c1-9b73-c83ea3104c99/undefined

Right now, many people in the US start on salaries that are not large compared to this sum of 7200 USD per year, and certainly there are a number who earn salaries comparable to what Andrew Yang proposes to give to everyone. And this suddenly makes everything very hard. Because human beings are good at short term optimisation. We have talked about how everyone seems to want things now rather than to build something; it is ingrained into our current psyche. And this applies very well to work. Why would you want to work when you could get money from the government for free that will allow you the time to (fail to) climb to the top of the Pareto distribution for music or art. This explains why, for example, in Cuba where all pay was basically equal until 2008[138] and is still very similar, there are a lot more people who want to be musicians than sanitary engineers. But the problem compounds when you factor in the collapse of productivity that this would bring. As less and less people are willing to take the jump into employment, people will become less and less qualified to be employed. Skills are generally gained on the job and not at University or any other training organisation and need to be practiced in order to maintain them.

The data seems to bear this out. It should not be surprising that these issues exist if you can simply put yourself in that position with a gedanken experiment even for a second. In Finland, where the experiment had gained almost unprecedented attention worldwide due to numerous factors, the whole thing was accepted to be a failure[139]. The hope had been, that because this UBI was offered regardless of whether these people had a job, that this would give them an increased incentive to get a job and have substantially more money without the fear that they would lose the UBI the minute they did. This was an attempt to counteract the usual negative incentive in European developed countries where entry level jobs are usually paid at levels that are only 1-2 times the amount of money individuals can get just from claiming benefits. However, it just wasn't enough. People who didn't want to work just decided to do things we would generally regard as hobbies and therefore they put themselves in some of these pareto distributions that are so

It is well documented, for example, that in the present environment, those who cannot find work within a period of, say, 6months, are then in a downward spiral because the fact that they have not been working for 6months makes them out of touch with their old connections and they are therefore less likely to find employment. It is worse than this, because the evidence suggests that the time off work generally serves to destroy the confidence of those affected such that they become willing to accept jobs that are not as good as their previous jobs. This has a massive psychological effect on human beings because humans are far better at dealing with a situation that is initially bad and gets very very slowly better than they are at dealing with a situation that is getting steadily worse even if, overall, they are better off in the second situation. The human condition is such that we always see things getting worse as a failure that is far more devastating than starting out in a bad way and continually improving. In a sense, we are simply extant as people in the moment, we tend to always romanticise the past and always assume that the future will be implausibly better than things currently are now. When that future is (and it is usually the case) not realised, we tend to have crises. Because as human beings, most of us do have far more confidence in ourselves than perhaps we should. We are scared, of course, but somehow always believe that things will be alright.

Ironically human beings have an amazing ability to believe that they are always the most important factor in any given event. Whilst politicians are well known for never blaming themselves, most human beings are not like this. When things go right, we tend to believe that we are geniuses, and that success is a causal result of our own perfect brand of leadership and vision. Conversely, however, we also believe that we are directly responsible for failures and these failures are entirely because of us and when we fail the tendency is to suddenly believe that we didn't have the skills or that we weren't good enough. But of course, usually quite the opposite is true. Failure usually equips us with experience and therefore we do

[138] http://news.bbc.co.uk/2/hi/7449776.stm

112 https://www.euractiv.com/section/economy-jobs/interview/finnish-finance-minister-case-closed-for-universal-basic-income/

become better at handling the situation that we failed at. In addition, very often the exact circumstances that caused the failure were not under our control nor were the conditions that led to success. We need to understand that this is the case to pick ourselves up again. However, not having a job often reinforces the false logic that we are the important part of the equation. And all this means that sometimes very qualified people can end up failing in their career even though they are good at their job.

This touches on another, possibly the most important point that we have here. Human beings respond very well indeed to having a significant responsibility. This is because there is something very deep down inside almost anyone that wants to feel needed and necessary. It is not even that case that people feel the need to do something very important, just something that is required. It is having this responsibility that makes people feel that their days and years are worthwhile. This is especially true in societies that are more secular in nature. The Christian always felt in the past that everything they were doing was for God. But the atheist doesn't have that comfort, and instead might take solace in the idea that their job is contributing to the world. If people need your services, you feel valued, and in the end in some sense loved. There have been studies undertaken[140] that have identified that working past retirement age by even a year has benefits to life expectancy. Whilst working beyond retirement can also have detrimental effects the evidence in general points towards a job being something that keeps people alive. It is natural as when you have responsibilities and something to live for you focus hard to make sure that you do not let people down. This in turn leads to better outcomes, because the world is mostly responsive to action, and many problems are solvable if they are simply worked on. Very little is ever irreversible and irrevocable.

The true question progressives should be asking; "Why are the lowest wages so... well, low?"

I have some sympathy for a minimum wage. There are many people in society who really are not paid sufficiently well in general. These include particularly those who are involved in caring for others such as nurses, but frankly also include people who do jobs that the average person really would not want to do. These include things like toilet cleaners all the way to the police who are often in danger especially in certain areas. Society really should put a much higher value on these sorts of professions. Equally, it is fair that human endeavour should be worth a significant amount of money and here there are vast inequalities indeed. For example, the stars of a movie can arguably be said to contribute far less than they get proportionally speaking compared to those in say post-production. The same is true for pop singers and reality stars and all manner of people.

So, a generous minimum wage is reasonable thing – the cost of human labour really should be higher. But this is where things become difficult. If I am an employer like McDonald's and someone tells me that I need to double the wages of my employees, I suddenly become much more incentivised to automate my restaurants. I start buying machines that reduce the need for people so that if I can halve (or do even better than that) the number of employees that I have, I can offset the additional burden to me. In fact, by having very high minimum wages, I force businesses both small and large to have as few people in employment as possible. I am pushing people directly into the cold and undead hands of "the machines". Recently Amazon, the company owned by Jeff Bezos (currently the richest man in the world) announced that it would have a minimum wage of 15 dollars an hour. This was greeted with great enthusiasm by the socialist leaning types, however as the New York Times declared[141] some workers were very concerned that they would be out of pocket due to the loss of bonuses and stock options. The employees that are worried are some of the most loyal and best performing (hardest

---

[140] https://www.health.harvard.edu/staying-healthy/working-later-in-life-can-pay-off-in-more-than-just-income

[141] https://www.nytimes.com/2018/10/09/technology/amazon-workers-pay-raise.html

working) that the company has, and typically would not be management but would be those that are aspiring to be in the middle class and better themselves; those who most reflect the American Dream.

The increase in productivity over the last 50 years has been something that has never been experienced since the industrial revolution. Yet if we look at wage growth over that time it has utterly failed to pick up. The question then is why is that? Discovering the answer is very pertinent because if wage growth since around 1968 had been in line with the growth of productivity, it is arguable that the lowest wages would be around 15 dollars maybe even 20 dollars an hour, higher than even today's minimum wage advocates would like. This would mean that even the lowest paid workers could be earning 50,000 USD a year (assuming 20 dollars an hour with 10 hour shifts daily and 250 working days a year being 5 days a week with 2 weeks holiday) which is above the average US income currently. Ironically, the reason that wages have not moved in line with productivity is partly due to illegal immigration into the US and partially due to some of the central bank policies that we have been talking about.

The movement of illegal immigrants into the US has been an exceptional phenomenon for a first world country. Whilst there are always problems with illegal immigration into any country that provides significant services for its populace, since 1990 there has been a particular, and a very direct push by those on the progressive left to make illegal immigration appear both less of a problem and somehow not a bad thing. Of course, progressives do not believe this for one minute, and President Trump demonstrated this when he dangled the idea that illegal immigrants should be bussed right away to the so-called sanctuary cities. The outcry from those who supposedly advocated for open borders was palpable. The phrase "one rule for me but another one for thee" comes to mind. Apparently illegal immigrants should all be placed somewhere far away from the gated compounds of the elites, but ideally just within commuting distance so that there are plenty of serfs available to clean for them, perform gardening services, and maintain their mansions, all at a bargain basement price.

This narrative of the progressives on immigration is aided and abetted by a leftist media who removed the phrase "illegal immigrant" from their coverage and instead used "undocumented" which of course simply implies that this is someone without a US passport but with every right to live in the US. Again, the sophistry is exceptional. The US now has almost the entire media and one of the two major parties, the so-called Democratic Party advocating for something like genuine open borders. Now open borders could perhaps be made to work in some countries. But this would only be countries that offer no social safety net whatsoever and no public services. Not only that, but the country itself would have to have no cohesive identity in the first place. Given that the US has the most comprehensive and ingrained constitution that defines the country, and is also a country where the government provides a lot of different benefits (food stamps, various medical programs, rent subsidy programs such as section 7 etc.), it is impossible to get open borders to work. And the irony is that everyone recognises this. When the Trump Administration suggested that perhaps those who arrive to claim asylum should be bussed directly to Democrat controlled sanctuary cities, the very democrats that argued a wall on the border was immoral [142] turned around and screamed most vehemently against the idea[143]. Clearly, everyone agrees that open borders are a disaster, it's just that the Democrats think that if they can get enough illegals into areas that currently vote Republican, then they can ensure they regain the presidency and stay in office for the rest of their lives. This is an utterly cynical tactic from a group that argue for a long-term view towards tackling what they believe to be the biggest problems of our time such as Climate Change, but then again since when did progressives have to be consistent?

[142] https://www.theguardian.com/us-news/video/2019/jan/04/immoral-nancy-pelosi-on-trumps-border-wall-video
[143] https://thehill.com/homenews/house/438639-pelosi-calls-wh-migrant-retribution-unworthy-of-the-presidency

In further examples of Sophistry, the argument is made that because legal immigrants to the US have been shown by various studies to perpetrate less crime than natural born citizens, that illegal immigrants must also have this characteristic despite the fact that the exact opposite is true even before you take into account that illegal immigrants commit a crime simply by being in the US illegally. Here the Latin phrase "Falsus in uno, falsus in omnibus" is very apt. This is an expression of the common law idea that a witness who is unreliable in one thing cannot be said to be reliable in other accounts. The analogy applies to illegal actions. One who is willing to do a certain thing illegally is more likely to do illegal things when it comes to even bigger issues. How anyone could possibly not understand this is beyond my ability to comprehend as it is the very basis of almost every correctional system in the world. We detain people not just to punish them, and really not primarily so especially in progressive circles. We detain them because they would quite simply be expected to repeat their crimes in the normal course of events if they are not shown the error of their ways. In the same way, illegal immigrants if they are willing to do something that they know is a crime once, they will be willing to commit crimes again.

Regardless, however, of whether you think that illegal immigrants magically become perfect citizens on arrival into the hallowed ground that is the US, what cannot be doubted is that illegal immigration will lower the costs of labour of the most unskilled. This is because illegal immigrants typically cannot access credentials that would pass scrutiny in the compliance department of any major company, and therefore even if they are highly skilled, they will only be able to find work in the most menial jobs. This in turn puts pressure on the amount that menial jobs pay because many illegals are working those jobs. Simply because of supply and demand, the cost of labour plummets and this has a knock-on effect on those who have higher paying jobs. To give an example, no one likes to clean toilets (at least no one that I know of). Because of this, the laws of supply and demand would dictate that all things being equal, the pay for those who are to clean toilets should go up further and further in order to bring in more aspiring toilet cleaners. The fact that you don't need too many skills to be a good toilet cleaner should be countered by the fact that no one likes to do the job, and therefore a typical toilet cleaner should be paid better than some low qualification office jobs. And yet this is not the case, because of illegal immigration and the rush to the bottom. Until this is stopped in an effective way, it will not be possible for any menial worker to have a fair shot at the American Dream.

The presence of illegal immigrants also interferes with something that is good for society in terms of who does the jobs at the bottom. Generally, as we have mentioned before, if you begin your working life at McDonald's as a dishwasher, you do not expect to keep doing that over time. The menial jobs at the bottom are meant for teenagers who have no experience yet in order to learn the value of hard work, and to help contribute to their cost of education. But if these jobs are being given to those who are working illegally, the lower wages will dissuade more teenagers from taking on those jobs and bettering themselves in the process. Not in terms of skills necessarily, but certainly in terms of humility and the appreciation for hard work. What is also seldom thought about is the fact that, in the west, even if you don't go to university and drop out of high school, there is no reason to expect to have to work in a menial position for the rest of your life. In the worst case that the only work you find is dishwashing in the fast food industry, diligence and time spent will certainly get you promotions, and you will go from dishwasher, to cook, or to sales, and then maybe to management in the franchise, and eventually maybe you get to own a franchise of your own. This may take a while, but if you persist you will do significantly better than you might have expected when you first started out. But if you do not do those menial jobs to start with you might fall into a trap where it is more convenient initially to collect benefits, and therefore you find yourself 10, 20 or even 30 years down the line with no experience at all and no skills because you didn't make the first step. This is very problematic, because by this time you will be so far behind everyone else that you really have no option but to do the least attractive jobs.

Whilst the movement of illegal immigrants to take lower paying jobs does affect wages significantly as we have said, this is not the whole story because, as always, the Central Banks are also involved. In the past, the money supply was controlled by one thing only which was growth. If companies and businesses began to do well and make money with increased productivity the excess returns that would be made would find themselves back in the real economy from the consumption of workers who received increase pay, and shareholders who received larger dividends etc. This would almost immediately lead to increasing inflation as the demand for goods and services began to pick up. This link has effectively been cut by the money supply manipulations of the central banks. Now even though the money supply globally has massively increased, the amount of money that is being used day to day has not. Much of this money that has been pumped just sits on the balance sheets of the various central banks and thus the inflation indices which have relatively little direct asset price exposure stay benign, but assets become overvalued as the market tries to take into account the increase in the money supply.

The one thing that has really held back the first world from falling over the precipice during the last 50 years has been massive increases in productivity brought about by the development of modern-day computers, and the internet and the associated newly created pareto distributions. This has been extremely fortuitous as this began to occur just about at the same time as the breaking of the last vestiges of the gold standard by President Nixon in 1970. But to talk about the gold standard we have again to go back to understand where it came from and why it was important. We will do so now.

Silver and Gold standards.

In my safe at home I have my coin collection. It is not an exceptional collection at all, but I have invested a reasonable amount of time in it even though the cost to replace it from a monetary perspective is not high at all in numismatic terms. It basically consists mostly of Japanese 1 Yen silver coins from 1870 through to 1914. The coins are not in great condition because finding those coins in an uncirculated format would have cost far too much for me to consider spending on coins. I also bought them mostly on eBay to save money[144] However, I do have one example for every year of circulation of the 1 Yen coin, so the collection is worth a couple of thousand dollars (for those who care about this almost half the value comes from the 1875 1 yen which was the year of the lowest mintage – it's in awful condition with chop marks but still valuable for its rarity, and my examples from 1879 and 1874 are both ex jewellery and therefore damaged so are not worth much even though they are rare).

The 1 Yen silver coin was minted almost exclusively during the time of the emperor Meiji (明治). The famous Meiji restoration is named as such, because de facto power throughout Japan was consolidated back to the Emperor at the time. Whilst there was always an Emperor in Japan, and the Imperial House of Japan (sometimes referred to as the Yamato dynasty) is claimed to be the oldest continuous hereditary monarchy on earth[145], the power of the Emperor fluctuated significantly at different times. Prior to the Meiji Restoration, the de facto ruler was the shogun of the Tokugawa shogunate that had been present since the early 1600's. The shogunate system had been established as an attempt to quell the warring tendencies between different Japanese clans that had been prevalent throughout much of the first Millennium. Japan being a country with a huge amount of mountain and forest (even today rural Japan is breathtakingly beautiful), it was very difficult to maintain order without modern day technology, and therefore the shogunate system was the "best of a bad lot" of options to keep the rule of law whereby each clan was responsible for a particular area and they all swore fealty to the shogun who had overall control even though the Emperor was still officially the Emperor. However, with the arrival

---

[144] eBay is a fantastic way to buy things like coins with one caveat – you absolutely must be able to tell what is genuine from the fakes (some of which are very good) otherwise you are likely to get fleeced. Because eBay has protection against fakes, if you can identify a counterfeit in hand, you will be fine as you can always get your money back from eBay if you could not 100 percent say that it was a fake in the photos before buying or if you were sent a substitute coin which I have been sent various times.

[145] The family traces its roots back to the Emperor Jimmu who was supposedly a direct descendant of the Sun-goddess Amaterasu and essentially became Emperor on February the 11th 660 BC in Yamato which is now just east of Wakayama and known as the Nara prefecture close to the southern coast of Honshu.

of Commodore Matthew Perry[146] in Tokyo bay (although Tokyo at the time was still known as Edo), it became clear to many in Japan that Japan was far behind the west and that therefore a top down approach to development of the country was required for Japan to "catch up." With support of various leaders such as Sakamoto Ryoma[147], the Emperor Meiji was essentially able to assume control by decree rather than with a bloody battle having ascended to the throne on February 3rd 1867, and oversaw the transformation of Japan from its feudal roots, to being a market driven economy.

Prior to the time of Meiji ,silver and gold, as well as electrum (an alloy of silver and gold) were distributed in small rectangular bars (sometimes known as Samurai money) but from 1870, the decision was made to go to a decimalised silver standard with a 1 Yen coin issued weighing 416 troy grains (all 1 Yen silver coins except the first issue in 1870 have 416 and 1 Yen written in English to show this) of 90 percent silver (26.96 grams). This was in order to very closely match the weight* of the original US silver dollar weights as mandated by the Coinage act of 1792. These in turn were mandated on the basis of the average of the weight of circulated (and therefore slightly worn) Spanish silver dollars which were the universal currency for trade mainly for Chinese goods through the Philippines (as China would only accept silver for transactions and wouldn't accept any other currency in use.)

So, from 1870 Japan was on a bimetallic gold and silver standard[148] and 1 Yen was Pari passu with the US dollar. But even by the end of the year Japan was in a scramble to switch to the gold standard (which it did in 1871) as a result of global events set in motion by the newly created state of the Federation of Germany precisely because it had been pegged to the US dollar.

The US was forced, not even a decade after the end of the Civil war (in 1865) to come up with another Coinage act – the Coinage act of 1873. The act of 1792 had essentially made the US on a dual silver and gold standard i.e. bi-metallic. This meant that a 10-dollar gold coin (called an eagle and being 16.04 grams of pure gold) was defined as well as a 1-dollar silver coin (being 24.1 grams of pure silver). This essentially pegged not just the US dollar to precious metals, but gold and silver together. The peg was therefore at 1.604 grams of gold per 24.1 grams of silver or an exchange rate of 15.0249 between the two. Unfortunately, however, silver and gold are not the same thing and as demand for silver changed there was new pressure on this peg. The changes in silver demand came from Europe and specifically when Germany ceased to mint the Vereinsthaler (or Thaler for short) just two years after the formation of a united Germany in 1871. The decision was made to go to the gold mark which we talked about before and was converted at 1 gold mark for 3 Vereinsthalers. This converted Germany from a de facto silver standard country to a gold standard country.

This was one of the first real financial shocks for an increasingly global economy. This is because suddenly with Germany on a gold standard, there were real problems for the countries that were on a bimetallic standard, owing to the reduced demand for silver in Europe. Why did it do this? Well supposing that silver in Germany had stayed at the same price as it was before Germany had converted to the gold mark. The citizens of Germany would, in this case, begin to sell all their silver to convert to "hard" currency in order to be safer especially if their silver holdings were just holdings in the currency of the day. This would cause the price of silver in the free market to begin to fall. So, capitalism being capitalism, some enterprising soul seeing this would do the following; they would take all the silver they

[146] I would make a Friends joke here, but sadly I cannot think of a witty way to connect this with Miss Chanandler Bong.
[147] A famous Samurai who was assassinated just before the Meiji restoration itself took place.
[148] Monetary Changes in Japan Author(s): Garrett Droppers Source: The Quarterly Journal of Economics, Vol. 12, No. 2 (Jan., 1898), pp. 153-185 Published by: Oxford University Press Stable URL: http://www.jstor.org/stable/1882117

could get cheaply and buy US dollars for example making sure that they bought eagles and not regular dollars. As more and more people caught on, there would be a run on gold versus silver dollars in the US. And this is the danger that all the countries with bimetallic standards faced. Suddenly everyone who could would be arbitraging them and the only way to fix the situation would be to do one of two things (actually three things if you include going off any standard into fiat currency); either convert entirely to the silver standard or switch to the gold standard.

And thus, it became manifest, that the US was forced to convert to the gold standard in the Coinage act of 1873. This further depressed the price of silver which hurt the US as part of the original reason that the US was on the bimetallic standard was because it was a miner of both silver and gold. Notice that here we really see what the key to the global economy really is. It is not that there were really many parts of the world with no contact whatsoever in the past (at least not in terms of significant economic output), but that these connections were very loose in terms of temporal effects. That is, information in the past travelled so slowly, that the effects of an economic collapse in a single state or country were not really that relevant to the world in general. Of course, an economic failure would have some direct result in terms of reduced trade, but it would not affect all the nations on earth and might not even be that relevant regionally speaking; if people don't hear about something it essentially nullifies its effect. But with the advent of the telegraph in 1832, followed by widespread adoption by many countries, and most critically the connection of those systems together, which took place between 1850 through to the end of the 19th century (Australia was finally connected in 1872, and the Pacific Telegraph was completed by 1902),the world was really global for the first time. Before this, it would typically take 70 days for a letter to reach Australia from London and therefore communications were so slow that economic events were very well insulated in the medium term. In fact, as has been documented, the finance ministers of Europe would often spend their summers on long distance expeditions to see how things were going perhaps in the US or even further afield, something which they continued to do well into the 20th century.

For Japan this was sadly not the end of its troubles. Being a country very close to China, Korea, the Philippines, and Russia, and not having established sufficiently high levels of trans-pacific trade at this time, Japan was still under pressure to make silver its standard. The first thing that Japan did was try to imitate the US and create a trade dollar in 1875 which was slightly heavier than the extant 1 Yen coins at 27.22 grams (420 grains) and the same as the US trade dollar. The purpose here was to flood the East Asian markets with Japanese silver, to subvert the dominance of American silver (both US and Mexican). This was an abject failure and only just over 3million (3,056,638) trade dollars were ever minted. Ironically this has made Japanese trade dollars still in existence worth well over 1000 USD dollars if in reasonable condition today.

At the same time Japan was minting 1 Yen coins with the old 416 grains weight again starting in 1875[149], because only 50million Yen in gold had, in fact, been circulated in previous years. Eventually, there was capitulation in May of 1878, whereby Japan went back to an explicit bimetallic standard meaning a fixed rate of exchange between silver and gold. It was worse than this though, because at the same time the 416 grains 1 Yen was declared to be of equal value to the 420 grain Japan trade dollar. This meant that the rare trade dollars were taken out of circulation very quickly as they were de facto worth more than the 1 Yen coin in terms of silver content. However, Japan had not yet established a central bank and would not do so until June of 1882. This meant that the government had also issued a very large amount of fiat or paper currency that was nominally equivalent to the metallic currency but traded at a discount. Eventually, Japan decided in 1897 to revert to a gold standard. This was again partly a

---

[149] only 139,233 were minted in 1875 which means that the coin is immensely valuable with very low quality and damaged examples still trading at over 1000 dollars, and uncirculated examples easily commanding 6 figure prices at auction.

response to what happened in the US and a recognition of the fact that the Qing Dynasty in China had been increasingly unstable in terms of the money supply.

So, we see that throughout the latter third of the 19th century, the entire world basically oscillated between the gold, silver, and bimetallic standards. The lack of homogeneity in an increasingly globalised world (albeit one where the velocity of information was substantially lower than today) pushed everyone towards a gold standard alone starting at the beginning of the 20th century. Any thought that this was going to last was shattered by the advent of the First World War when Germany and Great Britain as well as various other places. But in the US, it not only was able to maintain the gold standard, but due to supplying the allies with various resources during the war, the US essentially switched with the UK as the dominant economy post WWI. The US then entered into what seemed like a golden age of expansion in the 1920's despite events such as hyperinflation in Weimar and other such difficulties in Europe. But then the US experienced the Wall Street Crash and proceeded into the quagmire that became known as the Great Depression.

The US default? Never!

We all know about the Great Depression. A myriad of movies, pictures, and primary sources have described in graphic detail what life was like, the dust bowls in the Midwest, homeless or unemployed men selling apples for 5 cents a pop on the street, banker suicides, and huge lines in the soup kitchens. We also know about the New Deal, a collection of mammoth projects and entitlements designed to spend the way out of the Depression. However, what little know about is that the US effectively defaulted during this time. They did this not by refusing to pay back borrowings in dollars, but by coming off the gold standard and then back on at a different level.

The US repegged the dollar to the gold standard as part of FDR's approaches in the New Deal. This happened whilst the US was still feeling the effects of the stock market crash of 1929. Although this is not one of the things that we can focus a lot of time in our discussions, it is certainly instructive to learn more about it. At a minimum it is worth reading one of the shorter pamphlets on the even such as "Black Tuesday" by the Charles River Editors. That will give you at least a good basic understanding of the issue and then you can choose to look at some of the deeper analyses that are out there.

What is important to note for us was that the crash of 29 as well as the breakdown in financial conditions post the reversal of the over-optimism that was characteristic of the 1920's led to the Great Depression. FDR's attempt at dealing with the Great Depression included his big idea of the "New Deal" which was essentially a massively protracted works program that involved huge infrastructure projects as well as a whole bunch of other measures. However, FDR was hampered by one thing. The US at that time was still on the Gold Standard. Because of this the government was not able to devalue the dollar and gain a competitive advantage versus other developed economies. FDR circumvented this by essentially repegging the dollar. He did this in two stages that really were a very powerful example of bait and switch.

The first thing that FDR did was sign an Executive Order[150] in April 1933 that effectively stopped anyone from owning significant quantities of gold. The idea behind this was that the hoarding of precious metals was something that had been going one since the Depression started and that this was inhibiting the US economy by artificially sterilising the money supply. So, FDR signed into law Executive Order 6102. You can have a look at one of the bills that were posted to declare this order on the Wikipedia entry on the subject. This order basically limited private holders of gold to 5 ounces of gold at the maximum with some exceptions for jewellery as well as those who owned gold coins whose primary value was

---

[150] https://upload.wikimedia.org/wikipedia/commons/a/a1/Executive_Order_6102.jpg

numismatic. This of course meant that only those hard-core collectors of numismatic rarities were exempt which clearly was a tiny fraction of the gold in circulation.

The consequences for non-compliance were indeed quite dire. This could be either a 10,000 USD fine or 10 years in prison, or even both. This meant a fine of 500 gold double eagles, significantly more than any normal saver of gold was likely to have been hoarding, and in today's money would be worth around 750,000 USD simply from the value of the gold alone. Moreover, this also applied to holders of Gold Certificates who effectively owned paper that was convertible to gold at the fixed peg. This would have applied to many different people as the paper cash was more convenient than the physical gold for purposes of transactions and other things.

The deadline for returning all the gold in your possession, which would be replaced by Federal Reserve dollar notes, was the first of May 1933, and led to significant issues for both banks and individuals. The coup de gras however was to manifest itself in 1934. During the previous year, the exchange rate between gold and the dollar was undergoing a great deal of flux with the price being set by the government seemingly at their whim (somewhat akin to the current CNY fix). As a result, private credit was pretty much drying up and this was the excuse that the government used to effectively take money from savers with no compunction whatsoever. But further calamities were to befall the hapless US public as, with the Gold Reserve Act of 1934, a full devaluation of the dollar occurred. Before Executive order 6102, the price of gold was pegged at 20.67 dollars per troy ounce. This of course automatically made the gold double Eagle worth exactly 20 dollars (since the gold in a double Eagle was an alloy). Post the Gold Reserve Act, gold was revalued to 35$ per ounce of gold.

What this effectively did was to devalue the dollar directly with the cost coming from all the holders of paper money in circulation. One way of looking at this of course given that the US was on the gold standard is that the US government technically defaulted on their obligations. The US government had not honoured what they had promised to do and something which had already been banked on. And whichever way you cut it this is not something that should be forgivable Now often something like this has unintended consequences. The issues here were that there were many private contracts in existence as well as a number of de facto government entity contracts that specified that payment would be made in gold. Of course, since holding gold was now totally outlawed, the question was how payment would be made, and this was dragged all the way to the SCOTUS.

The supreme court did not support the rights of the individual to own and receive physical gold. The argument went as follows; whilst it is true that the bond required the delivery of gold, any gold given would have to be confiscated immediately due to Executive Order 6102. Therefore, to avoid this the bond will simply pay out its nominal amount. One justice did dissent here arguing of course that it would be easy to provide the US dollar amount that corresponded to the bond notional at the actual gold peg to the dollar of 35$ per ounce. So, the US has already defaulted on its debt in some sense. And sadly, it wasn't the only time in its history that something equivalent to a default had happened.

The end of the Gold Standard.

But by the end of the 30's the US was looking at something new. The spectre of war had yet again descended on the world, and whilst the US continued to mint silver "peace dollars" until 1935, by that time it was clear that bad things were happening both in Europe with the rise of Fascism in both Italy and Germany, and the extreme persecution of the Jews.

World war 2 for the US started of course with the bombing of Pearl Harbour. The day that "would live in infamy" was regarded slightly differently by the Japanese Admiral Isoroku Yamamoto who certainly believed that Japan was unlikely to be able to win any extended war with the US. Whilst the famous quote attributed to him; "I fear that all we have done is to awaken a sleeping giant and fill him with a terrible resolve" may not be of sound provenance, it is definitely apt.

The US was an exceptional manufacturing powerhouse, able to provide virtually the entire supply chain to the US military complex with ease. And of course, the US was able to do things that the other actors on the WWII stage were unable to do. That is, huge monstrous endeavours such as the Manhattan Project which was a staggering thing in the context of the time due to technological limitations. In fact, the Manhattan Project was one of the great accomplishments of mankind despite having such devastating consequences.

But something was different at the end of WWII versus the end of WWI. The role of the US during the first world war was almost entirely that of the banker. The US had hardly participated even at the end of the war. It had not declared war on Germany until the 6th of April 1917. Thus, the US was in the war for less than 2 years and the list of casualties demonstrates this. As a result of its role as a banker, and because its losses were minor compared to many of the other participants (the US for example lost 110,000 men compared to almost a million for the UK and colonies, as well as 1.7million for Russia), the US came out of the world war in a relatively far better position than anyone else.

For WWII the situation was not quite so clear cut. Whilst it is true that the continental United States remained free of the scars of war, the toll of the sons of Liberty was significant with over 400,000 military deaths which was more than those suffered by the UK, and only just lower than the combined (both military and civilian) deaths that the UK had. Because of this the US was not quite in such a good position in the years post WWII vs the rest of the world. Although WWII had effectively brought the US out of the Great Depression through the huge industrial output marshalled for the war effort, it did so at a cost of a massively weakened fiscal position. This coupled with both the cost of rebuilding Europe (via the Marshall Plan), and the drain of the Cold War led to an economy that slowly, but surely, began to weaken and wane even if it was imperceptibly so.

A huge quantity of the wealth and treasure of the United States was expended during the Cold War. Much of this was spent on things like the Space Race. Around 25Billion USD (the equivalent of just under 200Billion today) was spent in getting the US to the moon. This cost was just that of the Apollo program and didn't include the previous Gemini and Mercury programs as well as the various other exploratory missions that NASA undertook. At the height of the moon program, the funding for NASA was around 5% of the entire US budget a staggering amount. The US was also spending huge amounts of money on military programs on everything from ICBMs through to above top secret "black projects" that even today we have little idea what they were. I personally like the idea that the US has developed the TR-3B antigravity plane, a supposedly 600-foot wide craft that hosts electro-gravity technology years ahead of any vehicle the US has declared exists![151] The Cold War also saw an exceptional nuclear race between the US and the Soviet Union culminating in the testing of the so called "Tsar Bomba" which, when test detonated in the autumn of 1961, yielded around 50 Megatons of TNT. That is the equivalent of exploding 50 billion kilograms of TNT, and as a comparison the "Little Boy" atomic bomb that devastated Hiroshima in WWII was a mere 15 Kilotons less than 1 3,000th of the power of the Bomba. The cost of nuclear development was also exceptionally high for the US, and in the 50 years between the end of WWII and the end of the Cold War, the US spent nearly 10 trillion USD on nuclear weapons in terms of current USD values. That represents around 50% of current US GDP. A truly exceptional figure.

Well, all this spending had to be paid for and it was not going to be pretty. The US was going to go off the Gold Standard even in principle, and President Nixon did this in 1971. To all who had been following the US economy this was not surprising, and really occurred in stages. Firstly, the US ceased to mint 90% silver dimes, half dollars and quarters after 1964. Furthermore, the US silver certificates (basically US 1dollar notes) were no longer redeemable after 1968 and were replaced by federal reserve

---

[151] I did some theoretical and experimental investigations into electro-gravity tech myself. The first approach I undertook was to investigate how much more efficient a model aircraft plane can be made to be if the leading edge of the wing were to be heavily electrically charged.

notes. As such, the official exit from the Gold standard was practically assured. And as soon as this happened, as soon as the US was no longer obliged to give gold to holders of US dollars, and thus a huge number of dollar holders instantly lost significant amounts of real money. Quite expectedly for anyone who has read this book, there followed a decade of exceptionally high inflation in the US culminating in a print of 14.76% in April of 1980. This was something blamed on the oil crisis and other things, but of course, it was a direct result of the US exiting the Gold Standard. The US dollar was massively devalued and therefore, not surprisingly, both Gold and Oil became far more expensive in dollar terms. And it was this inflation that began to take us into the Prosperity mirage that we have lived in up until today.

The beginning of the Prosperity mirage.

The 1960's and 70's were periods of great change across the Western world. Some amazing things happened, and some abominable things happened. This is often the case with great change. The digital revolutions that began in the 80's and continue till today were but a glimmer in the eye of some far-sighted visionaries and not quite even that. But the basis of those revolutions, the Integrated circuit and the Transistor were already invented at the end of the 50's and 40's respectively. What was changing however were certain social ideas. The great changes were of course the Civil Rights movement, along with some similar changes in other western countries where segregation was not enshrined but where there were still significant biases against those who happened to have more melanin than others.

The awful things that happened during the 60's and 70's were the beginnings of things like the collapse of the family unit, and the abomination of state sanctioned abortions. This slaughter of innocents in the name (ironically for some organisations) of something that a sick mind might call "family planning" is a truly evil thing that the founding fathers of the US, and the great minds that shaped the United Kingdom would certainly have considered a true anathema and quite rightly so. Even the conquistadors when they saw that the Aztecs were willing to sacrifice their own children were horrified by these practices, what would they have said about the practice of abortion.

The breakdown of the classic nuclear family was also something utterly deleterious to the US and to the rest of the western world. The effect was only really seen properly over time and we are only now coming to grips with some of the terminal issues that this has caused. The lack of a male role model in the household has meant that delinquency amongst young men especially has skyrocketed and this is not hyperbole. In terms of the statistics, around 23 percent of children live in households with only one parent in the US now[152], and this has been accelerating. It is also one of the biggest indicators of poor success in later life, as well as delinquency itself. It is also a particularly good indicator of poverty in the future. And the left was steadily breaking down the idea that two parent families were good from the start of the 60s.

But the Prosperity mirage had begun and was already making things look far better than they were. With the collapse of the gold and silver standards, the US and other western countries began a great experiment in an almost fantastical amount of credit growth. There seemed to be limitless possibilities in terms of where the world could be. In Japan we have already talked about the massive credit expansion and excesses in the 1980's, in the US and the UK we saw huge property price rallies, and in the rest of Europe we also saw the same thing a little later on in the 1990's and 2000's.

Instead of growth being predicated now on real things being achieved, on the success of hard work, as well as innovation, growth had begun to be dependent on the expansion of credit. The expansion of the money supply and the continuous creation of credit meant that a lot of people who had bought houses or stocks before the expansion became instantly far richer by really doing very little. But this increase in "value" of assets meant that they also yielded far less in terms of returns from dividends or from rentals.

---

[152] https://en.wikipedia.org/wiki/Nuclear_weapons_of_the_United_States

This also meant that investing in such things involved more and more risk, because if the value of your asset went down, it would now take far longer for you to claw back that value through the yield (either of rents or dividends or whatever other income the product produced).

Today we are used to highly expansive credit, and as we have discussed, we also see almost no return from saving money meaning that there is a total disincentive to save and solidify our personal fiscal positions. We are pushed again and again to spend, spend, spend. And this is very hard indeed because, when push comes to shove, almost every "developed" economy is bankrupt.

Everybody is bankrupt:

So, are we really saying that the entirety of the western world is bankrupt? The answer is a resounding yes. At least in terms of what has been promised versus what can be delivered and this is the key. The result of all this is simply that there will be defaults either explicit or in the form of hyper printing of money to the extent that the value of whatever currency you own is reduced by 70, 80, even 90%. Already the so called "developed" world has undertaken every single form of taxation that is reasonable and even some that are not. To take the UK as an example. The highest rate of tax is 45% which is large but not ridiculous. However, on top of this there are all the hidden taxes. National insurance is 2%, council tax varies per property but is not insubstantial. Then there are additional taxes on anything and any service that you want to do. For example, stamp duty for houses can be significant with an additional charge of 3% on any second property purchased as well as the stamp duty itself which can be over 10 percent for the most expensive houses in aggregate. Then there is VAT which is charged on almost anything and now stands at around 20%. This along with things like service charges at restaurants all add up to a huge amount of passive costs that the consumer must pay.

In the US things are even worse with 2016 (pre-any Trump administration reductions) levels of Federal combined with state taxes at around 55% at the highest levels, and taxes of around 10% on services depending on the state. This all adds up to a huge drain on the consumer and this is what is driving the collapse of the middle class.

And just in case you think that this might not apply to the world. The total debt load (not including unfunded liabilities that are implicit rather than explicit) of the world right now if you include all household debt as well as all government debt and all corporate debt is 250 trillion dollars[153] now. To put that in context assuming a world population of 7.5billion, this means 33,333 dollars of debt for every man, woman, and child alive today. Or to put it another way, this means that the debt to GDP of the world is approximately 300%. But of course, that doesn't include the huge amount of unfunded liabilities that are extant. The US social security system, for example, is projected to deplete its entire asset base by 2035[154]. This is enough to be hugely problematic, but it is then abundantly clear that as soon as the coffers have been wiped the entire program in perpetuity is unfunded. That means the liability that will exist in 2035 is equal to the value of the program for the rest of time discounted to 2035. This must be funded eventually somehow, and it is clear that it cannot. Just look at the numbers. Taking the factsheet from the Social Security Administration referencing the month of June 2019[155], the numbers total 85.8Billion for the month. Assuming this is a typical month which is not unreasonable the total is around 1030 Billion annually, so let's say 1 Trillion for simplicity. Now assuming a long term risk free return rate of 5% which is very ambitious given that current 30yr Treasury yields are far closer to 2%, this would imply that the total value of the unfunded liabilities in 2035 will be around 20 times this which is 20Billion dollars assuming that there was no increase in the entitlements and that the population drawing benefits is static. Neither of this is true (everything would be far higher given current

153 https://www.bloomberg.com/news/articles/2019-12-01/the-way-out-for-a-world-economy-hooked-on-debt-yet-more-debt
154 https://www.barrons.com/articles/social-security-deficit-reserves-check-benefits-payroll-tax-51555958282
155 https://www.ssa.gov/news/press/factsheets/basicfact-alt.pdf

demographic projections), but even if it is, the value of this program in terms of liability is at a minimum very close to the total current US Federal Debt, and comparable to the GDP of the entire US in 2019. If we assume long term yields are 2% instead this exposure more than doubles in terms of present value. And this is just an example of the unfunded liabilities that the US government has. Of course, this doesn't just apply to the United States, similar things are true of many different countries and their entitlement and benefit programs. There just simply is not enough real money to go around.

These issues would also be surmountable in the first world if immigration was essentially stopped, as the demographic reduction would cover some of the problems associated with forward liabilities, but this will never happen due to the entrenched leftist ideas of "diversity" (ironically of everything other than thought) from the global elite. And one further problem with bringing in a large number of immigrants who are unskilled and often from the third world, is that there is the propensity to bring over the economic and political systems that they effectively fled from. And that, unfortunately, means bringing over the ideas of Marx and his views on socialism.

The evil that is socialism.

The dictionary definition of socialism is that it is "a political and economic theory of social organization that advocates for the means of production, distribution, and exchange to be owned or regulated by the community as a whole." Specifically, however, socialism is in Marxist theory a transitional state that exists before the full realisation of communism but post the overthrow of capitalism. To date most Marxists would argue that no country has ever achieved true communism and therefore countries like nominally communist China are, in fact, socialist and gravitating towards the ideal state of communism.

Now you may be forgiven for thinking that with current tax rates, many of the worlds most developed economies are approaching socialism and here is the dirty little secret of progressive governments; that you would be right in thinking this, at least in part. But there is a key difference between a state which has heavy social programs but has an engine of growth that is capitalist, and a state where both the mechanism of wealth generation, and the redistribution are socialist in nature. The truth is that many of the worlds governments now have socialist like social programs to redistribute the wealth, but the growth that got them that prosperity in the first place is not socialist in nature, it is pure capitalism. So, when Bernie Sanders claims that countries like Denmark, Norway, or Sweden are socialist, he is demonstrating a profound misunderstanding of the nature of those countries. So much so, that the Prime minister of Denmark felt the need to correct him in a speech given at Harvard[156]. What countries like Denmark or Sweden do is have light regulations, a good business environment, but very high levels of income tax or VAT to be able to redistribute some of the wealth but this system always has a critical problem; the remit and scope of the programs always tend to increase more and more. The government in question often finds they need to provide more and more money to accommodate this "mission creep" of the social programs and this puts them into even more debt. They then are obliged to raise taxes further and further to accommodate the lack of resources to pay for each of these programs which are in any case steadily increasing. They can only do this if the economies concerned are increasing steadily, and this can only really happen properly in a market economy. And this is where socialism just cannot work, because again, we are dealing with human beings and not agents of goodness.

Socialism is a simple idea and one that might seem to make sense on the face of it but only really for a moment. The idea is that wealth should be redistributed evenly amongst the populace such that everyone ends up with equal outcomes. This is the general mantra of the mainstream left – or at least the current manifestation of it, whether it be the Democrats in the US or the Labour party in the UK. But socialism goes further than this. Not only do you socialise the wealth once it is created, but over time you socialise the means of production as well so that the worker becomes the ultimate beneficiary

---

[156] https://www.miamiherald.com/opinion/op-ed/article215553335.html

of their work. The whole thing is a mirage or illusion in and of itself. It gives people the idea that as the workers in a factory they are the ones that are creating everything and therefore they deserve all the profits that are generated also. That might make sense but only if the workers were also prepared to accept the losses associated with failure. This is the reason why a salaried worker does not earn as much as the boss of the company who owns it. The salaried worker can always leave and go to another factory if the company that they are working for begins to fail, but the owner cannot do anything of the sort. The owner lives and dies by the success or failure of his or her enterprise. For the risk that the owner is taking they do get a large chunk of the benefits of success, but this is how it should be. For not every worker would be willing to work the same amount in a factory that is owned by the workers. One bright fellow might see that his co-workers were already doing a great deal of work and that the amount of produce that is being created wouldn't really go down significantly if they instead of working at their peak started "bunking off". Again, because human beings are not always the good and responsible agents that they like to believe they are we can see that it is quite likely that several of the workers would begin to have the urge to contribute less but still keep the same for themselves because there is no one to push them towards service. They will get as much as anyone who works hard so why should they do so?

The glib mantra of Marxism "From each according to his ability, to each according to his needs" sounds utterly wonderful at first glance but because it is predicated on human wholesomeness, fails at the very first hurdle. In the same way that human beings are not, in general, true agents of goodness, Marxism can never really leave the drawing board because it is axiomatically false. Do you remember the steady state fallacy that we talked about much earlier? The SSF applies here too. In this case, the SFF is in thinking that just because a country becomes socialist and it seems to perform reasonably for 10 or even 20 years, that this means the system is working. Well, no. The fallacy here is that you have to see what happens when other people's money runs out. If you just spend the money you appropriated from the rich for a few years you can make things look good initially as you continue to devour that treasure, but very quickly this is expended. This is obviously because you don't have an engine for creating value, you have simply taken it from those who have. And because of this you will always run out – if that value was created in a capitalistic system, however, it would have been able to grow naturally, and potentially provide enough for everyone if it was sufficiently well nurtured (and not stifled with prohibitive tax burdens and pedantic regulatory burdens for example). You see when human beings become involved in enforcing sharing, the nature of human beings kicks in and you see their evil coming out, and there is no longer the zeal to better yourself, but the desperation from seeing there is a finite pie that is getting rapidly eaten up and consumed, and where the need is simply to survive a day at a time.

Venezuela, a modern-day Kafkaesque nightmare.

Just barely 20 years ago, Venezuela was still being touted as the poster child for a successful socialist state. 15 years ago, I was looking at the oil warrants tied to Venezuelan par bonds as interesting potential investments, and many analysts were arguing that Venezuela would surpass Brazil as the real powerhouse of South America. But that was precisely because Venezuela able to look good as it continued to spend the money of the populace. This is where the Steady State Fallacy kicks in. Venezuela had (and still has) an abundance of proven oil reserves (bigger than those in Saudi Arabia for example) and has an almost perfectly favourable climate[157] with no real natural enemies. Caracas was and, to some extent, remains a beautiful city. And yet the country embraced socialism and within a few decades people had descended to literally competing with dogs on the street for scraps from the rubbish bins[158].

---

[157] Except for a tendency to generate thunderstorms, the climate is as close to ideal as it can be with temperatures seldom being colder than 15 degrees C and rarely higher than 30.

[158] http://www.educationviews.org/new-video-shows-people-dogs-eating-out-of-trash-in-venezuela/

Socialist states that begin rich are like someone with a spending habit that starts off with a large bank account due to perhaps an inheritance, or a lottery win. Initially they will not see much of their wealth reduce as maybe they are receiving interest from investments or other things. But over time things will get worse as their principal reduces, and they are able to make less money from investments due to their spendthrift lifestyle. They might survive in the style that they are accustomed to for a decade or even more but eventually they are unable to maintain their way of life. The same with the socialist state. Initially they might tap into their existing resources and seem to be doing well. But over time the fact that their labour force is no longer as productive as it could be, begins to drain the coffers, so the state starts to borrow heavily from the Capital markets. The markets initially accommodate the borrowing with low interest rates, often with investment banks fawning over the state to bring their offering to market, but over time as the debt owed grows, lenders will only accept larger and larger rates of return, and the borrowing of the state becomes entirely unsustainable. At this point in time it is already the end of all things, but the state can continue to survive somewhat by going to the next level of craziness and printing money. As they print more and more money, we see the hyperinflation that we looked at in the case of Weimar or Hungary and finally we end up with the Venezuela that we know. At this point, all the socialist sympathisers that initially lauded the great Venezuelan example begin to decry the management of the state arguing that Venezuela is failing due to corruption, despite the fact that in the 1950's Venezuela was the fourth richest country in the world.

Let me give you one other prediction that will happen whenever the next socialist state fails. Everyone on the left will begin to argue that that state which failed was not socialist. They will use pretty much every ad hominem argument, which really is no argument at all. They will also point out flaws in certain logical arguments that no one in their right mind would never make regarding capitalism. One such argument pointed to Zimbabwe's failure and argued that if you could use Venezuela as an example of why Socialism doesn't work you can use Zimbabwe as an argument that capitalism will never work. Now, unfortunately, Zimbabwe was never run post-independence as a capitalist country in anything but name, and Robert Mugabe the long-time President who died in 2019 was a socialist who blamed most of the woes of Zimbabwe on a capitalist conspiracy. But let us assume that someone has properly identified a failed capitalist state, they really have proved nothing. The corollary however is that whilst there are plenty of capitalist economies that have succeeded, there are no examples of any socialist country succeeding even over the medium term, zero, zip, nada. And let us not forget that Socialism itself is supposed to be replaced entirely by a Communist utopia soon enough under general Marxist principles. Again, we have example after example of failed socialist states. And the failure is not just measured in poor financial performance of the state. It is counted in blood – invariably that of the most innocent of the populace, those that stared evil in the eye and didn't blink.

Almost all of us (except for certain racist monsters) can all agree that Nazism and the ideology that it stood for is utterly evil, but for some reason the ideologies of the extreme left can be regarded as "cool" and somehow righteous by vast swathes of the populace . And whilst it is true that the fascists came up with the greatest evil of all time in my opinion, namely the systematic attempt to remove the Jewish people from existence in what they sickly termed "the final solution", we must never forget that the socialists and communists killed huge numbers of their own people in the 20th century. The monsters of Stalin and Mao Zedong come out top in another Pareto distribution – this one a hideous one of utter evil – that of the most people killed on the orders of one man. There are of course debates on exactly what the numbers are, but even if you take the low estimate of 49million people Mao[159] was responsible for more deaths than all the other people on the top ten list put together (Kim Il Sung the grandfather of Kim Jong Un of North Korea for example killed 1.6million making him number 9 on the list of evil)

[159] http://www.popten.net/2010/05/top-ten-most-evil-dictators-of-all-time-in-order-of-kill-count/

Of course, it is hard to be absolutely and categorically certain of all such numbers but if the hideous number of deaths from the horrible ideology that is Socialism and Communism are going to count for anything we should listen as they tell us in a resounding scream - "No more." Yes, we are looking at economics but if we ever forget human consequences in what we talk about, then we are no better than those people on the streets who hold the banners declaring their support for the "Socialist Worker" or some such publication with the hammer and sickle in red and gold. If anyone were to parade with the swastika we would, quite rightly, have them arrested; we should treat socialist and Communist symbols with the same righteous indignation. And yet we accept without any concern someone who wears a T-shirt with Lenin or Che Guevara or any other Communist "icon" plastered upon it, and it is certainly no anathema at all to express Communist or Socialist sympathies, leanings, or even declare openly that your only goal is the destruction of democracy and Capitalism in one fell swoop.

So, whenever any of these socialist states do fail, the clarion call comes from the left to claim that they are not socialist and that in fact corruption, or sanctions, or the US, or Donald Trump was responsible for the demise of what could have been a great utopia eventually. They forget that they were all supportive of these states when they were in their transition period - i.e. when they were still spending other people's money and that money had yet to run out. They also don't realise that corruption is an inextricably linked property of Socialism in the real world. And this is all because the left now no longer fails to discern evil. It can no longer identify true evil and it has become infected by the very same insidious force, and the reason that it became evil in the first place was because it thought that people were basically good and then drew the conclusion that evil things were good because they were done by "good people". The problem is of course that people are not good - we are all evil inside.

The lie of goodness.

People in general are not good. This maybe comes as a surprise to us in this century but would not have done so to those living 100 years ago or earlier. At that time, many read the Bible and from that book you can see that the nature of man is evil rather than good. These days we live in an age of political correctness whereby the assumption is that humans are basically good overall and that most people try to "do the right thing". In such a world, speech becomes equivalent to violence because the political elite see the world through a lens that assumes the general public is a group of innocents who need to be protected at all costs from the few who are bad and say mean things to them i.e. criticize them. Effectively the agency of human beings is no longer "a thing".

The scientific evidence just doesn't bear that out, but people throughout history have been unwilling to confront the idea that human beings are not pure agents of goodness. The Chinese philosopher Mencius (382-303 BC) tells the story of how an ordinary person feels if he sees a child fall into a well. Any person, Mencius argues, will feel alarm and distress — not because he hoped for anything from the parents, nor because he feared the anger of anyone because he failed to save the child, nor again because he wanted to enhance his own reputation by this act of modest heroism. It's simply that, Mencius says, "All men have a mind which cannot bear to see the sufferings of others." Certainly, it should be evident that most people would want to be able to help in a case such as this, but on the other hand this is a situation where the risk that the person seeing the child in distress has is limited. In fact, one could argue that society might look very badly on someone who chose to do nothing (France for example has the Good Samaritan law that requires anyone seeing someone in distress who is able to, to assist). But what if you have something to lose from acting? What would you do then? What if to rescue the child you would have to sacrifice yourself for sure?

For me the situation of the depravity of the human condition is very clear. I would take the argument employed by Paul Washer and others. The argument is to conduct a "gedanken" or thought experiment. You do it by thinking of what you thought about in the last hour. Now assuming you were not asleep or simply concentrating on your work, you will have thought various and rather diverse things. Now ask yourself would you be comfortable if anyone even your closest friend or husband/wife could hear and see your thoughts in the last hour. Which of us, if being honest would not do virtually anything to prevent that? I certainly would how about you? And for what reason would you want people not to know what you were thinking during that hour? Simply because you were thinking such evil thoughts that you would be horrified if people could see this. Your entire façade of a reputation would simply collapse into dust if everyone you cared about could see what was truly inside, if everyone could see the machinations of your dark and poisonous heart.

So, the myth of the "goodness of the human condition" is debunked in one fell swoop. You might say well, "Maybe I am atypical – there are others who are much better than me". Well you may be right, but I can tell you one thing, if there are such people, they are likely to have two specific qualities. Firstly, they will be deeply spiritual and most likely Christian, and secondly, they are very likely indeed to have no interest in politics at all. And the truth is that you, as a human being, are likely indeed to be typical. Or to put it another way, the Bayesian probability that at least 99% of human beings are bad given that you are bad is significant once you have found 100 people who you know, and all admit to being bad without one being good.

Socialisms dirty little secret – evil.

Well you might say. We agree that all human beings are basically bad but isn't there a chance that there is one human who is not bad, and if so, could we get him or her to lead a country into a socialism that would eventually really become the utopia that so many people in the past gave their lives for. Well here is the real problem with socialism. The whole idea of socialism is evil in and of itself. It is truly wrong to believe that everyone should have equal outcomes in their lives because not everyone on the planet is the same by any means. And by this I don't mean just in appearances or physical abilities. I mean in terms of interests, in terms of what people value and in terms of the willingness to contribute to society.

If people who could contribute more than others see that their contribution does nothing for them at all because in the end the system will lead to equal outcomes then you never will get anything that improves the world; no innovators, no entrepreneurs, no independent thinkers at all. You will end up with just a very grey world where human happiness doesn't exist and the populace either resigns itself to slavery or, due to the nature of the human condition, rebels against the elite that administer the place. At the end of the day there is another, rather more wholesome reason, that people should never prefer equal outcomes. And that is simply that as human beings we just don't all value everything equally. In the same way that we don't all enjoy the same things and we certainly don't ascribe the same sort of utility to the same things. I for example would not see any value at all to playing in the NBA even if I could, I just wouldn't care enough. However, I would be very happy indeed to be an archaeologist if I could magically deal with my fear of insects, and basically my acute hypochondria that anything I might dig up might be infested with bacteria that haven't seen the light of day in eons and might be resistant to even the most powerful antibiotics. Equal outcomes would do away with everything because it would mean that people would essentially be forced into living a life that was utterly grey. And that, of course, assumes that those who get to decide who does what are benign god-like people who never have grudges or favourites, or even make a wrong decision even just once in a blue moon. But the overlords will never be benign, because as we have seen it is within our very nature to be evil.

There is another thing about equal outcomes that is abhorrent, and it is that you are enforcing a breakdown of the 10 commandments. The most obvious violation is stealing – equal outcomes is a forcibly facilitated stealing plain and simple because that is the very definition of what enforced redistribution of wealth is. But then there are other things – you are not supposed to "Covet thy neighbour's ass". Well demanding equal outcomes is, by its very definition, a philosophy that encourages people to covet. Then indeed you are also putting this principle above God because that is what you must do to always enforce equal outcomes which violates the first commandment. This is not even to mention the commandments that you end up breaking to accommodate this such as the lying that you are obligated to do in order to justify such an evil system. Finally, of course, more murders have been undertaken in the name of Communism and Socialism in the 20th century than in the name of any other system, religion, or cause.

Equal outcomes for unequal effort should indeed be an anathema to human beings. It is not morally good or righteous at all to have this. It is like forcing everyone to have a single hourly wage regardless of performance and effort or the skills that they have developed in their lives. Equal outcomes would mean that Einstein, Shakespeare, Leonardo da Vinci, and all the others would simply have never existed in history because they would have utterly failed to flourish. Why? Because no one would accept that they should be famous or be allowed to affect the thinking of other people. They would simply be another grey face in the sea of grey faces that would never appear in the history books. In fact, there would be no history books with equal outcomes because history would no longer be necessary. Everyone would be able to see quite clearly that the past is the future, is the now, is the forever. In the world of equal outcomes, everyone would sink to the role of the lowest common denominator not the not the star. George Orwell makes this argument somewhat more eloquently in his excellent work 1984. As he says: "Everything faded into mist. The past was erased, the erasure was forgotten, the lie became truth." When everyone is "equal" in terms of all their human properties, there is no need for history because everyone was and always is equal and therefore history is entirely homogenous with no real events. So really history doesn't exist in this socialist utopia. This is a terrible idea not only philosophically, but also in practice.

Again, we have an obligation to help those who are either mentally or physically incapable of labouring. This group which includes both the physically and mentally handicapped is the **one group** that we should be protecting. I found it heart-breaking when I heard a recent question asked on the Andrew Klavan show[160] one of the podcasts produced by the conservative network the Daily Wire. The various presenters of the different shows on the network take it in turn to answer questions from subscribers and this time it was the turn of Andrew Klavan to answer one. The question was that of a person who was about to become permanently disabled due to some (unmentioned) condition. The person was asking whether it was hypocritical for him to take benefits given that he was entirely against big government and benefit culture. Mr Klavan dealt with the question in the best possible way with compassion and without demagoguery. He basically suggested that the subscriber might want to change a little his ideas about social benefits when it came to those who really could not do anything to help themselves rather than those who simply didn't want to do so, which was exactly right.

The reason I felt so sad here is that this was and is the whole point of social benefits, but no one seems to realise it. That in a civilized society we are both obligated and able to look after those that have become disabled either through illness or through war or any other unfortunate circumstances. The whole point of not offering universal benefits is to be able to provide generously, even perhaps abundantly, for those who are in this type of position, whereby through no fault of their own they are unable to fend for themselves and their families. But the assertion that Socialism and Communism make is that everyone should have those benefits and because they don't acknowledge the evil and selfish nature of man, they totally fail to understand the simple concept that human beings when given things for free and unearned will simply stop working. And therefore, they are doomed from the very start to fail as systems of government. This is because essentially every single axiom of socialism is both morally and empirically wrong, including those of the morality of the left.

What's in an infinity stone.

Avengers infinity war brought might not have seemed like it, but it exposed the evil of socialistic utilitarianism in the character of Thanos. In this epic movie you essentially have Thanos (and his minions) against The Avengers et al. The Avengers fall into the traditional roles of the goodies and Thanos is the archetypal baddie. This has been building up since the Easter-egg at the end of the first

---

160 https://soundcloud.com/andrewklavanshow

Avengers movie where Thanos is revealed and has been further alluded to in the Guardians of the Galaxy movies as well as other Marvel productions in the MCU[161].

But during the movie there is a twist. Thanos thinks he has a plan to make things better for (according to him) the fullness of the people in the Universe, but unfortunately for him, throughout the movie the Avengers rail against his plan. Interestingly enough, a number of left leaning (some very left such as Vox[162]) publications came back with the retort that perhaps Thanos isn't in fact a complete mentalist (to use the British euphemism) and that maybe he has a point. The idea here is that Thanos is a utilitarian and therefore sees the overall good of society as being predicated on how happy everyone is in that society. The idea of utilitarianism is simple; you evaluate the overall good of the life of every person by using some metric (such as net wealth) and then do things that increase the sum total of that good overall. A utilitarian is therefore allowed to do anything that achieves an increase on the sum of the good and thus a utilitarian should be perfectly fine with killing people if the increase to the utilitarian metric of the remaining ones is sufficiently high to negate the loss of the good in the lives of those who are killed. You can obviously see that this logic will lead to some quite toxic events and Thanos is very eager to do exactly that with a "genius" solution to the problem of universal overpopulation which seems to be endemic to the entire multiverse.

His direct answer to the problem of universal overpopulation is simply to destroy 50% of all created creatures and therefore giving the 50% who are left twice as much in terms of resources and so according to him the sum total of utility in the multiverse would actually go up (if you accept the reasonable assumption that having a significant surplus of resources in a world previously starved of resources actually gives people a far happier life perhaps greater than that of two people in a starving world). This is clearly hellish and should appear abhorrent to almost everyone. Well it turns out that some people, and the progressive left specifically, believe that Thanos has a point. For example, a Vox writer[163], came up with the following argument. I have the link below, but I will briefly summarise it. The overall theme is that there are two schools of thinking when it comes to the definition of the the greater good. Whilst this isn't true, let's assume that this is the case. The argument is that the two schools are the utilitarian approach that we have described above, and the Kantian approach named after Immanuel Kant. It should be noted that Vox doesn't bother with any of the thoughts that might come from the great Christian thinkers with regards to ethics for example, despite the existence of plenty of thought that comes out of that school which would illuminate the discussion here. Nevertheless, let us look at the thoughts of Immanuel Kant on the matter.

The Kantian approach says basically that human beings (and therefore in the case of the multiverse any sentient being as imagined in the Marvel Cinematic Universe) are a unit having essentially infinite moral value, and that there is never any reason to sacrifice one person for the good of others. This is essentially the point of view that Captain America is espousing throughout Infinity War. The Vox commentator argues that both moral approaches when taken to absolutes turn pathological. This is clearly obvious given the utilitarian ideas, but to me it is hardly clear that the extreme Kantian approach (other than in certain specific cases) is pathological at all. Let me explain what I mean.

Well, to begin with, Immanuel Kant[164] whilst being a great secular philosopher was simply distilling the commandment to "do unto others as you would have them do to you" from the sermon on the mount.

---

[161] MCU being the Marvel Cinematic Universe.

[162] Vox claims to be "middle of the road" but an extensive perusal of their content as well as the background of their writers and presenters demonstrates quite clearly that they are very left wing indeed, and certainly sport very little diversity in the only area that really matters; thought.

[163] https://www.vox.com/summer-movies/2018/5/17/17343442/avengers-infinity-war-captain-america-thanos-sequel-moral-dilemma

[164] Kant's Philosophy was that of transcendental idealism, whereby all experience is something that is fashioned into a narrative by the mind. In this philosophy it is impossible to question the nature of things like

Given that Vox is clearly leftist it is understandable that the wish would be to justify some utilitarian approach[165], but the argument that Kantian ideas are de facto destructive is disingenuous precisely because the ends never justify the means as we are human beings and our actions don't just have consequences on others, but they have consequences on our psyches and our souls.

The real problem with the utilitarian approach is twofold. The first is that you would have to actually be omniscient to properly assign the correct functional utility to the world – you otherwise would miss the world of highest utility, and you may actually fail to come up with a world with a better true utility function than the one that you replaced. In fact, unless you could more than double the "happiness" of those who are left by whatever metric you have selected to represent true utility, you will certainly get one with a lower overall utility. And it is arguable that simply doubling the access to resources for someone won't make them twice as happy as they were – we see that even with human beings whereby many people are functionally relativist when it comes to their wealth. The example here is with someone who owns the cheapest two-bedroom apartment on 5th avenue with a full view of central park. That person or family are extremely rich by any metric in absolute terms (and in fact if they moved to Westchester county just 25 miles away, they could have a 10,000 square foot mansion), but they are likely to be amongst the poorest of their neighbours. The fact remains that they are poor compared to who they see day to day and who they will generally identify as their peers. This means the certainty of increasing utility simply by giving more resources quite suspect at least in practice.

The second, related, and entirely intractable problem with the utilitarian approach – certainly as far as Thanos is concerned – is that you can only be trusted to generate the maximum utility even if you are omniscient and omnipotent if you are also infinitely good. And here we know that Thanos is not perfectly good because it is manifest in what he is doing that there is something bad. Before embarking on the quest for the Infinity Stones Thanos was perfectly happy to invade world after world and systematically exterminate 50% of the population, despite the fact that at that time he certainly could not have had laid claim to being omniscient, omnipotent, or anything of the sort. To expect someone to suddenly change just because they became infinitely powerful is the ultimate height of hubris. Not only does it never happen, in fact the exact opposite is true. The phrase coined by the first Baron Acton[166] "power corrupts, and absolute power corrupts absolutely" is a reflection of this fact, although it is also an irony because in reality corrupt people tend to seek power and therefore that authority simply reveals their corruption in the same way that a very small man who wants (for some reason) to kill all his fellow man has no hope to do this unless he has weapons which give him the power to do so. So Thanos is entirely unqualified to make those moral decisions by his historic behaviour and lack of compassion. In some deep sense, those who have the greed and desire to find the Infinity stones do not deserve to wield them. The Soul stone itself, cannot essentially be acquired without effectively disqualifying the person who seeks it from ever being morally justified.

So now we are back to the moral problem of the left. That problem is not just that sacrificing lives in the name of Utopia or utility is wrong (although it is), but that the left is demonstrably not worthy of the power to do this. Captain America is right not because humans are good or moral but simply because they are not anyone else's property. No-one has the right to ask even a single human being to die for the greater good because they are not their property. Human beings may sometimes choose to do so

---

time or space because the mind interacting with them convolves their true nature with its own and that the ability to filter this adjustment to finesse the absolute true real meaning of the concept does not exist.

[165] That, after all was the whole predicate of Communism, Socialism, and the teaching of Marx.

[166] John Emerich Edward Dalberg Acton (1834-1902) delivered an address entitled "The history of Freedom in Antiquity" which is a true classic, pointing out much of what I say in a more concise form. Sadly, I only read the transcript after I had nearly completed the manuscript. If I had read it before I wrote my script, the book might have turned out quite differently. This is even more depressing considering that the speech was made almost 100 years before I was born in 1877. https://acton.org/research/history-freedom-antiquity

because it is their right as moral beings with agency to sacrifice their own self, but they are not allowed to force anyone else to join them. And, by the way, if you disagree with this premise then, to be logical, you should be quite comfortable with the abhorrence that is slavery. Is that what you or anyone you know really believe?

And Thanos finally goes to show himself as the ultimate leftist – he doesn't even think of sacrificing himself to his glorious cause. This simply rips off the veil and lets us see him for who he is. Even though he eventually gives up his power, he is really sacrificing nothing as he was not even willing to do to himself what he did to everyone else. And of course, it is not just that this hypocrisy is palpable, but even worse he isn't only a hypocrite who says to himself "well I am just weak and useless, and I cannot live up to my own standard, but I do believe in that standard at least as something to aspire to despite my failings". That would of course question his ability to fully correctly analyse things in a utilitarian manner which is my first argument against utilitarianism, but Thanos is much worse than that, demonstrating extreme levels of hubris. He believes that he truly suffered greatly to achieve his "great goal" because of his "sacrifice" of Gamora, and that therefore he does deserve his reward for this. The hubris of both never questioning his ability to fully calculate correctly the metric of utility, as well as the idea that he has suffered and sacrificed and therefore he should not be rubbed out of existence, says immediately that Thanos is indeed the evil scumbag that was pretty much obvious from the start. As a good heuristic for life; if someone is willing to conceive of doing things which **you** would find abhorrent, then they are almost certainly very evil, because **you** are most likely quite evil yourself.

So, when you are tempted by the thought that "Castro is a great man" look to yourself and ask if you would even want yourself to have the power that some of the dictators in the current world have? Ask yourself why you would ever accept that and notice that if you did have all that power it would be tempting to try and do certain things. You might begin thinking that you could be benevolent and good, but then you would find the temptation to cut certain corners is there, to help your family, maybe your friends, and eventually you wouldn't even recognise yourself in your behaviour because you have become so accustomed to getting your own way that you still think you are doing good and always rationalise every selfish and evil decision as such. Like the proverbial frog we have mentioned, who doesn't know that it's getting boiled in water because the temperature is only increasing very slowly, you manage to rationalise your actions and your behaviour until it is too late, and you cannot reverse what is happening.

Did you ever notice that, anecdotally at least, that people who drive a Prius are often very bad drivers? Certainly, this is somewhat of a generalisation, but various commentators[167] have noted that someone who drives a Prius is often just a terrible driver. There are many reasons that have been cited, but my personal view is the human condition again. These people feel that they are "saving the planet" by driving a Prius versus a gas guzzling SUV, and because of this they become somewhat pious (Prius?) regarding this. Therefore, they no longer feel the need to drive in a conscientious manner because they feel they are already done "their bit" to save the world. This reason is exactly mirrored in the issues that exist once people get into the habit of recycling. Whilst before they might be quite careful about their use of various containers or packaging materials (for example using a glass bottle that used to hold mineral water to hold filtered water in the fridge), when they know that their discards are likely to be recycled they simply stop caring so much and end up using more packaging over time. Furthermore, that is exactly the attitude that those who advocate for socialism tend to have. There is a good reason that conservatives give a lot more of their money as a percentage of income to charity[168] and it's just another reflection of whether there is an understanding that people are fundamentally evil. When you think everyone is like you, and you know yourself, you realise that you must give to charity more as the government will not distribute fairly or correctly. Furthermore, your charity begins to be to specific

---

[167] https://medium.com/@Nostradommie/7-reasons-why-prius-owners-are-bad-drivers-a860c318b1d7
[168] https://www.philanthropyroundtable.org/almanac/statistics/who-gives

people who you know or hear about rather than organisations. I don't mean to say that giving to organisations is bad per se, it is just that it is easier to empathise with a specific person even if you have never met them. You cannot fight against your nature unless you understand what that nature is. Conservatives coming generally from the "human beings are bad" Judeo Christian point of view understand themselves far better and therefore push back more aggressively.

We are quick to accuse some people of being totalitarian. When President Trump criticizes the press, we should not suddenly reach the conclusion that he is some sort of intolerant dictator, rather we should think about whether he is right. Because it is self-evident that the press is not being supressed. If President Trump was a dictator like Hitler what would happen is that he would never send out an aggressive tweet, he would simply use troops or assassins to silence dissent. The fact that Saturday Night Live is constantly able to mock President Trump with impunity[169] and that over 90%[170] of news stories that talk about the President portray him in a negative light means that the idea that the President is a modern-day warlord in the style of Genghis Khan is frankly laughable. We should also look at the truth of the situation compared to dictatorial events in history; the fact that almost the entire "mainstream" media is against President Trump shows precisely that he is not a dictator. If it were otherwise the case, the press would be the first thing that would be compromised. Instead the press is "free" but not fair. The press is broadly leftist (some outlets incredibly so) and willing to compromise its reporting in order simply to propagate the agenda of the left. If they had read their history however, they would have to conclude that the mobs of the left are currently far more like the fascists of post Weimar Germany than anyone but the very extreme (and lacking any significant numbers) of the right. Both those guys are abhorrent, but the ones that are most dangerous are the ones with larger numbers, and who are primarily not being condemned by the left, and specifically the fourth estate. But it is not only the press that is doing this virtue signalling. This has become endemic in that great engine of entertainment that is Hollywood.

Hollywood has stopped telling stories.

Since I was a kid, I was always excited by Hollywood. I loved the stories that were always so beautifully executed. I loved the fact that the production values were top notch and how the stories told transported me to either another time, another place, or even a whole new reality. But here is the thing. If you look at the stories that existed around the time that I was growing up in the mid 80's and early 90's, you can see that by and large they were still actual stories. These stories often had messages and allegory embedded in them, but at the same time there were many parts of the stories that essentially were just story telling – where there was no message and it was unclear what the meaning might be. "Star Wars", for example was a standard fairy tale set at a different time. Indiana Jones also was just like that. The show the "Big Bang Theory" makes light of the fact that the role of Indiana Jones in "Raiders of the Lost Ark" was essentially redundant, and in this utterly misses the point. The point is that actual stories that are intended to be stories have a whole bunch of things that don't directly add to the main plot. This is why we enjoy them so much because we cannot be sure what is critical to the story arc and what is perhaps just an aside, just something that happens in the story and not anything with greater meaning.

The same goes for Comic Books. There is a reason that superhero movies are some of the most popular of all time, and that the stories and the cannon of the MCU (Marvel Cinematic Universe) represent the stories that were in the Comic books during the gold, silver and bronze ages of comic books. Today, the entire Comic book industry has been taken over by the politically correct, neo feminist, neo Marxist brigade, and fans are leaving Comic books in their droves. This is not because

---

[169] Having somehow failed to use the golden comedic opportunities of the Obama years such as the various "bathroom" crises that took place.

[170] https://www.washingtontimes.com/news/2018/may/8/donald-trumps-polls-improve-despite-90-negative-co/

there is any problem with women superheroes; Wonder-Woman and Supergirl are some of my favourite characters[171] but because of the need to take anything that is popular and whitewash it with the blandness that is leftist, progressive, socialist dreariness.

Today's modern-day allegories are all coming out of Hollywood and they do very little except drone on the mantra of the left. But at least Hollywood is in a country with freedom – therefore the movie industries of countries which are not free produce films that are overwhelmingly unattractive. When entertainment industries become simply a propaganda arm of a certain ideology, rather than reflecting a whole host of different ideas (God forbid that there might be a story from an orthodox Christian perspective!) which is what reflects the values of freedom and liberty. But Hollywood is becoming exactly this even though the freedoms exist; Hollywood and the media as a whole just spend their time advocating for the (far) left as if the right, or even centrists, just didn't even exist in the US or the rest of the world

What the political spectrum really looks like, and why is there no road to Utopia?

When we think of a spectrum we tend to think about a comparison to the spectrum of light. In short, we think of the spectrum as a bar from left to right. We see the Communists and Marxists on the left and associate the far right with supremacists and Nazis. However, the true position is not like this at all. The spectrum is much more like a colour wheel, where the extreme left and the extreme right meet right next to each other. And the reason that they meet is that they are basically the exact same thing in practice. They have to be so because they both advocate a totalitarianism whereby the entity that governs (either the state or supposedly the people but not actually the people) replaces God and becomes the moral yardstick by which all good and bad is measured. And of course, this means directly that those that govern can never be criticised because they become the arbiter or all moral truth even if their system is something logically incoherent such as "there is no arbiter of moral truth". This exposes another of the great false axioms of the left, the idea that morality can simply be intuited ab initio that somehow you can figure out what good really is through a form of deductive reasoning as human beings. And that leads to thoughts of Utopian societies.

Throughout history, we have seen those on both the extreme right, but particularly the extreme left that espouse the idea there is a potential entity that can exist, and which was historically named Utopia. Utopia comes from the book by the same name by Sir Thomas More and what is most prescient about that name is its etymology. It stems from a combination of two Greek words which together mean a place that doesn't exist[172]. The key here is that Utopia will never be real because we are not morally capable as human beings of constructing it. We cannot ever live up to any morality that is of any value i.e. one that is such that we would be willing to sacrifice our own self interest to really preserve it. Some humans might be able to do that, but as a species we cannot do so. The Christian would argue that this is obvious due to the original sin of human beings, but if you do not believe in God, you should still be able to look at the statistics from all the failed states that claimed to be taking their citizens at least to "equity". These states have largely not only failed, but never demonstrated even a few decades of "success". The final irony of utopia, however, is the changing of utopia to eutopia. These days, these words are synonymous, but their Greek origins are utterly different. Eutopia is a combination of two Greek words meaning blessed place as opposed to utopia meaning no place, and it is this word that has been co-opted by those that want to force feed us the idea that we can achieve perfection simply by tinkering a little bit with the Socialist, Marxist, or any other universal formula.

---

[171] However, I must say I detest the PC neo-feminist, hyper-left, political ideology oozing throughout the Supergirl series on tv right now to the extent that whilst I used to like Supergirl more than both the Flash and the Green Arrow, I watch those two shows and no longer watch Supergirl.

[172] The Greek words are ου and τοπος (I have left out the breathings) meaning not and place respectively, hence literally, utopia is no place.

The swapping of responsibilities for "rights" and the misidentification of evil by the left.

We are bombarded at this time with the idea of human rights. The left more so than anyone essentially places everything they believe as something that is a "right" rather than anything else such as an aspiration or a goal. They like to do this in order to short circuit any argument that whatever they are arguing about is impractical or too expensive or simply unfeasible. They argue from the emotional side and therefore appeal to the heartstrings and what they really want you to do is to agree that people have all these rights because they know that the logical question once there is consensus that human beings all have a number of right is "so how can we give everyone these very important rights". And then comes the coup de gras. The answer is "government is the only agency that can give people these rights and can make sure that they have them. And the only government that is designed to do so is socialism". This is the ultimate circular argument that completely removes the point of rights existing in the first place. They were always meant to exist so that humans could fulfil their responsibilities not as an end in themselves. The responsibilities to their families, to their friends and to the world in general.

Anybody on the left who is trying to be objective should acknowledge that whatever the failings of conservatives or classical liberals, they do a fairly good job at least in the West of identifying true evil and standing up against it. From the conservatives of the early Republican party that pushed back against slavery, through to those who railed against Hitler, and Communism, to those who correctly noted the problems stemming from the Soviet Union and other extreme communist type regimes, there is a grand tradition of properly identifying and pushing back against things that are malevolent and bad.

But the record of progressives on the left in terms of identifying and combatting evil is utterly awful. The biggest failing is in misidentifying the socialists and communist dictators of the 20th and early 21st century. If we look even at present leftist leaders, we see those who claim that they can lead us to better things but have historically sympathised with the most heinous criminals. Look at the support that Bernie Sanders showed for the Venezuelan dictator Nicolas Maduro (the successor to the abominable Hugo Chavez), or Jeremy Corbyn who openly espouses something very close to communism right now and who happily calls people like Hamas and Hezbollah as his "friends"[173]. This is not true of everyone on the left at all (and conversely it is also not true that all conservatives have been perfect at identifying evil), but statistically speaking, there is a genuine issue that the left has in identifying evil. This again really stems from the failure of the axiom of the left that human beings are "basically good". When you have this as a fundamental axiom, you fall into trap after trap that a powerful demagogue beckons you to. Therefore, a Hitler could seem benign and potentially moral to a large swathe of the British intelligentsia in the 1930's as people who hold this axiom as a deep truth long to give such charmers the benefit of the doubt. There is one other reason that the left fails to identify evil however, and that is the tendency to classify every human being as having innate personal characteristics that are a product of their skin colour and ethnicity. This is because the left is axiomatically racist – racist essentially by design.

Racism and the Trolley Problem.

Racism is a dirty and evil thing. It represents the worst in human beings and it also denies the truth which is that there is only one race, humans. There are 4 races of giraffes because those four species do not interbreed. This is not true of humans at all – we are all simply one race and just because we might look superficially different from each other this doesn't make it any less true. Identifying with someone else simply because of the amount of melanin in someone's skin is the ultimate in a pathetic form of neo tribalism and does no good to anyone in the long run. It is what people like Martin Luther King and many others fought against time after time, being something that doesn't belong in any civilised

---

[173] https://foreignpolicy.com/2018/10/03/jeremy-corbyn-has-a-soft-spot-for-extremists-ira-hamas-hezbollah-britain-labour/

society. But progressives love to categorise people by groups. They are the true racists and I can demonstrate this very easily.

If you want to know whether you are a racist, you can try a very simple thought experiment that is related to a philosophical issue called the trolley problem. The trolley problem posed in the most simplistic way is what would you do if you were in the following situation. There are 10 people tied to a railway track and there is a runaway trolley (or single carriage train) driving along the track. The trolley will kill them all and there is nothing you can do to stop it. However, you **can** flick a switch at a point on the track and put the trolley on a secondary track where there is a single person tied to the track. If you push the switch, then that person will die instead of the 10 others. Because this is a theoretical and moral problem, there is no solution of the form of the "Kobayashi Maru" that you can take, nor can you sacrifice yourself somehow. You simply have those two choices. If this sounds to you entirely like the Thanos Utilitarian versus Kantian problem, it is because it is extremely close to that although in this case some of the arguments are more obvious and a few are more nuanced. But for our purposes it doesn't matter what you would choose, we are interested in something else here. So, spend some time thinking about the problem and have the answer in your head. Now you are a racist if your answer will change depending on the colour of the skin of the people involved. Someone who is not racist will never change their answer to the trolley problem contingent on skin colour. But the progressive will change their answer because to them there is a race-based totem pole of "power" despite any mathematical analysis of the opportunities or not of different people in the West according to their skin colour says very clearly that there is no institutionalised systemic racism at all. This is the only **useful**[174] definition of racism; where you put one skin colour above all others, no matter how well-meaning you might be. If you think that certain groups of people with a different amount of melanin to you must have special consideration (either positive or negative it does not matter which), then you are a racist, and there is no other way in which you are. Because racism is about behaviour and attitude, plain and simple. And anyone who advocates for racist behaviour regardless of any hoops they seem to jump through such as arguing for the "minority" or for the "intersectionally disadvantaged", or any other manufactured term is a racist too. And here is an axiom for you that should be self-evident; the skin colour that you or I have, says nothing about who we are inside and anyone who claims that it does is lying, plain and simple. Let us treat everyone the way that we would wish to be treated regardless of what the optics of our corporeal frame might be.

St Valentine's day massacre.

Valentine's day 2017 was rather nice for me. I bought my wife flowers and a card and cooked us a special dinner. I rarely cook and am not very good at it but for some reason my wife loved this dinner. Then just before we went to bed, I saw an article[175] online entitled; "Even on Valentine's day people would rather have money".

Apparently, in a survey, over 50% of people would prefer 1 million dollars a year for the rest of their lives versus meeting the love of their life. This is more than just an example of human greed. There is a genuine concern currently regarding financial in stability that is much more than simply a result of changes in social conventions. Whilst it is true that the moral standards of the average person are dropping significantly in recent years in G7 countries, it is also true that people are far less safe in some

---

[174] And the only definition of racism that is not, in and of itself, racist.
[175] http://www.msn.com/en-us/lifestyle/relationships/forget-love%E2%80%94even-on-valentines-day-people-would-rather-have-money/ar-AAmVG4f?li=BBjnvnR&ocid=spartanntp

ways than they were before. There is significant evidence that over 40% of households in the US would not be able to pay an unexpected bill of 400 dollars[176]

This seemed a surprise to the writer of the article at the Washington Post, but it really should not have been. This is a direct result of the fact that there exists a much bigger "safety net" coming from the government than ever before. When the safety net is large, human beings tend to care less about ensuring that they don't need the safety net. Look at it this way, if you are at the top of a 100-foot tower, and the only thing below to break the fall is a small bucket of water, you are much more careful not to fall than if you were wearing a safety harness and there was a huge trampoline below you.

But once you fall into the benefit trap, it is hard to get out. This is because you often need to work very hard and for a long time to get into a better situation in all aspects of your life – working your way to an achievement takes time – unless you are employed in a job that pays a lot of money from the get-go (which would usually mean years of study or other such work without pay to get there), you will often not see it as being "worth it" for you to work long hours for a very slightly better ability to buy things. And as we have seen, the middle class is disappearing which reduces the ability of someone beating the poverty or benefit trap to transition away in perpetuity.

Human beings are truly creatures of habit and once we get into bad habits, we find it terribly hard to change. My first year at Goldman Sachs involved 3 months of training before we got anywhere near the trading floor. The training started every day at 7am and for the first month at least getting to work on time was utter hell. I had been used to waking up when I wanted (which was very late indeed), working well into the wee hours of the morning. I rarely woke up within an hour of the time that I had awakened the previous day and I was almost never awake at 7am whatever happened. So suddenly I had to be up at a set time and needed to be in the office on pain of losing my job and this was far harder than any of the other things that happened to me at Goldman. Everything else was a walk in the park compared to getting into work; I was just used to getting up late and without any consistency. In the same way, once human beings get used to something like being out of work, they find it very difficult to get back to it even if they do find a job.

Once humans do have a job though, they often get into the habit of working very hard. I saw that in myself and this changed my perspective on things very radically. When I first joined Goldman Sachs at the turn of the century, I was expected to be in the office for training from 7am sharp. Not only that, but it was expected that time would be spent on the trading floor both before and after training which ended at 5pm. As such, the work required huge amounts of time and I fully expected myself to find it horrific and impossible to do. The very thought that I would have to be at a specific place day in day out was anathema to someone who had previously seen "the lab" where I worked as somewhere nice to go just to hang out and think a bit about Physics when, and if, I wanted to. The immediacy of the financial markets was something that scared me quite a bit. But, very quickly, within days really, I had transformed my attitude. I was suddenly doing all this work without anyone asking me to. My line manager didn't really mind if I wasn't on the trading floor all the time, but I was still there day in day out. I never really had to do anything by force, I just wanted to do it. This was because this was my job, and the satisfaction simply from a job well done made me want to continue doing it. Work was not a chore but something that represented something about my identity. If I could do my job well this was important to other people and therefore this made me happy to work hard. I have seen the exact same thing in countless other people, in a whole host of professions including things that people might find boring or disgusting like plumbing or waste disposal. There is something that drives you when you realise that you do matter to other people through your job, and this is something of great value to

---

[176] https://www.washingtonpost.com/news/wonk/wp/2016/05/25/the-shocking-number-of-americans-who-cant-cover-a-400-expense/?utm_term=.74a92ba2c454

untold numbers of people. Hard work does make you feel good, and it is the responsibilities that go along with this work that enrich your life and give you value. But given that much of the world is currently obsessed with green, it is interesting that almost every government seems to want cold, hard, cash to somehow go away.

The wars on cash and interest rates.

Have you ever wondered why in the late 19th century or early 20th century when a dollar was worth say around 50-75 dollars compared to today there were 1000 and even 10,000-dollar notes available? In fact, in the gold certificate issuances of 1934 a run of 100000-dollar gold certificates were printed. So, in the past, you could walk around carrying the equivalent of up to 5 million USD in today's money in your pocket[177]. Yet somehow today many businesses don't even accept 100, or 50-dollar notes for cash.

In addition, countries across the world have made significant moves to remove high value bills from circulation. The arguments are always the same. The governments always seem to argue that large cash bills are not traceable and therefore they can be used to fund organised crime, and terrorism. Now whilst this is true, the sacrifice of getting rid of cash for law abiding individuals also has the consequence that the central banks are free to experiment undertaking ever more draconian, and strange, behaviours. We talked before about the concept of negative interest rates and how pointless they are, but if cash is no longer valid then central banks are entirely free to dwindle the mismanagements of a government by imposing negative rates on everybody. They can do this only if people cannot take out cash and put it under their mattresses as it were. If people could do this then they could effectively beat the negative rate issues by getting a rate of 0% at "chez individual" And this is why governments desperately want to implement their currencies into a digital framework so that they have the ability to tax at the source as espoused and championed by MMT. When they can do this, they think it will lead to ever increasing prosperity and productivity. But because they have fallen into the MMT trap they do not realise that this war on both cash and interest rates will cause such high inflation that there will literally be nothing they can do to stop it. In some sense this inflation is already there.

Supposing that you are a very hard working and fortunate person to have been able to save 1 million dollars for your retirement. Then the question might be, for how long could you afford to live on that retirement? Let's say that you can live on 50,000 a year. Then that 1million can last for 20 years. But of course, whilst life expectancy in the developed world is around 78 years, the actual life expectancy if you have already achieved age 65 is, in fact, around 84. This is a result of applying something called Bayes theorem to life expectancy. In the simplest terms, because you have already lived for 65 years you are clearly someone who did not suffer from premature diseases and therefore it is more likely that you were fitter than average in the first place and therefore you will live longer than would have been predicted at your birth at which time it was not known whether you were genetically fit or not.

So that means that if you live as expected you will probably have just enough. However, the uncertainty of your life is high so there is a decent chance that you will not just live to be 84 but you will live to be 94 or maybe even 104. Now 104 is 20 years **more** than you can afford and so you need either to spend less or, hopefully make a return on your money saved by investing it to counter-balance the amount that you spend each year. The whole thing is worse when you consider that inflation increases the amount that you need to spend each year for the same lifestyle. This is all very depressing and because of compounding you will end up needing a lot more to survive.

"Lavish inflation" and the aspirational question.

30 years ago, the world was a very different place. The internet was a very nascent embryonic environment still, and the majority of people were not connected. Even the so-called experts called into

---

[177] Though it should be noted that the hundred-thousand denomination bills were really meant just for banks to replace the gold that they government was effectively confiscating at the request of President Roosevelt.

question the potential for the internet as more than a passing fad and this was in 1995[178] In 1988, if you were not at a university the only way you could connect to the internet was through a modem that you hooked up to your physical phone line with an "acoustic coupler" which if you never saw one you can of course easily search for photos, but you can also see one demonstrated in the great movie "war games". These modems transmitted at such slow speeds that you would have to wait minutes for one photo to appear, and you could never download anything at all

30 years ago, almost no one had a mobile phone and only extremely few even had a phone built into their cars. 30 years ago, few people had gaming computers and the Apple Macintosh had only been created 4 years before. Even the Commodore Amiga which essentially allowed the populace in general to have a computer that you could actually do some reasonably complex things with was just barely out there in the world having been launched just a year earlier in 1987. Now in the last 30 years inflation in the US (and pretty much every other western first world economy) has appeared to be almost irrelevant compared to what happened in the 20 years before that.

Despite the indications and economic claims that inflation has remained remarkably benign, and even the argument that it is too low for a healthy economy, the inflation related to so-called luxury items has exploded. This has happened to such an extent that simple garments in the form of a thin coat can cost 5,000 USD and more. As an anecdote, on January the first 2015 I happened to be in Las Vegas. Going into a high-end shopping mall in a vague attempt to find something interesting to buy I noticed two things. Firstly, that you could buy a reasonably large studio apartment in the building above the mall for 250,000 USD, and secondly that the lovely white mackintosh type ladies coat in one of the vitrines was on sale for just below 5,000 USD. This means that you could get the apartment for 50 coats. I know which one I would prefer to have especially as the apartment is likely to still be around in 20 years. Given also that the cost of materials of such a coat are a vanishingly small percentage of the overall cost, it is genuinely frightening to see something that would have cost a maximum of 500 USD 20 years ago now retail for 10 times the price. The price at which clothing retails mirrors extremely well the supply and demand in the market exactly because of the limited costs of materials. Because almost every aspect of a high-end clothing range is to do with the value ascribed to it by the consumer and not with costs of manufacture, these are very good indicators of inflation amongst luxury products. The same is true for shoes, and especially so for handbags.

Let's look at the retail cost of a couple of examples to see what I mean starting with a pair of Prada classic stiletto pumps (technically glossed black textured leather pumps), which for those who don't know (and everyone should know) are the possibly the definitive high heel shoes. In 2000 this pair cost around 150 dollars – I know because I bought my girlfriend one at that time. In 2020, the cost of these has shot up to 675 dollars. Now this represents a 4- fold increase in the price over a 20-year period. The same picture emerges when you consider Chanel bags. According to a survey by baghunter.com[179], the Chanel Medium Classic Flap Bag which has been available since 1955 (so hardly a novelty) has more than doubled between 2010 and 2020 (from 2850 to 5800). These bags are not limited in terms of supply at least in theory and so there should really be no expectation that these prices outperform inflation, and yet they clearly are. There are countless other examples of luxury goods that have seen these sorts of stock market like price increases and these all contribute to an inflation phenomenon that is real but shouldn't really be, as in the case of Chanel bags, an almost entirely equivalent and hand made version of the design (sans the symbol) could be made at less than 5% of the price by a master

[178] http://www.newsweek.com/clifford-stoll-why-web-wont-be-nirvana-185306

[179] https://baghunter.com/pages/chanel-bag-values-research-study

leather craftsman by hand. To me, that is real luxury, but for why so few people think this way, you cannot do better than "Deluxe, how luxury lost its lustre" by Dana Thomas which is a fascinating read.

So, what we have is not inflation in the things that people need to subsist; food, clothing, shelter, basic schooling, basic medicine etc. But what we have seen is an exceptional amount of inflation in things that people want or aspire to. In terms of the best medicine, the best places to live, the best clothes, the best places to live, and the most prestigious schools. This is in addition to the explosion in things that we never thought that we needed but that now we do. When in the past people were happy with "I love Lucy" shown once a week, a few books, and their religious life, people now want experiences that replace their religion. They want to see things and have the best of everything because everything they see in the cinema, and on their television, and on their iPad tells them of all the things that they should have. Again, the immediacy of everything changes the paradigm.

We started with being able to see new films in Cinemas only, and before television even old films could only be seen in cinemas. Over time however, Logie Baird created television and movies slowly crept into the home. As technology evolved, we obtained the ability to store tv shows and even films on video tapes, and later video disks and DVDs, and finally Blu-ray. But as we have seen, storing programs on hard drives and digital downloading would supersede even this, and finally the state of the world now is that very few even store such movies themselves, we now either stream in real time from various services or we store purchased movies and tv shows on the servers of those who provide that digital content.

So, whereas even 30 years ago, you might have to wait a few days for the movie you wanted to watch to come back in stock at your video store you can now instantly stream everything you could possibly want, with the only issue being the price point at which you purchase this intellectual property. If you are willing to wait, you can get the same content on one of the current streaming subscription services a year after this appeared in theatres, but this is generally not what most people aspire to unless they don't particularly like films. The movie theatres themselves have reinvented everything too. Now, there are a number of chains where you go to the theatre and can expect to pay up to 100dollars a head for the film and restaurant quality food served at your lazy-boy seat as you watch. Again, the lavish experience makes this far more costly than in the past.

Now, of course, you may be like me and think that, for the most part, luxury goods are a waste of time and maybe this should not apply to you, but let's think about what the inflation metric should track. It is intuitively very clear that, central banks should be tracking an inflation index that mimics the cost of living in a given country. But when we think about this it is also obvious that there exists a myriad of ways to define an inflation index. We could, for example, go for an extremely basic index that tracks the cost of simple subsistence with no luxuries at all, with nothing but the most basic healthcare, food, and lodging. Such an index would look at rent, the cost of the most basic of necessities such as bread and the cheapest (non-organic) vegetables, as well very limited healthcare and schooling. We could, instead, take an index that includes nothing but the best; the very best education, private healthcare with the best doctors and specialists, luxury clothing, only organic produce, owning and living in a luxury house or condominium, and so on and so forth with different combinations and metrics. As you can imagine, the index that is currently used is somewhere in between these two extremes, but what may not be quite so obvious is that the inflation indices in most developed nations track inflation that is closer to this subsistence level than the luxury level. We have already mentioned that the indices have substitution effects that mean that generic products can be substituted for the leading brand for example, and we have also talked about the fact that house ownership is not assumed.

Now I would argue that, in a developed economy, such as that of the United States, the inflation metric should include much more aspirational components, such as home ownership, and better healthcare and education than just the basics. After all, everyone aspires to the American Dream, do they not? And given this, we should use a metric that reflects this much better otherwise what is the point of this statistic in the first place? This is something that I would term "aspirational inflation" i.e. an inflation index that includes much more than just basic subsistence living. And indeed, when we look at such a constructed index, we see that the implied inflation from this theoretical aspirational inflation index would be significantly higher than the inflation indices that are used, with much of this coming from the price of property. Not targeting this sort of inflation index has meant that interest rates have been set lower than they should have been, which has contributed to the buying power of savers being further reduced, eroded, and placed into the coffers of borrowers. This means more money to the rich and by extension to corporations who were able to borrow at better levels and therefore make more profit. This has, of course, contributed to income inequality, but not because of capitalism, but because capitalism was interfered with by those who essentially belong to the Idiocracy.

Why capitalism works.

Capitalism is the single best idea that has ever occurred to man regarding economics. It is the product of thinking that came out of the Judeo-Christian point of view. But a lot of people do not seem to understand what capitalism is or even how it can really exist hand in hand with Judeo-Christian values. And this is mostly the fault of the left both politically and in Christianity. Because the left lies about what capitalism does. Capitalism is brilliant. It has brought literally billions of people out of poverty in the last 100 years. No other economic system can really say that, but capitalism is fundamentally a child of the west. The idea of capitalism is very simple indeed. That if I want to provide for myself and my family, I am obligated to work for it. I am obligated to provide "goods" for which I am able to trade with others for their "goods" that I might need and therefore I don't need to actually obtain those goods by myself. This has several obvious implications.

Firstly, that I am obligated to work. This sounds almost trivial, but it is a key idea. It is what keeps the engine of a capitalist economy from stopping. It is the absolute core of what is important. The second implication is that I am also obliged to work on producing things that others value as otherwise I cannot get the goods that I value from those who produce them. This leads to the third implication as a corollary because I am therefore extremely incentivised to work either on things that I am good at, or things that I believe that I can get good at sufficiently quickly to ensure I can eat, or stuff that I have an interest in that are also valuable to others. It is the inverse of the issue that we saw with the Welfare state. With the Welfare state, the danger was that it was directly subject to corruption, but capitalism has the inbuilt defence against this, which stems from the fact that practice at something makes humans better and that we all have given strengths and weaknesses. This means that no man (or woman) is an island and that we need the skills of each other to survive.

Now note that the "goods" that we are talking about do not have to be physical. They can be anything at all. They could be entertainment, such as a comedy act. They could be getting rid of garbage. They could be writing a book. Or of course they could be producing something such as growing apples or building houses. And the coolest thing about this system is that it is self-regulating by nature. Why is this? Well if for example there are very few bakers in an economy, the products of each baker working become more and more sought after and they can command higher and higher prices for their breads and baked goods. However, after a while people see that being a baker pays well and more and more people decide to become bakers which means that there are more bakers to cover the demand, and this puts a downward pressure on the cost of baked products. As the demand reduces, some bakers (the ones who produce the least tasty goods or who manage their business less effectively) decide to switch to selling different goods, and this reduces supply, which stabilizes prices again. The same is true for anyone offering a given service, and for all people who work. Essentially in a capitalist system everyone is CEO of their own little brand or business whether they in fact work for themselves or whether they work for a large Multinational Corporation. Whatever they do for work, they are obliged to provide a quality service to pay for the services of others. And because of this you also get much better products produced. If people were forced to do just what was allotted to them by some system, you would never have the diversity of product or the brilliance of things that have been made that you have in the capitalist system. This is because people do a better job when they are interested in what they are doing or writing about or making. They are far better at it when they have a direct investment in the outcome, and this keeps them trying to attain a better and better performance.

In some sense, capitalism is the ultimate competitive environment where everyone can win. You don't have to be the smartest human being, or the strongest, or anything at all. You simply need to work hard and do something that you find interesting but that produces something that other people want. If you can do that, you are likely to do well and benefit from the system. Notice that this doesn't require anything other than hard work and ability and this makes it resistant to abuse from those who have been given material and other benefits through birth for example. Also, because several occupations have skill sets with lots of different qualities in common, there is a good chance that you can change your occupation to adapt to find a niche that isn't currently occupied.

In a mathematical sense, capitalism effectively negates the shackles of the pareto distribution because now there are many different pareto distributions that each can lead to success. Not only that, but the number of pareto distributions available is highly diverse which means that some of them have lots of winners (who tend to win less and sometimes a lot less than those in other distributions), and others have very few. This is because capitalism allows for growth of entirely separate enterprises, and because it aims to make the barrier to entry as low as possible, it makes it very easy for someone who fails in a certain area, to make a switch to another without a significant cost. Also, because the requirements of people for certain things are often different, capitalism presents many different niche markets where it becomes possible to be at the top of the pareto distribution simply by being the only one in a small market. And there is a pareto distribution for everything for grocers, greengrocers, bakers etc. A top down system could never really achieve this because it would be too hard to identify such niches easily because they also change over time. Another way to look at it is that capitalism, by restricting nothing basically allows for every single possible pareto distribution to exist (and to be created) and because there are so many it becomes possible to allow almost everyone to be at the top of one of those distributions if they work hard enough, and that means that we have nullified the constraints of that distribution. The solution to the inequalities created by capitalism is to have more pareto distributions for people to be able to "play". Capitalism 2.0 if you will, is simply to have more and more of these pareto distributions available. In fact, bringing people out of poverty is linked to how many of these pareto distributions exist. The more choice that is available in terms of product, the more natural redistribution of wealth accelerates. Imagine in the past, when the only things that were available were food and (if you will forgive my crudeness) sex, and land. The great emperors of the past didn't really have so many things to spend their gold on. They could build great palaces of course, but eventually there wasn't anything to do other than to hoard gold and gems. Scroll forward to today and there are so many different options in terms of entertainment and things to aspire to for anyone such that even the very richest person in the world does not have time to do everything. Well, this means that wealth is likely to be better distributed because there are so many more choices that one can spend their money on. People who travel to glorious holiday destinations are redistributing their wealth there. People who buy computer games likewise, and what they are really doing is providing capital and financing for yet another pareto distribution "game" which allows yet another person to succeed. And that is why each revolution in turn, the renaissance, the industrial revolution, the electrical revolution, the computer revolution, and finally the rise of the internet, are all simply different aspects of the same thing. They all spawn more and more cornucopias for wealth to flow and flourish.

Socialism tries to deny that pareto distributions and evil exist, but capitalism accepts that they do and attempts to correct for pareto by presenting so many different ones that its always possible pack up and try another "game". And as we have seen, in the case of evil, the answer that capitalism prescribes is competition which pits the greed of a producer against that of other producers and leads to lower prices. And of course, as we have seen, not all pareto distributions are quite as drastically steep as others. So due to capitalism, there is always plenty of room at the top. Another way to look at this mathematically is , if what you do is dictated from above and everything is redistributive, there is only one single pareto distribution, and you can bet what kind it is - that of the tennis player not that of the doctor or lawyer. A single very, very steep peak with whoever is in charge of central planning at the very top - the ultimate dictator. Capitalism coupled with technology brings a broad range of pareto distributions and everything is better.

Well how does that square with the Judeo-Christian approach? Unsurprisingly, very well indeed. In the Bible it is made clear that we all have a responsibility to provide for our families and to work hard. This comes from the book of Genesis just after the fall where God requires man to work so that: "...In toil you shall eat of it all the days of your life. Both thorns and thistles it shall bring forth for you. And you shall eat the herb of the field. In the swat of your face you shall eat bread..." Further to that, one of the Ten Commandments is a requirement to "Honour Your Father and Mother". Clearly this doesn't just mean be nice or respectful to them but is a requirement to honour them both by accepting guidance from them and providing for them when they are at an age where they can no longer fend for themselves. This is again something that is relevant to capitalism because that system requires us to take de facto responsibility for our own lives and part of that responsibility is to provide for the greater family and the community rather than just ourselves.

But Capitalism came naturally from the West. It is something that seems to exist because of Western Culture and Civilisation not the cause of it. And this leads us to ask the question where did the West emerge from in the first place, was it cultural, was it something evolutionary? Is it an amazingly happy accident, or was it going to happen anyway regardless of how things developed?

What is the West Predicated upon?

Many have argued that the West is a product unique combination of three things. The first of these would be the logic typified by the period of the flourishing of the great thinkers of Ancient Greek; Socrates, Plato, Aristotle et al. The second of these would be the statements made in the Bible particularly in the New Testament about the value of individual humans to God and their intrinsic worth leading to the emergence of Christianity. And the third would be the focus from the Old Testament regarding the rule of law, as well as the spreading and mixing of these ideas within the Jewish diaspora that existed in the Greek and especially the Roman world. I say especially the Roman world, because much of the traditional ideas about the rule of law were always present in Rome from the start of the Republic itself.

To understand how this combination happened we need to travel back in time again to the time of Alexander the Great. It may surprise you to know that, apart from biblical and related texts, we have very little access to ancient documents from say two or three thousand years ago. Indeed, until the dead sea scrolls, we had very little except purely biblical texts. This is to do with the fact that papyrus and parchment decay very easily. Even vellum which is animal skin doesn't survive well except in the driest of conditions. So, we are fortunate to have some relatively

In the works of Flavius Josephus, we see a description of the entry of Alexander into Jerusalem. When we think of Alexander, we imagine the sacking of Persepolis and other such acts of destruction, but according to Josephus, as the conqueror approached Jerusalem the Sanhedrin essentially came out to meet him and left the gates open. They also showed Alexander the prophecy of Daniel where his empire was described. He knew at this time that this was indeed his own empire and not something else. Alexander had a feeling that the God of the Jews was not just some regular god, but someone very different. He instinctively knew that this was the Great I Am, the awesome Yahweh and not something more akin to the Greek myths that had had grown up with. At least according to Josephus.

Most historians do not agree that the account of Josephus is historical. This account they say is too good to be true, and several of them also claim that the book of Daniel was not extant at that time. I personally disagree with that statement, and I believe the preponderance of evidence is that the book of Daniel did indeed exist, and it would have made sense that Alexander felt in awe of the Hebrew God whose prophets had pre-empted his miraculous conquests. However, regardless of whether things happened exactly as Josephus states, the upshot of this is that the Jews were well treated in the empire of Alexander, and even when it broke up. As a result, the Jewish diaspora was able to spread throughout the Greek speaking world. After Rome conquered Greece and its colonies, the diaspora remained and if anything grew.

So, the Greeks brought logic to the table, and the Jews brought Judaism and later Christianity. And the Roman empire brought this all together and under the emperor Constantine made the empire Christian. For over a thousand years, Byzantium carried the candle in terms of preserving the light of the Judeo-Christian ideals through the traditions of Orthodox Christianity. Rome and the Catholic Church did the same in the west of Europe. And then, as the Renaissance, and the reformation occurred, the torch was handed over to Great Britain which gave the world the great gift of an exceptional structure of English Law. The culmination of around 2700 years of Greek logic, and 3500 years of Jewish followed by Christian theology resulted in the fruit that is the Constitution of the United States, along with the Bill of Rights, and the Federalist Papers which together effectively defined the United States as it aspired to become. And the development of the west really is a journey, a journey that moved ever westwards, initially just a little bit but then further and further. Beginning with the results of the Exodus and the Torah leading to the founding of the ancient state of Israel in Jerusalem, moving through the Jewish Greek speaking diaspora initially focused on Athens and Asia minor but rapidly spreading west to Rome. Then moving further west to England, and finally being perfected in the New World with the current best realisation of a Republic, the United States of America.

The US is now the west. The US alone preserves the Freedom of Speech and enforces it as such. The United Kingdom has lost some of these freedoms, as have many European states. In the UK, the reason for this is extremely nuanced but has to do with the fact that the UK has never had a constitution beyond Magna Carta which of course is more than 800 years old.[180] What the UK does have is the tradition of British Common Law which was the foundation of the ideas that brought about the US Republic. But the US may not always be the "City on the Hill", and this is noted by John Adams, the direct successor as President to George Washington in a missive that he sent to the Massachusetts Militia on the 11th of October of 1798, just 22 years after the signing of the Declaration of Independence. In that letter, he makes a very clear statement: "Avarice, Ambition, Revenge or Gallantry, would break the strongest Cords of our Constitution as a Whale goes through a Net. Our Constitution was made only for a moral and religious People. It is wholly inadequate to the government of any other." This is fascinating because it was clear even to the Founding Fathers that the US could only function properly as a Republic if there was an understanding that there is a greater authority who effectively supersedes everything. In a sense we are back at the Higgs Boson, not without reason called the God particle. But we don't need a Boson to breathe life into the Constitution, we truly need an Almighty and not just any God, but the Judeo-Christian God.

This is something for everyone to bear in mind and it is not something that can be dealt with easily and would probably require a tome at least as long as this book simply to make out the basic arguments regarding this.

Atlas Shrugged.

In her 1957 dystopian tome (the first edition had 1168 pages) Atlas Shrugged, Ayn Rand described in great waves of polemic discourse her beliefs in aggressive individualistic utopian capitalism. The story is essentially the adventures of those looking for the answer to the question "Who is John Galt" The ethos

---

[180] The Magna Carta, which is regarded as the first and really only attempt at a British constitution (even though it was really a contract between the King and his barons drafted by the Archbishop of Canterbury, and therefore not really very relevant for the general public), was signed in Runnymede which is just a little southwest of London on June the 15th 1215

of her thoughts is very nicely contained in the pledge that John Galt, the main protagonist of the story requires for anyone wishing to live in his utopia: "I swear by my life, and my love of it, that I will never live for the sake of another man, nor ask another man to live for mine."

I don't know about you, but this scares me a lot. The thought of this scares me because this is utterly wrong. It is against everything that comes from the best of us and it is against the principles that the US was founded on. The whole idea of the Judeo-Christian tradition is in fact that human beings do give their life in service of others and the entire concept to me is anathema.

But there is one important lesson to take from this. This is that there is always the danger extant that the government does become too powerful. The other danger is that the government in an effort to remain in power will make promises that are not appropriate for a government to make and that the infrastructure (that people now call the "Deep State"), or if you are being more sanguine simply the bureaucracy, will make every attempt to subvert any effort to reduce the extent of the power and influence of that government unless there are specific laws that properly prevent this. Furthermore, those laws need to be enforced. And this is the real issue that Ayn Rand does have a point about: that the government spends taxpayer's money keeping other citizens who are perfectly able bodied and able to work.

It is even worse when you consider that however wrong this statement from Rand is (it is the sort of ethos that ends up in fascism), the opposite of this is even worse. This is because asking others to live for our lives is genuine evil distilled. It is the mantra of the far left essentially and it is the mantra of communism. Only, communism and the left hide this by emphasizing equality. In fact, not only do I see social security for those who are unwilling to work as being unacceptable from the point of view of taxpayers, I also advocate that it is a much worse thing than even that.

The reason for this is that people who take things like unemployment benefit simply because they do not find the work that is available for them acceptable are, in effect, stealing. And the worst thing about this is that they are stealing from the needy. From those through no fault of their own are not able bodied or do not have the mental capacity to work and earn money. The reason that we cannot provide a reasonable standard of living to those in society who are genuinely less fortunate is that our society has become diseased with the idea that we should be providing finance to citizens simply for being alive.

This has no precedent that ended well. We have been through the mathematics of it. The world simply cannot afford to support itself when a significant fraction of its people, are essentially, unwilling to contribute. Again, the very fact that there exist programs that are not conditional on the willingness to work changes the entire landscape of reality for the human condition and when such programs are stopped or curtailed[181], this basically forces people who are inherently self-serving (sometimes in good ways such as feeling the need to provide for their family) to change their overall strategy.

And this is where we should mention somewhere where we should be spending much more. Those who are disabled, and mentally incapacitated and otherwise unable to work through no fault of their own are owed a far better standard of living than what we currently provide for them. In a very real sense, those who are able bodied and perfectly capable physically and mentally to work are taking the bread from the mouths of those who are significantly disadvantaged in those respects. The answer is to focus on those who have been truly dealt a bad hand in terms of health, ensure they are looked after as well as possible, and then allow everyone else an equality of opportunity that allows them to perform to the limits of their potential. Those who really want social justice, or as I refer to it, simply justice, should advocate for these people rather than the able-bodied populace who simply doesn't feel like working.

Is it an op-ed? For some everything should be an op-ed.

---

181 http://dailycaller.com/2014/04/24/caps-on-government-benefits-in-the-uk-spur-self-employment/

Democracy dies in Darkness is the motto of the Washington Post. It is indeed a good one to remember. However, this once venerable newspaper is in fact part of the problem. It has a reasonable circulation of just over 300,000 in terms of the physical paper, and a much bigger one in terms of online viewing. However, it has long since given up on reporting the news of all things. In fact, so has (almost) everyone else. Much of what is today news is just regurgitated results provided by a group known as AP. You probably haven't heard of them. There is a chance that you know them by their formal title The Associated Press.

AP was created back in 1846 in order to socialise the costs of covering the Mexican American war for five New York Newspapers. It made sense at the time because travel was very difficult and costly, and because every reporter was likely to see and experience similar things and therefore sharing the costs would make sense. The whole idea was smart because it meant that it would be possible to have more investigative reporting overall because you didn't need to have a reporter from each newspaper present at every event and could therefore cover far more incidents and newsworthy occurrences than you would otherwise. Of course, you would miss out on a few scoops, but overall everyone would benefit for this in terms of coverage of things like wars.

But the AP of today basically has the monopoly on news. Over time, it was realised that almost all reporting made sense to be socialised by the media. This sort of worked for much of the 20th century as the focus was generally on gathering facts, and opinion pieces (which were not as common) could be written having also given the facts of the matter. But as the internet began to kill the traditional newspaper reporting model by killing paper newspaper circulations, the AP became more and more critical to reporting across the western world. In the past, the New York Times might have a reporter permanently in Boseman Montana for example to report of whatever went on there. These days the AP takes care of that, and over time, due to cost cutting and other things, news outlets have begun to use the AP report ad verbatim. And the obvious problem applies. The number of investigative sources has been reduced to just one, so if that one reporter is not being honest, or has a bias (and everybody generally does), then it is very unlikely that the view of the news that you see is objective at all.

And the AP does nothing at all to disguise the fact that it is essentially at this point part of the PR branch of the Democratic Party. Their Twitter feed is exceptionally depressing. When Iran accidentally shot down a plane from the Ukraine inside its own territory, the AP immediately decided they should blame this on the US and President Trump despite the fact that, on the day of the accident – which of course was the day that Iran decided (and generally failed) to send a couple of dozen rockets into US bases in Iraq – the US did not fire a single piece of ordinance[182]. When the AP has essentially become a generator of op-eds it has singularly failed in its purpose.

I stand instead with Patrick Henry who at the Virginia convention declared "Give me liberty or give me death" and that includes the inalienable right to say whatever I want to say. As has been stated many times by many writers; "I may not like what you have to say but I will forever defend your absolute right to say it"; to be clear if you believe anything other than this you are a Fascist or a Communist. However, from the press we should not expect overt bias. The press should very seldom give any form of opinion on anything, and those few times should be regarding tragedies such as earthquakes and other such acts of God. The press as individuals of course are entitled to their opinion and liberty, but if they do provide such opinion and "analysis" of what they say, they should be clear and say they are no longer journalists but opinion writers. There is nothing wrong with being an opinion writer and advocating your own ideas, but you should never pretend that this is journalism. Of course, it is often extremely difficult to try to contain biases, but for factual reporting, I would argue that it is just not that hard. You simply report the events that happened and leave it at that. You need to singularly resist the temptation to analyse what happened and trust that the viewer or reader is intelligent enough to come to their own

---

[182] https://twitter.com/AP/status/1215453319768035328

opinion about it. Anything else represents a supreme amount of hubris essentially claiming that the opinion of the writer is necessary for the people to understand what is happening. The only people who in the form of normal discourse should be taking this approach are kindergarten teachers talking to their little charges about things which do indeed need explaining.

Democracy or bust?

We have talked already about Greek (and particularly Athenian) democracy and how it is a pillar of the West. So, it really is democracy or bust for the West, but not because of the intrinsic merits of democracy itself – at least on its own. Democracy is, in fact, a spectacularly bad way of governing people if you are able to make just one little assumption. That assumption is of course to assume that people are generally good. But we know from the arguments we have made that people are not good at all. We have talked already about Greek (and particularly Athenian) democracy and how it is a pillar of the west The Ancient Greeks knew that when they came up with democracy as the way of governance. They understood the evils of the populace (Athens was one of the most aggressively militant places on earth before democracy and continued to be problematic even post that.) and understood how power can be used for ill. So, they came up with a democratic process with the view of making things as transparent as possible so that there was the least chance of corruption coming to the fore as there would be so many eyes on those that were tasked with governance. It is analogous to the way that a distributed ledger relies on absolute transparency to prevent hacking.

Democracy recognises that human beings are not generally good but also notes that they want to be seen to be good, if possible. We call this "shame" – we don't want to be seen to be bad people. This is the whole basis of the current evil that is "virtue signalling" whereby some company decides to cancel some sponsorship it does because it gives them a better reputation. Virtue signalling is truly abhorrent because it is simply done for public brownie points. It is the equivalent of the pharisaic trumpets blown at the temple when a rich man donated a sum of money to the coffers. It is not just hypocritical, as it bows to the loudest voice which is very seldom the correct voice. The one who feigns outrage is often the least affected.

So, democracy uses our badness against us at least in theory and ends up with a less bad outcome than would be the case if the most rich and powerful were simply allowed to reign supreme. It should also be noted that the Greeks also chose many of their administrators by lot; roughly speaking of the 1100 council members around 100 were elected. In addition to this, there were additional two term restrictions and other such things to effectively prevent dictatorship; not because the Greeks thought that dictatorship was bad in and of itself, but because they recognised that there was no human being who could be a benign dictator.

How do we mitigate mob rule?

One of the big arguments against democracy and a correct one is that having a fully proportional democracy can essentially encourage policies in politics to be at the mercy of a bunch of plebs. This is clearly a concern. We know again and again that the majority is not always correct. That mobs can and do form and that it is our obligation to defend the rule of law against this, and we need to prevent the "Tyranny of the Majority" in our systems. So, in order to do this, various countries have found ways to have a hierarchy that was both democratic, but at the same time at least somewhat robust to the whims of many uninformed people.

You see one of the axioms that are required for Democracy to be the least-worst form of government is that the populace, the "hoi polloi" who have the vote need to be both highly intelligent and adequately informed. The second is a key concept and is part of the reason at least that Athenian democracy had so few people eligible to vote. It is completely pointless, for example, for a huge percentage of the voters on any given matter to be ignorant because this negates the idea that everyone knows what the right thing is, and the democratic process shames them into doing just that. If there exists a huge swathe of people who either don't care enough to find out, or just don't quite understand that situation, they may well be voting for what they deem to be the best thing but they might be unable to recognise such a thing when they see it.

There was also the possibility, that humans being evil might still sanction in the majority some evil ideas that, though unconscionable, were sufficiently subtle as to leak their poison to pollute the souls of the quorum of people. Finally, of course, the simple subconscious bias that the majority might have against minorities could (and have) lead to laws and dictates that entirely benefit the masses against the few. So, in the modern age, there were several attempts to have democracy but with a system of checks and balances that essentially try to mitigate the ability of the majority to fully control the situation. The British solution was to have a parliamentary democracy. This meant that you didn't vote for the people to rule directly, but you voted in your own little district or borough for an individual that would represent you and your interest. You would vote for a member of parliament and because that member was local to you, they would be able to listen to your specific issues and represent your little part of the world.

The Americans decided to create a republic, this being quite convenient due to the history of the colonies that would become the States of the United States of America. The US has two separate houses, as does the UK. In the upper house, the senate, each state would have two senators to represent it regardless of the population of the State in question. Therefore, right now California has 2 senators, and so does the state of Wyoming with around one 70th of the population of the aforementioned[183].

In the lower house called the house of representatives, the number of members is much more proportional to the population, though there has to be at least one from each state in the union. Thus there, California has 53 representatives versus seven states with just one member of the house. Balancing the wish to represent the people directly, and still have a genuine Republic, lead to the bicameral nature of the US legislative body. The nature of Congress came from the example of the parliament of Great Britain[184] where there were also two houses, with the house of commons being as described above, and the house of lords being unelected. In that sense of course, the two systems differ and indeed the perceived weaknesses of the British system were addressed by the construction of the bicameral system of the US along with the Constitution which is something significantly lacking in the United Kingdom to this day[185]

The key here is that the west attempted to create democratic societies both that followed the Judeo-Christian principles that were so important to so many of the contributors to those societies, and to provide representation with checks and balances in place to prevent tyranny and dictatorships. To shame us all into doing the right thing when it is extraordinarily tempting, even to breaking point, to turn aside from the righteous path and enter the dark wood of selfish entitlement. The Judeo-Christian ideals were steeped in responsibility, stemming of course from the deep desire of the Christian and the Jew to honour God and give Him glory. And because the Christians and the Jews understood the heart of the people, they were always looking for these protections against tyrannical and megalomaniacal rule.

In this way, the rise of Hitler and the second world war were seen by some as being proof that the way of the west did not work, that all these mitigants had been for nought because an atrocious dictatorship had been born from the ashes of Weimar which had been a democratic republic. But again, we see that the reverse is really true. The strongest democracies, those with the most mitigants in place, and those with the longest history of being an extant republic were the ones to resist the most. Those were the

---

[183] California has just under 40million people and Wyoming despite being the 10th largest state by area only has just under 575,000

[184] It did not become the UK parliament until 1801 when the Irish and British parliaments combined.

[185] The closest thing to a constitution of the UK is the Magna Carta which also inspired the Founding Fathers. This proto constitutional document was signed between King John and his barons in 1215 in the (then) village of Runnymede.

British and the Americans, but also a number of others such as the French and even the Greeks who had fought very hard to preserve a democratic state since they had regained their freedom from the Ottomans. All this should be obvious, because what is the point in surviving if your culture is non-existent? What is the point in freedom if you do nothing at all with that freedom, and if you do not see your society as being worth preserving, who is likely to do so? But those who preserved their democracies were generally the cultures that viewed their liberty and sovereignty as inextricably linked to who they are.

So, we see that the west comes essentially from Jerusalem, Constantinople, Rome, and Athens. Jerusalem which brought the truth of Judaism and Christianity, Athens that developed Republican and Democratic ideals, Constantinople that preserved Christianity against onslaughts from the East both physical and spiritual, and Rome which both spawned Republican ideals and also supported and grew Christianity in the west. There is one other source of the west, although this came much later indeed. That source is Great Britain, and specifically British Common Law. As we have said, there is still no British constitution but the country of Magna Carta that produced Shakespeare, Newton, and the Royal Society, did more than any other to put the principles of Christianity and the teachings of Jesus into practice. This includes things such as ending slavery and providing a system of jurisprudence that provided equal protection in terms of rights to all whether pion or a King.

So, the west is important, it is great in many ways, and freedom needs to be preserved. The US and the other major western democracies need to deal with a populace that is increasingly less Christian even though many of these states were designed and developed with Christians in mind at least in terms of the set of assumed axiomatic values. And so, we come full circle again with our thinking. We now know why the situation has become what it is. We know that the basis of the West was the Judeo-Christian values that can be summarised in the Ten Commandments and the Sermon on the Mount. But we also know that for these values to be raised up, venerated, in order to dominate behaviour, it requires to paraphrase Adams, a People who believe in them due to their reverence of God. But this hasn't been the case in the west for a very long time. For the last 150 or so years belief in the great pillars of Judaism and Christianity has waned radically. Just to take a single example, in the Census of 1851 in England and Wales it was estimated that on any given Sunday[186] over 40% of the entire population attended at least one church service. At the time the population of the country was around 18 million, and on that day, if you factored in people going multiple times in the day, there were over 10 million attendances. Compare this with the "record high" attendance for Church of England Christmas services in 2017 (being the highest of the decade) at around 2.3 million in a country with 3.7 times as many people, and we can see the stark contrast. If we compare just a regular Sunday this attendance is below a million and just goes to show how far from Christianity, the British people have come. But this is just as true in most of the rest of Europe, and a similar picture exists in the US also. And with the passing away of genuine believers, faith in the corollaries that emerge also tends to be extinguished. In the eyes of those who are postmodern, post religion, the ideas of Christianity appear parochial and therefore those in the west who don't subscribe to the religion are often tempted to simply exit the ideas which were a consequence of those religious beliefs. There are some who maintain these ideas as good in and of themselves whilst still advocating for staunch atheism, there are todays classical liberals, but there is also a huge cohort that simply wants an end to the ideas of the west and wish to herald in a new and glorious age of socialism, communism, and radical post-modernism.

And many of these postmodern ideas have contributed to the reality that we see today. Little by little, small bits of socialism crept into the systems of Europe and the US. These included significant overregulation of various industries, as well as extreme health and safety bureaucracy, and of course various slices of the economy being brought under government control as well as just a generally increasing amount of government oversight over almost everything. And we have already talked about

---

[186] Based on data from the 30th March 1851.

the benefits trap whereby people who become used to a certain level of benefits begin to see them as a right and not as an emergency measure for when things are not going well due to unfortunate circumstances. All this has gently nudged the west into having characteristic systems that are more socialist than before. And of course, this has caused some of the usual symptoms of a country infested by socialism albeit far milder than if the entire country had become socialist. But, little by little, even the west has begun to run out of other people's money.

They will try everything except true austerity to keep the system going.

The truth is that for the first time in History pretty much everyone is bankrupt and addicted to leverage. This may strike you as a great generalisation, but it doesn't change the fact that it is true. Even countries that optically have relatively little debt such as China have hidden problems in the form of the shadow debt that we talked about before. There is not one G7 economy that is likely to be able to stand the next 10 years without some form of default. Even those that might try to (Germany could be one of these) would have to go to such extreme measures in order to guarantee their solvency that this could not be politically contemplated by anyone even the radical right parties that are currently getting more popular.

There are other books and authors that will try to convince you that there is an easy way out. That somehow you can avoid all the bad things happening to you. The majority of these authors also publish periodicals that contain their trade ideas. Many of these are good and most of those that have seen what is coming are smart individuals and traders. And you will generally make money from most of what they say. However, there is one thing that these people, all these individuals, are not telling you and this is the most unpalatable truth. They are not telling you what anyone reading this book should be able to see now. That there is no going back. That when the financial meltdown comes there will be almost nothing left. That there will be a time when there is no trade in the financial markets that can be done to protect you, and that even if things look on paper as though they are protecting you, they will instead fail.

If there is one thing that we have learnt from looking at the pengo, or Weimar, or any of the other crisis realities is that the authorities will try everything to get out of the situation and they will also blame everyone but themselves. They will, instead of going for unpopular austerity measures in an attempt to reign in deficits to manageable sizes, simply push on with increasing the money supply ad infinitum. But this could only come from people who don't see a country as a company or like your family. We all know what we would do if we were in a large amount of debt but still had an income employment. The first thing we would do is not spend money on anything except the most critical things. We would effectively go to a zero deficit (and hopefully some surplus) mode to save money and deal with the debt. We might bring sandwiches to work instead of going to a food truck for lunch, maybe we will start walking to work to save petrol, or perhaps just stop paying for a bunch of streaming services etc. But those who subscribe to MMT think they are cleverer than the average bear... they think that this is the perfect time to throw all caution to the wind and create a cornucopia of (fake) prosperity.

This is already happening. The obsession with reversing "Climate Change" rather than just trying to cope with the modest change in average temperatures that even the most aggressive models predict will happen, partly stems from the fact that many politicians know (even if they do not admit it) that the developed economies (and some of the rest) are living on borrowed time. That there will come a reckoning very soon, and not from the climate. And this is the key that links all the apparently disparate topics that we have discussed. This links the push for Socialism, the Green New Deal and the Climate Change panic, negative interest rates, the games played with the inflation indices, the push against Capitalism, the Luddite like concern that technology will take jobs from everyone, the overextension of credit, and a number of other themes. Indeed, the Green New Deal as a plan, turned out to be nothing but a push for socialism rather than anything primarily designed to save the planet as admitted by the (ex) chief of staff of Alexandria Ocasio-Cortez, Saikat Chakrabarti[187]. This is exactly what H.L.Mencken who died in 1956 (a decade before the supposed environmental movement even got started) had in mind when he famously quipped " The urge to save humanity is almost always only a false-face for the urge to rule it"[188]

One of the primary reasons that all these concerns are even able to take hold in the mind of the populace is simply society living beyond its means and all of us, collectively, being unwilling to admit that this is the case. One hundred years from now, a historian looking back on our time will marvel at the idea that we were worried about the slowly changing climate when none of the g7 economies were living within their means. That we worried about not eating animals when we were willing to slaughter our kin in the womb to accommodate our lives, that our society was filled with "experts" many of whom were not even mildly competent at the subjects they claimed to have expertise on. And, they will certainly wonder how Modern Monetary Theory ever got started in the first place when a 10-year old (admittedly somewhat precocious) child could have figured out it was a description of a simple Ponzi scheme.

Meltdown.

When financial meltdown does occur, it will spare no institution. This is because every single institution in the world is inextricably linked to every other one. To put it another way, there is no Battlestar Galactica in our world. There is no system or institution that is solvent on its own out of the way of everything else. China is as dependent on the US as the US is on China, and indeed even more so. The UK may have Brexited, but it needs the EU from the perspective of trade as much as the EU needs it. We could go on and on, but the fact of the matter is that unlike the great depression in the 30's which was sorted out by a world war, this global depression will not be sorted out in this way.

This will be a time when every single asset in the world goes down in value versus the US dollar and the US dollar itself becomes worth a lot less. The ultimate collapse of the pride of life that is the world financial system. No one will be spared, not those with Bitcoin, those with Ethereum or any other cryptocurrency. Nothing will be worth holding. And don't believe that holding property or land will make much difference. The governments will come for the landowners, the property owners, and the farmers before the collapse gets properly underway. This is because there is no one else to go to and if there is no other choice whatever anyone has will be taken from them. There is no country to escape to because even those that are initially unaffected will be drawn into the black hole of the quagmire of financial ruin because again those countries are all interconnected. If there is one country that might escape this, it might be New Zealand both because of its current fiscal health and its geographical isolation from other nations as well as a relatively small population. However, this is just a guess, and in all probability even that country will be inundated by economic refugees and the spill-over of the Global Financial annihilation, for that is what it is.

Things may even become bad enough that there is an escalation to something close to WWIII perhaps with unconventional weapons being used. And in case you think that this is hyperbole, remember again we have never seen this level of indebtedness before. This is an unprecedented time in the world and during such times wars do tend to break out. And of course, the weapons of destruction that we currently possess in the world are orders of magnitude more powerful than even the horrors which were visited on Hiroshima and Nagasaki. One can only hope and pray that it doesn't come to this, and hopefully it will not, but this is clearly a concern when there is such a financial shock to the system that the structure of world organisation itself becomes crippled or is even destroyed entirely. Assuming, of

---

[187] https://www.washingtonexaminer.com/opinion/editorials/the-green-new-deal-was-never-about-climate-change-its-just-alexandria-ocasio-cortezs-excuse-to-destroy-americas-economy

[188] Appearing in Minority Report: H.L.Mencken's Notebooks published in 1956

course, that a physical global Armageddon doesn't, in fact, take place what might we see in the aftermath of all this?

What might emerge.

The thing that is really the most concerning regarding the coming ultra-crisis is likely what remains after the smoke has cleared. When such systems fail so palpably, the first thing that happens is that blame is scapegoated onto someone or something that is convenient as a stooge. This is for various reasons, but mostly because it is far harder to accept blame than it is to rationalise it onto something else. Just look at the financial crisis; how quickly did the public manage to divest itself of any tendency to claim "mea culpa", how readily were the bankers blamed for every possible ill related to it, and how fast did everyone forget that the US government ended up making a profit from its TARP and other programs in the end. No one was willing to take some personal responsibility for the debacle, and the same will be true to a greater extent in the ultra-crisis. More bankers will be blamed, more blame will go to individual 1%ers and maybe even the 0.1%ers. It doesn't really matter who will be blamed, no one will accept the truth. That the current failure to accept responsibility for one's life which has been indoctrinated into the minds of the young at University by the "progressive left"

But there is one particular scapegoat that will be the largest recipient of blame by the progressives. It will be capitalism. Capitalism, it will be argued, only works for a very short time and needs to be destroyed. Already we see this happening. There are calls for socialism to come to the rescue of a supposedly "failing" capitalist system in the inner cities in the US for example. The fact that it was the socialist undertones of policy that have been constantly undermining the power of the free market to properly work and provide a living for individuals. When the health and safety costs of a business are enough to drown it in both red tape and costs, that business will shut. When you are instructed to hire based on diversity rather than competence, your endeavour is likely to fail. And it should be obvious that capitalism does not work well with a top down control mechanism because it relies on self-organisation which is antithetical to top down economics.

But after the blame has been ascribed, then things will get even more worrying. The push will be towards two things. The first is some kind of neo socialist governance. This is scary enough in and of itself, but what is more concerning is that the policies that these governments begin to put into effect are going to become more and more informed by the Idiocracy, by social and political scientists rather than by pure scientific evidence. This will mean that political correctness will run amok when it comes to public policies. It has already begun in some corners of the world. For example, the woman who went to jail for daring to criticize the prophet Mohammed in Austria. This dovetailed with Social Credit system type technology using advanced facial recognition (provided by your friends in Silicon Valley), will bring the state envisaged in the book 1984 essentially to fruition

What can be done to fix all this?

Whilst I don't propose to have the solution to everything with regards to this reality there are things that can be done to cushion the blow. None of these things are particularly palatable nor are they necessarily the only things that can be done, but there is no question that to avert the greatest financial disaster of all time from happening things do need to be done.

There are many potential solutions to the problems that bug the world's economy. However, at this stage there is no remedy at all that does not come with a lot of pain. The debt that has accumulated worldwide is so pervasive that we have no hope for a very "soft landing". However, knowing there is a problem sooner rather than later is better than not knowing. This leads to the question (I would have said begs the question, though I am too scared of my logic teacher to go there), a natural one indeed, does Janet Yellen, did Bernanke, does Carey, do all those other "great minds" know how bad things are?

Despite the fact I would think them crazy, I very much hope that they do not. I don't like the idea that they might know and continue with ever greater credit expansion just because they don't want things to blow up "on their watch". But somehow, I suspect, that they know all too well the lessons of history, are staring down into the abyss, and just don't have the guts to go down there because they are scared that in this age of soundbites and nothing more, they will be accused of being the ones that caused this disaster just because they were the ones to raise the alarm. If they are such, they are both terrible cowards, and great agents of evil, because the longer they allow this charade to go on, the more people this will ultimately affect and more and more deeply.

Having said that, if we are looking for the best-case scenario, and assuming that all the heads of the central banks suddenly realise the crux of the matter, what is the best thing they can do? I will present something akin to a package that would, in my opinion, work to solve things with the minimum of suffering comparatively speaking.

Well the first thing to do is stop keeping rates below inflation and move from negative real rates to at least zero. This sends the signal without leading to an avalanche that they are, if not sane, at least aware of their madness. The next thing that I would want the central banks to do is to begin using the cash that they receive from their bond maturities as they arrive not to reinvest, but to pay for some real projects. For example, the US is in dire need of a proper rail-net. Whilst the US arguably has the current best in class freight system in the world when it comes to trains, it has horrendously slow and outdated passenger services which no longer belong in the first or even the second world.

If they could run trains at similar speeds to Japan, they would be able to send a train from NY to LA in 12 hours. That doesn't sound that great, but when you consider that the average flight from JFK to LAX is 6 hours, and factor in potential delays as well as the time taken to get to NY from JFK and the check in times, the train suddenly becomes very appealing especially in the form of a far more comfortable red eye service leaving LA at 5pm, providing you with dinner and a good sleep and arriving in NYC at 8am in time for a full day of business. This is before you consider the fact that you can freely walk around comfortably in a train, there are many less bumps in a train[189], and that a train could carry your car for example so that you wouldn't have to waste time fly driving. You could also do far more work in a carriage where turbulence didn't exist, and you had pretty much free access to wireless infrastructure at reasonable speeds (if you have ever tried to do anything on Wi-Fi whilst on a flight you will know what I mean). The economic benefits of such a full-scale network would be extreme for the US especially. This would significantly even out the advantage that the east and west coasts would have versus middle America. Even on the coasts, connectivity would become exceptional and improve almost everything including traffic on the infamous I-95 and I-405 on the east and west coasts respectively.

Now paying for a project such as a full rail net across the US would cost in the trillions of dollars. But you see the Fed **has** trillions of dollars which are right now locked up into the treasury bonds they own. If they were to begin to use that money to build real infrastructure it would both improve productivity, as well as stimulate growth. Why is this? Well when you build a project of this scale you need raw materials certainly, but a big cost would be in the services that you pay to manufacture the rail lines, the rolling stock, and the other infra associated with the service. All these services result in jobs for individuals and through this the economy is stimulated. Productivity increases because people now spend less time travelling and not working. Yes, they spend longer on the train, however, because a train is very comfortable, it is very close to being able to work from home or the office. Therefore, because you save check in and other delaying time (during which it is impossible to know how much time you have therefore the average businessman tends to not work at all) you end up working more. This is before you factor in the fact that the reduced pressure in a plane and higher temperatures tend to send most people to sleep for most of a flight whilst a train being on the ground is much more similar to

---

[189] This is true for the very high-speed train services because of the quality of the rails that need to be used to ensure safety. Ironically, the slower the speed that can be accommodated, the less smooth the ride becomes.

being in an office (if you don't believe me because you are used to Amtrak services, then try the Shinkansen in Japan, the ICE or TGV in Germany and France respectively, or even the fast trains in China. You will find that there are almost no bumps or difficulties on a train and there is generally plenty of room – except in China when there is never any room).

Am I saying that a new train system is the only thing that the US can do to begin to address its issues? Certainly not! I am simply giving an example of one potential approach to begin to deal with a problem of titanic proportions whilst not causing too much of a shock to the global economy. This is somewhat akin to the public works projects during the depression such as the Hoover dam that did indeed do a lot to stimulate the economy of the US. One could argue, and a number of historians have, that the US really only ended the Great Depression by having the second world war to fight. Whilst this is somewhat true, that option is no longer on the table for the US. This is because the US is so much in debt that even the Fed couldn't finance a war on the scale of WWII even though the US is still extremely unlikely to lose. In any case, the moral consequences of deliberately starting a war are far greater on a nation than any financial consequences they may forgo as a result.

Other possible solutions that could work but would have a much bigger jolt on the economy of the world would be a string of defaults. If all the worlds governments simply defaulted at once of their debt, things could pretty much reset themselves. Well that is the theory anyway, but in practice this doesn't work the way it would in the past. For us to begin to understand what default really means in terms of real-world consequences, let us go back to the past during a time that also appeared prosperous but was found in fact not to be so. Let us look to France and the times of the French kinds leading to the French revolution.

It is said that the storming of the bastille was maybe the most symbolically important event adjusted for the lack of importance what it achieved in and of itself. Whilst it will forever remain ingrained in the psyche of the French people as a great even where thy took down a monarchy and became a Republic, the consequences of the event itself were a freeing of a total of 7 prisoners none of whom were of any real import in the first place. This is a little like the people storming a north Korean gulag and finding that there are more guards than victims. I will present something a bit more all-encompassing overall, but for us to realise why it will work, we must first understand why capitalism works as a whole. Why? Because my plan for the western world, should anyone care to listen to it, involves getting Capitalism to do as much of the dirty work as possible. And that is a very good thing because Capitalism is nothing if not effective.

Resurrecting the American Dream.

The world is addicted to credit and printing money. There is never going to be a solution that gets us out without significant pain. This is entirely analogous to going "cold turkey" for someone who is an addict. Whilst I have little personal experience of addiction (for which I am extremely grateful), I was at some point in time forced to go on a significant diet because I was extremely overweight. I was essentially addicted somewhat to carbohydrates and sugars. I loved pretty much every form of cake, my personal favourite being cakes that fell loosely into the category of "chocolate fudge cakes" whether they truly contained fudge or not. Thus, during the Christmas of 2017, I went on a significant chocolate cake eating binge as this was my first Christmas for some time spent in Cyprus where I had access to my childhood favourite chocolate cake from a patisserie called Noufaro in western Nicosia. If you are ever in Nicosia, I would strongly recommend that you go to Noufaro and taste the "Sokolatina" which they create. It is, in my opinion, the tastiest thing this side of heaven. It is the only chocolate cake that I have ever tasted of which I can eat literally kilos of without feeling full.

Well this chocolate cake was my own personal kryptonite, my own personal QE and money printing. And getting off it was hard and painful. Every day of my diet I would be tempted by sweet foods and carbs and it was extremely hard to get off it. I felt that pain, and I can still feel it when I think about it. The problem is that this sugar was bad for me overall. I wasn't able to sustain the intake of sugar and remain healthy. And so too is the situation the same with regards to printing money and QE. And now if you have been paying attention you will be able to see intuitively at least that there is no way to get out of this mess that doesn't involve some pain. The numbers simply do not add up. But there are things that can be done to get debt back on track that don't attract as much pain as a full-scale default would. It is not about preventing a crisis, it is about making sure that the crisis we find ourselves in is not entirely pathological.

With this regard, some of the actions that President Trump has undertaken are good. President Trump has governed like the person he is when the hatred of the media is factored out; a President who is right of centre on most social issues as well as immigration and someone who is centrist when it comes to financial issues. This does not surprise me. After all, President Trump is fundamentally a businessman, used to making deals and not particularly conservative when it comes to monetary and fiscal considerations. However, his tax program was a good one indeed (and far better than anything that came out in the 20 years before). You may ask what is the difference between a tax plan that reduces government revenues and QE? The difference is that the tax plan puts money back in the pockets of the consumer and creates a genuine demand side economic stimulus and not just an asset stimulation effect. This means that the real economy is enhanced rather than just the bank balances of a few. Also, the Laffer curve is a real thing indeed. It postulates that when tax rates are too high (specifically when they are raised beyond a certain level that is not explicitly cited), this discourages people from working harder to earn more money as they know they are taking home less of it than before for every dollar they earn and therefore tax receipts are paradoxically . And broadly speaking, it is correct. In fact, it is mathematically provable very easily. Imagine that tax rates were 0% then clearly the government will never take any tax. Imagine also that they are 100%, then the same would be true as no one would work for free (or at least admit that they worked). However, for any other tax rate, there will be some amount of tax collected. Finally, as the tax rate can be incremented by theoretically any percentage between 0 and 100, the assumption is made that a smooth curve can be constructed between these three points. If this is the case, then there must be some tax rate where increasing the tax rate even a tiny bit further leads to a drop in the amount of taxes collected.

Now the exact causal reason for the Laffer curve working may be partly the assumption of discouragement, but it also is probably related to people focussing more of an effort on (usually legal) tax avoidance measures when they know that there is more at stake. The Laffer curve leads to something called Hauser's law as a corollary which is the claim that US tax receipts since world war II have been essentially just under 20% (Kurt Hauser in 1993 stated this was 19.5%). Whilst economists have pointed out that even 19% vs 20% of US GDP is a huge amount, the fact remains that this number has remained almost always between 15% and 20% over the last 80 or so years, and this is indeed good empirical support for the Laffer curve.

Nevertheless, even though the Trump administration has made a good start, the fact remains that taxes need to be further reformed with a complete reversal of capital gains taxes and income taxes. This will tax the very richest much more than those who are in the middle class and will be far fairer particularly in the US where those with very large amounts of capital are unfairly benefiting from policies such as QE. This will be tricky, because of course for capital gains taxes to contribute significantly, stocks and property prices need to be going up rather than going down. In addition, the legal loopholes that currently allow potential perpetual avoidance of capital gains tax with products that allow you to synthetically sell an asset without losing official ownership and therefore effective sell it without triggering the capital gains tax requirement would need to be closed. This will be an astonishingly hard problem in countries like the US given the complexities of the US codes of law, but it would not be insurmountable. One way would be simply to throw all the laws on the books at the Federal level in the bin and come at it with a new deck which is consistent with the requirements of the Constitution and the Amendments collectively known as the Bill of Rights.

The immigration issue is also an important one. Immigration to the US and Europe is a great thing if it involves those who are either very skilled, or who have extant financial resources, or are extremely driven. These three groups of people would significantly contribute to the economies of pretty much any western country. What does not work in large numbers is aggressive entry of unskilled workers. As we have seen, bringing in unskilled labour leads to a "race to the bottom" in terms of the value of unskilled jobs. In the same way that if you brought in a million financiers into Germany next year, you would expect salaries and compensation for those in the finance industry to drop significantly as there will be many skilled (subject to the ideocratic constraints we have talked about of course) financiers available for a limited number of roles. When the more sophisticated jobs are over resourced and the more menial ones are under resourced, income inequality will begin to shrink over time till it reaches a reasonable steady state – one where bankers will be paid more than the janitor, but they will not be paid orders of magnitude more.

Putting an increased focus on capital gains taxes, along with reducing the numbers of unskilled immigrants essentially transform the balance of power from Capital back to workers without compromising capitalism one iota. It is certainly not socialism or anything like it, but these two things will bring back the middle class far more aggressively than anything else. Essentially making menial jobs more valuable by using capitalism rather than working against it changes many things for the better. It will make some things worse of course.

Also, the culture of litigation that exists at this time within the United States and is creeping into other countries needs to be stopped. The cost of legal actions is a significant drag on any economy and makes it impossible to really do business in an efficient manner. In the same way that California is stifling entrepreneurial spirit by having so many regulations and requirements for someone starting a business, so does the litigation in the US make it extremely hard for businesses and individuals. You only have to look at the insurance premia that are paid by physicians (often in the millions of dollars) to know that litigation is one of the biggest reasons for the extremely expensive cost of medical care in the US. Again, if this doesn't change across the developed world, it will be very hard to properly maintain these economies over time.

The true solution to the problems of the world.

At this point we move away from economics or even mathematics or anything else that would be considered to be economic or scientific. Our problems as humans do not stem from the fact that we differ in so many different ways but simply because we all agree in principle; we all agree on our own selfish desires. Everyone wants more than their fair share, and everyone wants to give less effort than the average to attain what they want. And a further issue is that employers often do not give sufficient credit for how hard working or dedicated someone is. In particular, employers across the world seem to embrace what is really the cult of the "80:20 pareto" that the top 20% of employees are responsible for 80% of the profits associated with the company and thus reward their employees accordingly. If this was really the case, then surely it would make sense to exit 80% of the workforce and replace them with other employees of the 20%. In fact, this is nonsense and companies are completely unfair to behave in this way and is an example of the failure of the Pareto principle which is wrongly used here to defend the 80 20 rule itself. As we have said, with regards to the Pareto principle, yes indeed 80% of the decisions are made by 20% of the people but, in reality, these people are often interchangeable with the other 80%. This is particularly true when the Idiocracy is dominant i.e. where merit and competence is less important than intangible things. The CEO for example is all too often credited with successes and is very quick to claim market conditions affected their failures. Whilst the CEO is the most important position in a given firm, the reality is that it is extremely rare that a CEO is so much better than any other. It is also true that there are always people in a workforce that contribute more than others, but the key is that most of them contribute more as a function of their role in the company rather than because of some innate capability. Thus again, being in a key role in a company can make that employee seem more important and effective than their abilities alone would justify.

Should you pay so much more for those in key roles if you know that the role itself partly defines how effective the employee would be? Well I would argue yes given that the contribution is bigger regardless of why and because you still want to have the best possible people in those jobs. However, what I am saying is that these key people shouldn't be paid many multiples of what those who are not in key roles are paid given that the role itself contributes. It is difficult to square this with the idea that the free market should also determine what people are paid, but it may be that a simple psychological change is sufficient to change perceptions of what CEO pay should, in fact, be.

I think that a more capitalist environment will improve the situation because again it would lead to companies that are more efficient. Those companies that overcompensate their top management will eventually lose out on the ability to attract talented workers at the bottom who will go to their competitors. And this will lead to a failing company and hence top management who are either removed by their shareholders or simply cannot be paid because there is not enough money available.

Ultimately however, human beings will always be too selfish for any man created system to really work. There is ample evidence that however much we claim "enlightenment" we as a race fall into the same traps that we have always fallen into. As individuals we are also identical to our ancestors in terms of evil. We are all touched by hatred and maliciousness. As the Bible says "For all have sinned and fall short of the Glory of God"[190] I ask you to think about this and the truth of it. During the 20th century much of the world lost God. A huge percentage of the globe turned from being God fearing to claiming that we can all live without Him. So many states have experimented with entirely secular societies where atheism was essentially the state religion. And one by one, all these states have either failed or have exceptionally difficult issues. The greatest massacres the world has ever seen have been officiated over by atheist dictators (Stalin, Pol Pot, Hitler[191]) This century, we have seen massacres and genocides inflicted by theocracies like the so-called Islamic state, but even there these people were not God-fearing in the traditional sense; they believed that God instructed them to kill others who were not like them. Such is the danger of a theocracy, but again not all religions are the same and some are far more peaceful than others, at least in principle.

The Cyprus Problem.

When I was a boy, my father would often talk about the Cyprus problem. This is something that was very close to his heart. The whole thing started many years before the invasion of 1974 but that was when the troubles that had taken place in Cyprus since independence from the UK in 1960, culminated into a full-scale invasion by the Turkish army. More than 40 years later there still is no solution and half the country, sadly remains occupied by the Turks who have now claimed the northern part of the island as an independent state.

My father was very much affected the things that happened during those years. At the time he and my mother were just recently married and living in Athens. He was a very up and coming researcher in Theoretical Physics as I mentioned before having written his DPhil Thesis on something called Superpropagators that was the dernier cri of Theoretical Physics at the time. But when the invasion happened, he had patriotism coursing through his veins and this thoughtful and mild-mannered Physicist (who almost never needed to resort to punishing his children because just looking sad made us do whatever he wanted) decided he would take the boat that was leaving from Athens to go to the war. Well my dad was late for the boat. For whatever reason he missed it and that was a good thing too because he would have been killed as the ship turned out to be deadly sinking somewhere between Greece and Cyprus.

---

[190] Romans 3:23
[191] Whilst Hitler initially claimed to be Christian, his conduct simply was not so, and after taking power he made it very clear that he wished to construct an atheistic panacea having described Christianity in private as "the greatest curse ever inflicted on mankind"

My father went home initially depressed, but when he learned of the tragedy that had happened, he praised God that he had not been on that boat. Just 11 months later, I was born... make of that what you will. But my father's experiences had some effect on his views regarding the Cyprus problem. As we sat and listened to my dad, all us kids (I have two brothers) would hear about the events in Cyprus and my father would always say something that aggravated my mother (who was the embodiment of righteous indignation regarding Cyprus and the invasion). He said that it was the fault of the Cypriots that Turkey got away with the invasion. Of course, I never really understood why till much later and then I realised that what he said was 100% true. You see the Turkish army did indeed invade Cyprus and that was evil and wrong. But on the other hand, the wave of extreme patriotism that swept through the island in the first half of 74 was the pretext that the Turks needed to invade. They invaded supposedly to guarantee the safety of Turkish Cypriots and, on the surface, they did need protection. The fact is, however, that they are still invading and the final consequence of this is that every Greek Cypriot living in the North lost their land and their homes and every Turkish Cypriot living in the South was able to keep their property. All because of the arrogance of the Greek Cypriots in wishing for enosis (or union) with Greece and causing troubles that gave the Turks the excuse to invade. My father sees what so many Cypriots have failed to see, that being "in the right" is not enough. If you give someone the pretext to do something wrong in the name of "what is right", they will do it and you will lose out.

The same has happened to the banks who have been made the scapegoats of the biggest crisis in the current age because of the greed that a few individuals in the bank had. The fines for LIBOR and for collusion in FX are all a consequence of the few bad players who never actually wanted to play the game the way it was meant to play. The people in banks who owned subprime were often not the ones who were supposed to be the experts on the securities, and the banks paid the price. And the politicians blamed the banks because it was convenient to do so. After all it is far less palatable to the individual to take responsibility for their own actions and admit that they bought a house that was not within their means and that they had made a mistake. It is far more straightforward to believe that somehow this was all engineered by a few expert financiers in order to create trouble for the world. The simple fact is though, that subprime would never have been a problem had people not believed in the mythos that house prices in the US would go up by 5% a year every year regardless of what happened, and that interest rates would never be higher than rates were at the time they were borrowing. And one of the surprising consequences of the financial crisis, as we have seen, was the further rise of the Idiocracy which is always a danger when the cause of something is not properly identified.

But the banks were also full of greedy people that were happy to push the product and not ask questions about where the subprime was coming from. Those people should not have just been fired but they should have been charged with gross negligence. Being part of the financial system is a very important responsibility and no one – not in the banks and especially not any of the regulators really took that duty seriously enough. Within the banks the so called "control functions" that were supposed to look at the traders' positions and ensure that the bank was not taking undue risk were also negligent. Again, it was not so much the risk, but the fact that the risk was in the wrong people's hands and for this the control functions need to take much of the blame. The onus is to make sure that those with the expertise in the markets manage risk. It was far too easy during the good times for sales people or quants or structures to become traders and when that happens there is a great danger because these people have not seen enough of the tough times to really understand the consequences and therefore they are not able to deal with those situations when they arise. Such people fall into the trap of believing that they really understand the markets and that they are always going to be able to tell which they will head.

These people are akin to someone who looks at a book partly covered by another, and concludes that the book must be a copy of The Bible because he can see the word "The" not obscured by the top tome and The Bible is the best-selling book of all time. He might be right, in fact that is probably even the best guess (all else being equal the most printed book should be the most likely – what are the odds for example of the book being "The Prosperity Mirage"?), but a lot of the time he would be wrong. And in the world of finance, being wrong even once can have very serious consequences for many people.

Going back to the risk managers for the moment. I knew many of them at work. They were generally very diligent and conscientious. Good people. But the problem with the majority of them is they could have never been traders. They didn't have the curiosity and ability to assess risk that a good trader has. And therefore, far from being a canary in the coal mine, they were often the last to see the risk. That doesn't mean a good trader is always right about a market move but notice the risk managers simply had to know when the risk was too much and therefore, they should have thought like traders, because a good trader does always see the risk even if they do not believe that the risk is real. Again, this is an example of banks wanting to have people who thought differently from traders not thinking that they needed people who had the same sense of the market as traders but who had to be cognisant about different **aspects** of the trades. So, a risk manager would, because of the role they were given, undertake a different approach to the trader in the bank but in terms of skill sets they needed the exact same capabilities and mindset as the traders had. But because management didn't understand this simple fact, they allowed the bank to hire risk managers that just didn't understand risk and didn't care about it.

The hiring of the risk managers was also shaped by greed. Good traders were relatively hard to come by and therefore their skill set commanded significant renumeration. But the banks were unwilling to pay that much for individuals who they saw as not contributing to their bottom line (which in itself was fallacious as a risk manager saving the bank from making a mistake that would lose them a billion dollars effective was making a billion for the firm) and therefore they hired people who had skill sets that looked superficially like those of a trader but weren't. It was worse than this because any individual who could have been a good trader but for whatever reason (usually education or appearance) was unable to secure a front office position (as we called traders and sales people) and had to settle for a risk management role would always be on the lookout to become a trader and would usually find a way to the front office. So, because of the gaping disparity between trader and risk manager, banks could never retain the good risk managers. Small wonder therefore that most traders were able to run rings around their risk managers who were unable to serve effectively as the control function that they were designed to be in the first place.

My father would always point out to me that the way to change things is never by doing the "macro" things. That the only way to make lasting change is through the small things that genuinely changed individuals. He would tell me that small contributions were always the way that things incrementally got both better and worse and that those who really thought that they could change things in a grand way were almost always disappointed. I never really felt that this was true when I was very young but eventually, I came to realise that he was 100% correct. That even the big changes that took place over time were essentially a product of a lot of tiny nudges that transformed the realities of a group of people ever so subtly. He knew the results of what we have seen throughout this book. He knew that the world functions by human beings all following their own desires and wishes, and that all the great things that have been achieved by the human race have been due to individuals and not because of some big government project. In fact, consider what you believe is the greatest thing that has arguably been done by a government. It is probably the Manhattan Project leading to the atom bomb and all of its "cultural enrichment". Or if you are feeling super charitable perhaps you might say the National Health Service in the UK. But individuals have created great art works, the papers of Albert Einstein in that glorious year 1905[192], and one of them, gave His life for the whole world 2 Millenia ago.

---

[192] Einstein had an annus mirabilis in 1905 publishing no less than 4 seminal papers in the German publication Annalen der Physik. As well as the ones everyone has heard of such as Special Relativity, Einstein wrote the definitive paper on Brownian Motion, which unbeknownst to him would lead to some of the greatest discoveries in finance such as the Black-Scholes equation which I use almost every day multiple times.

Of course, individuals have also given us the worst things in the world too, and perhaps far more of them than the good things. But like it or not, it is "micro" changes that govern the world and not some grand set of government initiatives. Until we understand and accept that individuals do not generally function as benign angelic beings, we cannot begin to understand the world. This is one of the great axioms of reality that we have been following. And the left completely fails to see that this axiom is true. And as we have argued, when you follow logic perfectly but one of your axioms is wrong you can create something truly savage and destructive. And the corollary of this should also be that Big Government is an awful idea. Because the more the government is involved in the day to day lives, the more the evil human beings that control it will be allowed to interfere to the detriment of the governed.

Parallels like chains linking people and events through time.

Throughout this account we have seen that, crises have abounded throughout history. It seems that generally financial crises and collapses tend to happen almost at the exact moment that the general populace becomes comfortable that the good times are here to stay. And it is not just the public who fall for this. As we have seen, the Wall Street Crash was presaged by the comment that the stock market had "reached what looks like a permanently high plateau."[193]

Even Charles Mackay who published "Extraordinary Popular Delusions and the Madness of Crowds" himself was caught out by a bubble – this time the Railway Mania that occurred just a few years after the book was published. And as noted by Andrew Odlyzko in his excellent paper "Charles Mackay's own extraordinary popular delusions and the Railway Mania": "He lived through several giant investment manias in Britain, yet he did not discuss them in his books. An investigation of Mackay's newspaper writings shows that he was one of the most ardent cheerleaders for the Railway Mania, the greatest and most destructive of these episodes of extreme investor exuberance." Of this Railway Mania, Odlyzko notes, no less an intellect than Charlotte Bronte wrote "very many are- by the late Strange Railway System deprived almost of their daily bread"[194] and here we can see the glimmers of the doomsayers of today regarding the various technological and robotic enhancements that are taking place at this time.

But there are a couple of great differences that we have seen between the bubbles of yesteryear and the issues that face us in the present day with the biggest being that the overheating is now no longer just in a confined specific asset or even asset class, but they live in pretty much every asset class in the world, and more importantly, they apply now to almost every major world government. Before, it was possible to move money to other countries to avoid the deluge, but at this point in time, right now, there is nowhere left to go. We have discussed the likely consequences of owning gold or silver as protection, but unfortunately, as we argued previously the first thing that will happen will be the confiscation of gold and silver. There are many ways to do this including imposing taxes. Property taxes will also be created in countries where they currently don't exist. Again, this will be the case because there is no other option for the governments. There is nothing they can do except more taxes. Remember that this will take place when the markets will no longer allow governments to print more money without punishing them to extreme levels.

Alter the understanding of "rights".

---

[193] ["FISHER SEES STOCKS PERMANENTLY HIGH; Yale Economist Tells Purchasing Agents Increased Earnings Justify Rise. SAYS TRUSTS AID SALES Finds Special Knowledge, Applied to Diversify Holdings, Shifts Risks for Clients.". New York Times. October 16, 1929. p. 8.

[194] M. Smith, ed., The Letters of Charlotte Bronte, with a Selection of Letters by Family and Friends: Vol. II, 1848–1851, Oxford Univ. Press, 2000.

There is a massive focus on people's rights rather than their responsibilities and using the word right is basically a way to mask the idea that the state should be taking over. We need to change this. No one who is physically and mentally able to work has a "right" to things. No one has an automatic right to a house, to clothing, to food, to education, and to all such things. They are all privileges that emanate from a successfully developed society, and from working hard in that society. I have argued that those who don't have an able body or the mental capacity to function are owed something approaching and extreme duty of care in any society that could remotely call itself civilised, and we certainly have an obligation to those who are not of natural working age (such as the very old, infants, and also widows and orphans), but in order to provide for this, welfare benefits for all need to be reduced to very basic healthcare, education, and pension provision and eligibility for more will need to be targeted aggressively. Not only that, but we will have to provide a lot more lavishly for those in the community who really are unable to deal with things as they stand. Again, this must apply only to those who are physically or mentally disabled, and this is a very small fraction of the population and cannot include those who are not significantly impaired. This is the only way to treat the truly disadvantaged is to be generous far beyond what can currently be provided, and there is no option at all other than to demand of the able bodied, and mentally capable, the responsibility that is to fend for themselves. If we can do this, we can also provide far better for those who have temporary difficulties. But certainly, universal basic income and any such plans are not the way to do it. Nor is socialism. The only way to do it, is to not provide anything universally, and give only to those who can do nothing by themselves through no choice of their own. Surviving if you are young and vigorous needs to be incumbent on yourself and needs to be a responsibility. It can be no other way, because the budget will not let you. And you would otherwise be stealing from the disabled and the disadvantaged. The government does need to be responsible for things like defence, policing, border patrols and the basic infrastructure of the country, and furthermore it should be allowed to charge companies and potentially individuals who are not taxpayers for the use of its infrastructure such as toll roads. In that way, the government does represent the interests of the citizenry. Immigration needs to also comply with this which means ending illegal immigration to the west and tightening restrictions on how legal immigration should occur.

The big lesson is that the numbers do not lie. They can appear to lie if you construct a system that deliberately hides those figures, but when they are brought out into the light everything is just a very basic mathematical tabulation. Everyone can understand the workings of an economy, and all can understand the basics of budgets as well as assets and liabilities. There is no gnostic path alluded to by Modern Monetary Theory that can magically make countries no longer subject to the basic laws of mathematics, just sleight of hand that can fool many people for some of the time but not everyone forever. This is the case simply because human beings must do this in their own lives to avoid bankruptcy. The truth is not different and only slightly more complicated when the same approach that you might apply to yourself is applied to any corporate, or any world economy for example. There is no financial magic formula to create wealth like the acolytes of modern monetary theory would have you believe, because finance, and financial instruments are only ever supposed to be facilitators for the real economy. Finance was always supposed to be the ladder that can be used to scale new heights, not the view that would result from getting there. Instead, we have turned finance into something that is its own end, but it doesn't have to be this way. The same with money. Money is useful when it facilitates real things, and it is a representation of value but only that. Finance doesn't create value by itself and those who act like it does are seriously misrepresenting the discipline.

But when finance is allowed to function in a capitalist system with little intervention, when the natural feedback systems of loss and risk are allowed to fully manifest themselves, finance can lead to very good things and can be the engine that allows for innovation, and world changing events. The important thing for politicians and the central banks, is to try to avoid the manipulation of money as much as possible. To allow the markets to dictate the risk associated with a certain government, not just for the good of investors, but for the good of every citizen such that they are able to properly see the health of their country and economy and can make the government of the day accountable to them. For all practical purposes, this means central banks returning to their generally accepted canonical mandate of controlling inflation. Not inflation defined by some antiquated measure that doesn't consider things like house prices, but a genuine measure that properly takes into account the different types of inflation including the "lavish inflation" that we have talked about before. It also means, central banks being prevented from adopting things like QE without some very well-defined reasons, and it also means that the central banks should ignore speculative markets such as the stock market. The best way to temper markets in a natural fashion is to make it clear that you will not come to their aid if a market overheats and then collapses. The central banks need to control only inflation and not accommodate governments that borrow too much and cannot repay.

And this is where another key idea needs to be considered. Not all growth is equal. Growth that comes from improvement in productivity is incredibly valuable and useful. Growth that comes from simple demographic changes can be damaging and deleterious to the functions of any country. The GDP numbers therefore need to identify where the changes are coming from. If they come from productivity everybody wins as the value that a given individual brings to the economy is growing and therefore individuals should, in general, see a corresponding increase in their own economic fortunes. But where GDP is growing simply from demographics we don't even know if that is a net gain for the economy because if that someone is simply taking from the system more than they put in in the first place GDP may be going up, but the net wealth of the country as a whole is going down. The focus needs to be on GDP gains from productivity and not those from demographics, and again this necessarily means a reworking of the metrics that are being used to properly identify these quite different sources of GDP growth.

Finally, we need to deal with the genuine Idiocracy that is occurring both in the universities and the outside world. People should not be promoted on the basis of being a man, a woman, a majority, a minority, or because they exhibit any other collective group characteristic. They should simply be promoted because they are competent, and demoted if they are not so. To get back to a proper meritocracy both in academic scholarship and areas of the real economy is extremely important. It is for this reason that, I always look fondly a at a postcard that a friend of mine sent me when I was just starting my undergraduate studies at Cambridge over 2 decades ago. He was a real scholar of literature and urged me to heed the words of Alexander Pope: "A little learning is a dangerous thing; Drink Deep or taste not the Pierian Spring." These words are a damning indictment of the present day Idiocracy that is a literal pandemic in finance and academia in general that we find ourselves up against at the moment and this must be reversed in order to allow technology to stay as a tool rather than transform into an impediment to rational and focussed thinking. It is even more critical in the days of AI and other technologies that the grasp of the basics of human knowledge and learning, logic, the scientific method, mathematics and history needs to be rock solid in peoples minds otherwise the Idiocracy will grow and fester. We need nothing less than a revolution in thinking in order to overthrow and destroy the Idiocracy that this literally killing our world. This will come only by talking about the difficult issues, the ones that no one wants to talk about and not accepting Sophistry and those types of arguments, and it also requires companies, governments, and a whole host of other entities to accept that only a true meritocracy can lead to real success, that diversity for the sake of diversity is about as valuable as an inflatable dinghy in the dessert.

And this is where I will leave most of my readers with what will at first seem to be an unsatisfactory answer, but I thoroughly believe it to be the correct one. The solution to every problem of mankind are to be found in one person and only one person. That person is Jesus Christ who I believe is both God and man, who died for all the evils that we have ever done or conceived and was gloriously resurrected from the dead. Ultimately it will be the return of Jesus that leads to a world that is perfect and equitable, but for the individual He will always be a solution to whatever worries and ails you. He is not easy to follow; He doesn't care about your status, or your contacts, or your experiences. He only cares about the state of your soul and it is only by having Him in your life that you can really have full hope in the future. Not necessarily in this world at all, but in the New Heaven and the New Earth which will be perfect and blessed and where all the tears shall be wiped away from our eyes.

Christ said "I am the way, the truth, and the life. None shall come to the Father but by Me". If there is even a tiny Bayesian chance that this is true, then we should all look at what He had to say far more closely than we have before. This claim is the most important ever made and it is a claim that could radically change your life; it did mine.

Summary of TLAs (Three Letter Acronyms) in rough order of appearance.

SPD	Social Democratic Party of Germany
Pengo	The Hungarian currency known as the pengö
GDP	Gross Domestic Product
PPP	Purchasing Power Parity
R&D	Research and Development
ATM	Automated Teller Machine, otherwise known as a Cash Machine.
CNY	Chinese Yuan (RMB - Renminbi)
USD	US Dollar
BOJ	Bank of Japan
JPY	Japanese Yen
OCP	One Child Policy
SSF	Steady State Fallacy
AI	Artificial Intelligence
IOU	I owe you
SAFE	State Administration of Foreign Exchange
ECB	European Central Bank
ICE	Intercity Express
SNB	Swiss National Bank
P&L	Profit and Loss
EUR	Euro
CHF	Swiss Franc
IMF	International Monetary Fund
MMT	Modern Monetary Theory
AIG	American International group
CDS	Credit Default Swap
ISDA	International Swaps Derivatives Association
ISK	Icelandic Krona
FX	Foreign Exchange
NYSE	New York Stock Exchange
LSE	London Stock Exchange

IRC   International Reply Coupon

TBV   Tulip Breaking Virus

SEC   Securities and Exchange Commission

HKMA   Hong Kong Monetary Authority

AI   Artificial Intelligence

P/E ratio   Price Earnings ratio

P/T ratio   Price to Turnover ratio. A metric advocated by some to represent a P/E equivalent for Cryptocurrencies.

AGM   Annual General Meeting

CBD   Central Business District

CalPERS   California Public Employees Retirement Scheme

FIDE   Federation Internationale des Echecs

UBI   Universal Basic Income

FDR   Franklin D. Roosevelt

ICBM   Intercontinental Ballistic Missile

NBA   National Basketball Association

MCU   Marvel Cinematic Universe

CEO   Chief Executive Officer

AP   Associated Press

LIBOR   London Inter-Bank Offered Rate

NSA   The National Security Agency of the USA

AP   The Associated Press

FDIC   Federal Deposit Insurance Corporation. Guarantees customer deposits in US banks up to the amount of 250,000 USD as of the time of printing

TARP   The US Troubled Asset Relief Program instigated in 2008 in response to the failure of Lehman Brothers